FULL CYCLE

THE HUMAN LOVE STORY

A Novel by
Ripley Webb

Author's Dedication:

To all kindred spirits who are struggling to express through the dark glass of human personality something of their own brightness

Published in Canada by
Marcus Books
Post Office Box 327
Queensville, Ontario
Canada L0G 1R0
(416) 478-2201

(Marcus Books is a trading style
of 703809 Ontario Ltd.)

Write for a free catalogue of
New Age and Wholistic Health books,
audio and video tapes, and other items.

First printing February 1990
Manufactured in Canada by Webcom Limited

Cover art work by: ∿

Yvon d'Anjou
P.O. Box 1013
Haute-ville
Quebec City
Quebec, Canada

CONTENTS

INTRODUCTION

Ripley Webb was born in Slough, England, in 1892, and he died in London in 1968. His father was a bank manager and church-warden, his mother a dedicated theosophist.

As a young man, Ripley Webb showed his independence of mind by leaving an unsatisfying job in a bank and travelling to South America to work on a sheep farm in Patagonia. This was the beginning of many years of travel and exploration in different parts of the world, including Afghanistan, the Himalayas, Pakistan and India. His adventurous spirit and enquiring mind introduced him to oriental philosophical thought.

He served with the British Army in France during the latter part of the first world war, and then spent 25 years as a professional soldier in the Indian Army. He reached the rank of Major and received a number of awards for bravery. Throughout his army career his optimism, integrity and courage were recognized and acknowledged by his superior officers and the men with whom he served. These qualities are later seen to be reflected in his writing.

Ripley Webb was able to carry out some of his most worthwhile research when he had to spend some time in England due to ill health. However, at the outbreak of the second world war in 1939, he was recalled for active service in India.

His army career ended when, after many years of living in the tropics, he suffered further prolonged ill health. Following extended periods in hospital, he finally retired from the Indian Army in 1943 and rejoined his family in England.

At the time of Ripley Webb's marriage he had commenced 45 years of study, stimulated by his own experiences and background, and particularly by his wife Violet's psychic gifts and inspirational writing. After his return to England he devoted his whole life to scientific and philosophic research and writing, loyally supported by his wife in all his work. For relaxation he turned to his beloved garden, where he found great joy and peace.

Ripley Webb was a Christian whose ultimate aim was to discover and reveal the meaning behind the spiritual evolution of humanity. He searched for the truth and challenged accepted ideas, trying to find an explanation understandable to all people, young and old. In a number of books and articles he set out his conviction that, despite outward appearances, humanity is subject to an overall guiding power: a God of Love, who cannot fail and who has always maintained a balance between Man's erratic self-will and his divine destiny.

We, his daughters, are happy that "Full Cycle", Ripley Webb's first book, has this new opportunity to reach a wide audience. We wish to express our grateful thanks to Daniel Menkin for his enthusiasm and effort, without which this book would not have been published.

M.J.R.
D.J.E.
London, England. 1989.

2

Chapter 1

GENESIS

Many, many years ago God called to Him one of his servants, by name Tendor, a spirit who had served Him long and faithfully and was now to receive a new commission. Into the arms of Tendor God placed a tiny flame, burning pure and bright with never a flicker, a spark of divine Love which was destined to travel through experience and learn of its Father's Love. Tenderly God's servant nursed this tiny flame, rejoicing in his heart that God had entrusted him with the task of guarding and guiding the path of this tiny babe.

As time passed, the embryo spirit gathered form and intelligence, scarcely discernible at first but gradually drawing to itself the substance of the Spirit World as an earthly seed draws the means to manifest as a plant.

Issuing from the Eternal Father-Mother of all Creation, the tiny spirit knew only perfection, lacking any form of experience. Only love and truth and beauty surrounded it, but it could not fully appreciate these as it had as yet no means of comparison with their opposites. One cannot paint a picture with only white paint! It is from shadow that we find the meaning of sunlight. If we had lived only in the Arctic, tropical heat would have no meaning for us. If there were no opposites to love we should take it for granted and be unable to appreciate it.

During its descent into experience the young spirit was forced to undergo the painful experience of parturition into its masculine and feminine characteristics. Thus there grew up two spirits, twin souls, to whom Tendor gave the names of Michael and Ann.

3

These heavenly twins knew not evil, knew nothing that was not a direct attribute of God the Perfect. In accordance with their Father's unscrutable purpose they were sent forth that they might partake of the fruits of knowledge and, after refinement by the fires of experience, *know* themselves to be pure and good through deep knowledge of the meaning of those terms. And because they were children of God they knew within themselves that they carried an assurance of their eventual return to the place that was theirs.

Through long ages Tendor brought up his children, for so he thought of them. As they descended step by step into denser and still denser form, he watched over the fashioning of the bodies most suited for the manifestation in each deepening state of density, for the Spirit World has as many distinct planes of existence as an onion has skins, each forming an outer protecting skin to the previous one and providing a means of contacting the experiences which that particular plane has to offer. These planes are co-existent with our physical world, invisible to our slow reacting sense of sight, yet as real and concrete as the invisible waves which carry our wireless programmes. As a spirit descends, plane by plane, into the depths of experience, a body complete with the organs of sense suitable for manifestation in that particular sphere, has to be donned in order that those senses may respond to the vibration of things comprising that sphere. Without such a garment it would not be found possible either to express oneself or to receive impressions in local surroundings, and the experiences in that particular plane would be fruitless.

Not so many years ago such an idea would have been ridiculed. But as we begin to understand something of atomic structure, that all matter is fluid, composed of electrons and protons in varying number and degree of cohesion, we see that spirit form is just as comprehensible as material form. This is no place for a scientific discourse but the facts are there for all to search and find, proven and accepted. The heresies of yesterday are the facts of today.

The earlier stages of spirit education are of too rarefied a quality to bear description here so we will watch the progress of Michael and Ann from the time they reached realms more approximating our own. So far they had acquired the elements of wisdom, the principles of truth and the significance of sanctity. The bodies which now formed their external covering were of etheric structure but of human shape. Certain organs found in physical bodies were non-existent or vestigial but otherwise the forms were almost exact replicas of human forms, the principal difference being in the density of the atomic structure, that is to say, in the composition of the atoms forming the etheric body and the relation of the protons to the electrons in those atoms. To Michael and Ann their bodies were as substantial as that of any mortal is to its owner and they would have laughed heartily at being described as phantoms. Like all others on their plane of existence they wore robes of handsome design made of a delicately textured material not unlike silk in its quality and sheen, though infinitely finer and in endless shades of colour of far wider range than is to be found in earthly existence. In the Spirit World an individual is known by the degree of light he radiates and by the colour of his garments. The divine spark within the spirit radiates so strongly as to cause the clothing to glow with an opalescent light which gives a wonderfully beautiful effect. The higher the degree of a spirit the finer are the colours he can use. It is not possible, therefore, for a spirit of a low standard of evolution to robe himself in garments of high degree any more than it is possible for him to endure for any time a state of existence higher than that for which he is equipped.

It was during their present state of existence that Tendor explained to Michael and Ann that Earth was destined to be the place in which both of them would experience the densest form of life. He had pointed out that their present habitat was the anteroom where dwelt those who were on their way to inhabit the dark star of bitter experience, an adventure that affrighted not a few of the more timid ones but which drew evolving souls as a flame draws moths in the night. These were aware that in this most material of all planes of endeavour they could learn all that their hearts yearned to know in a far shorter time than would be possible had the same experience to be undergone vicariously in a school less hard.

When Michael heard of their objective he was thrilled beyond measure as he always was at the prospect of some new venture. Ann took the news more quietly. Being in affinity with Michael, eternal feminine to his eternal masculine, she viewed anything that might involve their separation with dismay. The very thought of life without Michael was, to her, anathema; it was the negation of the first principle of their lives. For the love that bound these two was fundamental, having its roots in pure Spirit and as such it was unquestionable.

The two were living together in a house of their own design and construction. This dwelling was the subject of much tumult and not a little light-hearted merriment in their lives. In this plane of Spirit, house-building is scarcely less difficult than it is on Earth. On Earth thought precedes activity; in Spirit thought *is* activity. True, the spirit materials do not have to be manufactured or quarried and there is no problem of space or expense, for all the materials of the building are assembled by the power of thought. Lest this statement sound impossible to finite ears, let it be remembered that all substances have their atomic composition fixed by natural law. Steel, bricks, glass, wood, all obey a prescribed law. To assemble their etheric counterparts therefore, it is only necessary to know the formula for their atomic composition and to use the power inherent in all spirits, of ordering the atoms of the Spirit World to re-arrange themselves in the manner desired. This is done by concentrated thought. In mortal life houses are first constructed in thought and then the thought is transferred to paper, thus gaining the first semblance of form. When the plans have been approved materials are prepared and brought to the site; building can then commence. In the World of Spirit, from construction in thought to construction in material is but one step. The builder concentrates his mind on the quality, shape, colour, etc., of the material he wants and it assembles itself by atomic re-arrangement before his eyes. Each course of bricks, the fashioning of the woodwork, the correctness of angle or elevation, all are affected by the power of thought of the spirit builder. And in accordance with

6

his skill so is the result. But he has one great advantage over his brother in physical life: the spiritual house, being created by thought, can be "undone" by the same method. The beginner can "rub out" his mistakes and start again.

*   *   *   *   *   *

Michael's and Ann's first efforts at house building were subject to many "rubbings out" and reconstruction and they would wrangle happily together as they laboured, for all the world like two children building sand castles. It was noticeable, however, that Michael's was the dominant mind, especially in the exterior design, though he gave Ann pride of place in the interior decoration and furnishing. It is easy to imagine the pleasure to be obtained in the arrangement of colour schemes in such a home. One shade after another could be tried and compared, in materials resembling silks, brocades, damask and others unfamiliar to our earthly minds, conjured up, tried, discarded or altered as the mood dictated. There was of course no kitchen in this spirit home, for spirit bodies do not require to be fed. The rays of Spirit power which flow freely in the atmosphere do all that is needful in that respect. But in the main a visitor from Earth would find little difference from a modern, tastefully furnished house designed to the order of a cultured and wealthy occupant. From the first Michael had been the gardener. Though he had studied the subject intensively at the horticultural college he found it difficult to settle upon a suitable layout for the extensive grounds. Time and again he would "rub out" his previous efforts and start entirely afresh. So many attractive designs could be assembled and so many flowers, many of which have never bloomed on Earth, could be planted. In Spirit, flowers do not grow and die; there is no cycle of the seasons. If full blooms are created, full blooms they remain as long as the owner desires, drawing their sustenance from the all-pervading Spirit power and giving in return their lovely essences to the atmosphere. In all it was very good fun, and Tendor, who had his being in a higher plane than this, would drop in at odd times to inspect the work in progress and listen gravely to the

7

ideas that filled the eager minds of the young creators. For this is how education progresses in the land of Spirit, through the inherent desire of the spirit to create.

Inside the house they each had their own set of rooms. One room in each suite was designed so that they might withdraw and rest, one being used as a study or work room where they could be alone with their thoughts or their books if they wished, and a third for robing, where they kept the garments they used for special occasions. In the centre of the house was a long room running the whole length of the house, in which they would receive their visitors or occupy when they sought each other's company. There was not much furniture, the *decor* being mainly through colour schemes, aided by flowers and a few paintings they had done. But there were couches on which they could recline and chairs on which to sit. Tiredness, as such, is unknown in the Spirit World. But there is a form of mental depletion due to various causes which enjoins the remedy of rest and recuperation. On such occasions a spirit will be glad to retire into seclusion and recline upon a couch while rays of healing power are directed upon the depleted body, revitalising it. There is no sun and therefore no day and night, the light being provided by the all-pervading Spirit radiance. But a depleted spirit, or one who wishes to meditate at length will often withdraw within himself, building up a sort of misty cloud round his person which has the effect of shutting out all external influences. Anyone found thus is seldom disturbed.

Spirits are just as careful about their dress as when they inhabit a physical body. Though spirit robes do not wear out, a change in colour or texture is often made for aesthetic reasons while special excursions demand special robes. A descent into the realm of physical matter for whatever reason or an ascent into a higher realm for a temporary visit, will require a special robe of a lower or higher vibration to be consistent with the conditions to be found there. Low Astral influences can tarnish a robe and it has to be renewed, while one for visits to superior planes requires lengthy preparation and needs much skill. An existing robe can either be dematerialised if no longer required or stored in the robing room for future use.

There was a lake close to the house where Michael and Ann used to swim and dive happily together or with their friends. Distance being no object and climatic variations unknown, a visit to the seashore presented no problem. The waters of Spirit are always pleasantly warm and exhilarating and the drops dry off the body just as water evaporates from the human skin. Michael had a boat on the lake in which they sometimes made voyages. It was of graceful lines having neither sail nor engine for it was propelled by the universal motive power of thought. After some practice it becomes quite easy to propel a boat and carry on a conversation at the same time.

Movement on land is by two methods. The first is by walking as we do on Earth, but progress is effortless and can be speeded up as desired, far beyond the capabilities of an earthly body. When great distances are to be covered or another plane of existence is to be visited, the usual method is to concentrate the thoughts on the destination, hold that thought firmly fixed in the mind, and then take a leap into space, as it were, so that the spirit body follows the thought and arrives. There is a method used sometimes on Earth in equitation when training riders to jump. The instructor will say to the pupil: "Throw your heart over and your body will follow." It is something like that only easier because there is no fear of physical injury.

The education of Michael and Ann was progressively planned in consultation with advanced spirits who had made the subject their speciality. In the Spirit World education is voluntary like every other pursuit; in fact, the main problem is to restrain eager students from trying to absorb more knowledge than they are capable of assimilating. There is no fixed scholastic curriculum as in earthly schools, instruction being given more on the lines of our university training. The object is to provide a wide experience of matters pertaining to the line of evolution the student has before him, rather than mental exercises designed to develop mind and memory. Facts do not have to be memorized for it is only necessary to concentrate upon a question for the facts to come into the mind. This is done by tapping the Akashic Records. Every spoken word, every framed thought, every event that ever happened in the Universe, is recorded upon the screen of time at the moment

9

it occurred. By directing the thoughts upon some desired fact, an adept may cause laws of selection to work directing the enquiry to the pigeon hole where the desired information is recorded. The higher the development of the enquirer, the more profound will be the information thus obtained. Educational organization can therefore be concentrated upon the application of facts to life without the strain of collating or memorizing facts.

The instruction is far, far wider than any given on Earth. For example, spiritual mathematics have twice the octave of the subject as at present understood by human minds. Good government is studied but in principle rather than practice. Geography and its allied subjects are not confined to the terrestrial globe but embrace the Universe. The Arts are studied and expressed in terms of the undimensional aspect of the Spirit World. Perspective, for instance, will have a totally different meaning in conditions not subject to three-dimensional time or space. Moreover, the scope of expression is far wider for there are colours in use which would be beyond the range of physical receptivity together with infinite shades of each colour, growing in range and depth as the consciousness of the individual expands. Sound expands infinitely beyond the range of human ears and with the aid of thought transference instead of human speech, it is easy to realize that the field of expression is almost boundless apart from the state of development of the individual. Added to this is an almost infinite capacity for appreciation. Art in human existence can only be viewed through a keyhole; not until the individual is freed from human restrictions will its full beauty be comprehended.

Lost in wonder at all they saw, seeing with the untarnished vision of pure Spirit, Michael and Ann wandered at will through this land of marvels. There were halls to visit in which were shown the etheric counterparts of earthly machinery used since the dawn of history. Here could be studied the principles of applied engineering underlying each machine. Here would assemble scientists lately returned from Earth who were eager to study certain aspects of their craft which had eluded them during their incarnation. For it is in the realm of Spirit that the underlying principles of all great inventions have their genesis. When it is time for some great new invention to be externalized into the hands of mankind, some spirit incarnate who is judged sufficiently knowledgeable is chosen and invited to visit the laboratories of Spirit during his sleep state when the spirit is able temporarily to free itself from its mortal prison. Thus the conception is implanted in his mind, later to be externalized into his physical mentality through his creative faculty. It is not the fault of the spirit designers if the invention is used as a means of destruction instead of construction.

There were many classes for instruction in the Arts to choose from and at some of these the great artists of history would demonstrate their skill for the benefit of students. At rare intervals Tendor would thrill his charges by taking them to some vantage point whence they could witness the movements of the constellations of the Universe. They would stand in amazement at the prospect displayed before them, the endless array of stars and planets, evolving, changing, growing, decreasing, in perfect obedience to the cycle ordained by God.

It was while Michael was in his study examining a chart of certain planetary aspects of the Universe, that he sensed the near approach of Tendor. Hurrying out to greet his beloved guide Michael saw at once from his expression that he had come on no ordinary mission. Michael's eyes lighted in anticipation; he was always ready for something new. Answering an enquiry from Tendor he sent out his thoughts questing for Ann's whereabouts. He found that she was resting in her room. Though Tendor would have waited patiently for her to appear Michael impatiently demanded that she be wakened. Entering her room he found her reclining on the couch surrounded by the cloud-like screen which denoted that she was in the spiritual equivalent of sleep. With all his force he concentrated his thoughts in an endeavour to pierce the cloud. With no result. In the end Tendor took a hand and because of his powerful personality he succeeded. There were signs of movement in the misty cloud and, like a child pushing its head out of the bed-clothes, Ann's tousled head appeared out of its concealment. With one flash of his mighty mind Tendor acquainted her of his mission, then the two left her to complete her toilet and returned to the central room.

It is not easy to paint a pen picture of a human being; it is far more difficult to describe adequately a spirit being. To begin with, all spirits are of one age; there are no old folk or youngsters except those who have just returned from life on Earth and these gradually rejuvenate or grow up until they reach an age corresponding to our age of thirty or so. Then there are no imperfections of physique, for spirit bodies are well set up and proportionate. Yet there is no commonness of type, for it is far easier to distinguish character and it is this which makes the distinction together with the state of development of the individual. Although Tendor and Michael had the same well-developed bodies, there was a wealth of difference in their appearance. It was easy to see that Tendor was a being of wisdom and high degree, because of the character apparent in his august features as well as the colouring and radiance of his robes. In Michael's features was depicted the clear, eager innocence of youth. His eyes moved restlessly to and fro as if seeking some new thing, and he had not the assured grace of movement of the more advanced spirit.

Presently Ann appeared to join the party. In contradistinction to Michael's dark locks she was fair, and she wore her hair in the Grecian style, bound by a fillet. Her complexion was ivory-clear and delicately coloured and she had long artistic hands with tapering fingers. She was dressed in a robe draped in the Grecian style and cut with what we might call expensive simplicity. It was, of course, designed for her and created by those who make a speciality of such matters, though any spirit can provide himself with a robe by the mere effort of thought creation. But there are robes and robes, and a special robe needs special skill and instruction in its creation. The clinging folds of the garment showed off the lines of her figure to perfection and gave her added grace as she moved. The colours she had chosen were pastel shades of apple green and the colouring was skilfully used to accentuate the folds of the material. The effect was both charming and graceful, glowing as it did with her own natural brightness.

When they were all three seated, Tendor began to speak. It must be realized that in the Spirit World the larynx is used only for speaking to those who have just passed over. No one would dream of confining himself to the clumsy and limited mode of communication used by mortals, when the infinitely variable method of thought-transference is available. When we mortals wish to speak we first conceive of an idea. This may be a wonderful conception, say, the colouring of a sunset. We have to fit that idea into the bottle-neck of words, our vocabulary being ill-designed for such descriptions. Moreover we cannot be certain that the idea we wish to convey has in fact been transmitted to our listeners. In the Spirit World the thought is projected and received in its original conception, as if we had painted a good representation of the sunset and handed it to our listeners by way of description. Such freedom of communication is essential when one considers that not only are the spirit senses infinitely more sensitive than ours, but the range of colours, sound tones and other external stimuli are far wider in scope than anything we know of on Earth.

To the twins Tendor's voice came as a beautifully modulated range of mental impressions. He understood the art of painting a mental picture in a way that delighted the mind, for his powerful wisdom enabled him to people his pictures with living impressions. And he could present his hearers with a vision, lifting them up and carrying them with him into a world that had every aspect of reality except its concrete presence. It is quite impossible to translate such pictures within the compass of words. We humans are almost inarticulate in comparison with the artists of the land of Spirit.

He spoke to the two young spirits of their preparation for their forthcoming incarnation on Earth. He sketched for them the type of experience he thought would be best for the development of each of their characters. Always he stressed that whatever they decided must be to a large extent dependent on their own free will. Michael expressed little anxiety as to the future. It was an emotion he knew little of and that only vicariously, while the attractive prospect of experiencing through acute physical contact enthralled him. He was not aware that this urge was shared by all evolving spirits in greater or less degree, and was the motive power that impelled them through existence and kept them on their way back towards the Source from which they emanated.

"If you decide that you would like to have this experience now, Michael," explained Tendor, "an opportunity is opening up that I consider most suitable. I have discussed the matter with the Sages and we find that there is a thread in the scroll of Destiny that will bring you the experience best calculated to teach you the lessons you need for your advancement. There is also another thread which interweaves with this one that would be suitable for Ann. But she would incarnate some time after you, Michael, about three years of Earth time." He smiled reflectively as he added, "This time business. It is like a dragging chain about the feet of Earth folk; it sets a limit upon everything that they do and dominates their very minds. But try and remember when you get there that time is an attribute of human existence only."

"Why is it so difficult to remember these things when we are in human bodies?" asked Ann.

"If incarnating spirits could carry with them even a faint recollection of the joys and beauties of this sphere, it would make it impossible for them to remain in tenancy of a physical body. To drink deep from the cup of experience it is necessary to contact life in its lowest form of manifestation. In order to do this you have to slow down your vibrations to a very low rate and come under the cumbersome laws which govern that form of matter. To one who remembered what life really is, the ache to return would be so intolerable that no spirit could hold down an earthly body. It is a merciful provision of God that such memories are temporarily veiled."

Michael was still struggling with the implication of the time factor. At length he gave it up and decided to leave it to actual experience. "Tell us about the experiences we shall have," he begged.

"I will tell you this," said Tendor, smiling at Michael's eagerness. "Before you can come into contact with Earth experiences it is necessary for you to wear an additional body, an intermediate one between the one you are now wearing and the physical form that you must inhabit. The difference in the

14

rate of vibration of these two is so great that they could not function together in close contact. It would be like over-filling a balloon. Between the two there must be a soul body, or as some call it an emotional body, which functions in a higher plane than the physical, yet lower than the spiritual. It is at once a means of more easily contacting the mortal body and of forming a protection to the spirit body, to which it acts as a kind of cushion against the harmful influences of Earth. You will find it a very difficult body to wear for it is the seat of the emotions. It is the engine that will drive your physical body. It will try and take control and take you anywhere but where you want to go. You must learn to be its master and not its servant. That is done by exercising your spirit will through the etheric mind of this soul body, and if you are not careful you will find the soul body getting the message all wrong and doing something quite different from what you intended."

"It sounds terribly complicated," confessed Ann, with a little frown of puzzlement.

"I think it sounds marvellous," said Michael, his eyes agleam.

"You will find," continued Tendor, rather grimly, "that the mind of this soul body, through which you will have to filter your real intentions, will operate as readily for evil as for good. The object of this is to enable you to strike a balance between the Light of Knowledge and the darkness of ignorance." A sad little smile played about his features as he added, "The Powers of Darkness will see to it that you have the aspect of evil, or ignorance as I prefer to call it, well and truly placed before you."

"Supposing we fail to control this body with such a lot of names?" queried Ann.

"There is no such thing as failure. You have a test to pass, one which you have set yourself to accomplish. When you pass it depends upon the effort you make. If you do not pass the test in the experience you are about to undergo you will have other chances of doing so. You will always find fresh opportunities opening out before you. In time you will accomplish what you set out to do, however many distractions

15

may deter you from your object. The power of the Spirit can and will win in the end. It is like a powerful magnet drawing you on. You might even return to Earth if during your first incarnation you had created so many obstacles to your progress, made so many mistakes, that only in that same condition could you undo and overcome them. It is the effort that counts; the responsibility is yours. No other can accomplish your mission for you. The scales of divine justice are accurately balanced; there must be nothing owing if you are to progress."

"Will we be conscious of this emotional body?" enquired Michael.

"You will not be conscious of any body but your physical one," replied Tendor. "But you will be conscious of being swayed by your emotions. You may find them to be violent at times but remember that they are not meant to be utterly suppressed. Rather should they be controlled, like spirited horses."

"But," protested Ann, "I don't see how we can control this excitable body if our memories are clouded over and we cannot remember what you are telling us."

"You will know," observed Tendor with a tender smile. "There will be the Spirit speaking through you, the divine voice of Conscience. If you exert the desire to know and to understand what perplexes you, you will get the answer from within, for by enquiring within you will contact your real self, which knows. It is the power of the Spirit within you that you must try and tap, the power which accomplishes nearly everything for you here. You are apt to take that power for granted but you will find that the Earth folk often deny that such a thing exists, so cut off are they from realities. Many of them deny that we, as spirits, have any existence. Some deny that there is a God."

The twins gazed at their guide in amazement. This was altogether beyond them. If they had known the meaning of exaggeration they would have accused him of it.

"Remember," he went on, investing his words with all the force of his being, "that the driving force that will guide you safely through incarnation is the power of the Spirit. But you will not be conscious of it as you are here. You must try and remember to contact it within and let it flow freely through your being. Let it flow consciously through your three bodies, spirit, soul and physical. If you do not, the soul body may sway out of alignment with the other two and then the channel of Spirit power will become choked and the power distorted. Then the power is unable to flow freely and the soul and physical bodies will be starved. Eventually some parts of those bodies may become atrophied and illness or disease may result. Or the brain of the soul body, and later that of the physical body, may get sick from being insufficiently supplied with power and thus become unbalanced. The ideas which the spirit tries to get through will be distorted or biased because part of the brain is not working properly. In this way some fine spiritual ideal may be wrongly represented, inverted as it were. The results may be terrible and very far from what the spirit intended. Which shows that you must not judge entirely by appearances nor condemn another without knowing the whole circumstances. God reserves to Himself the onus of judging and condemning; no one else is capable of doing so not being in possession of the full facts."

Feeling that he had given his beloved children enough food for prolonged thought, Tendor now took his leave. It was characteristic of him that he always treated the twins with the same respect he would have shown to an advanced spirit. He never displayed his authority over them nor did he allow his parenthood by adoption to become possessive.

After he had gone Michael and Ann remained in thoughtful discussion on what he had said. For the first time the magnitude and the potentialities of the task before them came into prominence. Then, feeling that they were in need of spiritual inspiration and refreshment, they went off to a concert. Though music of any kind can be 'switched on' by thought processes, nevertheless concerts of many kinds are given which are eagerly attended. It is only necessary to throw out one's thoughts in order to ascertain when one is due for presentation.

This concert was held in the open, in some gardens designed for such entertainments. After a swift approach the twins alighted at the edge of the flower gardens which bordered the immense amphitheatre in which the concert was to be given and made their way through the banks of glorious blooms. These flowers are specially selected and arranged according to their quality so that the scents they give off bring the visitor into a suitable frame of mind for the entertainment which is to be given. Soothed and uplifted by the lovely scene, Michael and Ann reached their seats in the amphitheatre. At one end was the stage for the musicians who were already tuning their instruments. Behind them was a background of trees, surely the most magnificent drop scene that could be devised. The foliage was dense and of a dark green with the branches so intertwined that there was an appearance of solidity and yet there was the knowledge that they were alive, for the gentle breeze made an almost imperceptible movement among them.

Presently the conductor arrived and after exchanging greetings with the orchestra and audience, began to explain the melodies he was about to present and the symbology of their arrangement. Then he tapped with his baton and the first work commenced.

How shall the beauty of that scene be expressed? To compare it with earthly music would be like comparing a Festival Hall symphony with the strummings of a beginner. The spirit ear is attuned to a vastly wider range of sound than an earthly one and this fact alone makes it impossible to convey any conception of the heights that are attainable. It is entrancing to those who have an infinite capacity to be entranced, that is all one can say. But to the harmony of sound is added a new delight. It is beginning to be understood on Earth that the sound vibration of a note of music has its counterpart in colour. There are some incarnate spirits who can see these colours and interpret them, albeit they are a sorry representation of the original. But in the freedom of Spirit these colour harmonies are clear and lovely to watch. In the Spirit World the love of the Great Spirit is very near and dear to everyone, for a spirit knows the truth, that God *is* all these wonderful things that make up the joys of existence. But nowhere is the sense of the omnipresence of God more real than in the experience of a colour-harmony such as this. The audience is indeed bathed

18

in Spirit, and the experience is more of a Sacrement than an entertainment. So to Michael and Ann there came a glorious sense of easement and at-one-ment with each other and with all other spirits, a wonderful sense of Brotherhood, as they watched the lovely symphony of colour playing upon the dark background of living trees in consonance with the aural harmony of the orchestra. The lighter passages of music were represented by darting shafts of brilliant colour while the deeper notes and more sombre passages were seen as broader and slower moving bands of deeper shades. Throughout this melody of colour were golden threads indicating the *motif*.

By means of this kaleidoscopic display of sound and colour the composer was able to take his audience with him into unimagined heights. Through this expressive medium he was able to interpret the meaning of Spirit as it appeared to him, in a way that was impossible even through the free channel of thought-transference. The language of symbology is the language of Spirit in its highest aspect and only through artistic channels can it be expressed. When the last sweet notes of the symphony had died away through the trees the audience stood for a while in grateful praise of the Great Spirit for this lovely manifestation of Himself. In conclusion they sent out a grateful thought to composer, conductor and members of the orchestra for the part they had played in this spiritual treat. Then they made their way out of the crowded auditorium. There is no overcrowding in the World of Spirit. For one thing there is no need for haste, no last bus to catch. And there is none of that flatness which greets those who emerge into a workaday world after such a spiritual treat as Earth can afford. Those who desire can, of course, use the swift means of dispersal at their command and take instant flight to their homes. But on this occasion Michael and Ann preferred to make their way slowly out through the banks of flowers greeting friends and discussing the symbology of the symphony they had just witnessed.

Soon after this Tendor called to explain to Michael that he proposed to escort him to a higher plane for the purpose of making his decision regarding his forthcoming incarnation. Michael expressed himself ready to accept this responsibility and after certain preparations Tendor and he sat together in Michael's study. After a prayer Tendor took both Michael's hands in his and told him to lift his thoughts as high as he could. Michael did as he was told and presently began to feel as if he were being drawn out of himself. Then he heard Tendor telling him to open his eyes. Immediately he found himself blinking at the sudden increase in light. The Cosmic rays were much more intense in this higher sphere but after a few minutes he got used to the new conditions and began to look about him. He discovered that they were in a large building, standing under a central dome. It was of vast proportions, made of stone of a restful shade of grey-green, and Michael found that gazing up into its dim recesses was a comfort to his eyes. The walls were covered with a tracery of design which betokened a very high degree of skill, while the roof was supported by fluted columns, the design of which accentuated the height and grandeur of the hall.

Presently Tendor introduced him to a professor who had come to greet him. The newcomer looked Michael over keenly and then asked him to accompany him to his room. Here he underwent a strange sort of examination. The professor did not examine his body but produced queer-looking charts which appeared to record his progress somewhat on the lines of a horoscope. It was all quite meaningless to Michael, nevertheless from the charts the professor was able to give him a clear and lucid statement of his abilities and weaknesses, the conquests and the defeats which made up his progress to date. From the same source the professor worked out the type of problem that was likely to face him in accordance with his destiny, and explained the course of an incarnation that would be likely to provide the lessons he most needed. Deeply interested, Michael followed him to the end. Then he watched the other take up a sort of tablet in which he inscribed certain symbols which, he explained, represented the essential factors required by his incarnation. Finally, he got up and went to the end of the room where he inserted the tablet into a slot. Then he came back and resumed his seat.

"We shall have to wait a little while," he remarked, smiling at Michael's puzzled expression. Then he went on to explain.

"I will try and make clear what I am doing. You must understand that every incarnating spirit is doing so in accordance with his destiny which has been worked out for him by the Great Spirit, the whole thing being carried out by the Lords of Karma. These are great beings who are entrusted by God with the task of administering divine justice. It is they who consult the Akashic Record and weigh up the progress of each spirit and decide upon his further opportunities. They trace the destiny of each one of us, and there is no appeal against their decision. In accordance with that destiny, each spirit is allowed free will to progress according to his ability. So it is that you are allowed to select the manner in which you will learn the lessons the Earth has to offer you. Your destiny is recorded in our archives and the tablet I have just prepared will be received by our workers. By a process of selection they will abstract an incarnation which, according to destiny, follows a line that promises to provide what you require. When you see that record presently you will be able to judge whether you think you are ready to face the difficulties if offers; if you are not, why then we will find something easier." He smiled with a confidence that Michael found inspiring at this profound moment in his career.

"What about Ann?" Michael ventured to ask. "Will we have to be parted?"

"That depends entirely upon you," observed the professor. "Upon you and Ann. If you decide that you will learn your lessons to the best advantage by incarnating together then no doubt you will do so. There is no compulsion either way." As he spoke there was the silvery tinkle of a bell.

The professor got up and went over to the slot whence he took what appeared to be a roll, somewhat like the scrolls used in an automatic piano.

At his request Michael followed him out of the room and into another in which the bright rays were much subdued. Greatly interested, he watched the professor insert the roll into a machine he had never seen before. A moment later a screen at the other end of the room became diffused with rays from the machine. By manipulating certain controls the professor caused these rays to condense into a clearly defined picture.

21

As Michael watched, enthralled, he saw a number of threads of different colours moving endlessly across the screen into what might be a loom or weaving machine. On the other side of the loom appeared a piece of finished material woven in intricate pattern from the coloured threads.

The professor kept up a running commentary as the picture unrolled itself. He showed Michael the thread representing the incarnation suggested for him, and to his intense relief pointed out another that might be selected by Ann. He showed how their threads met and crossed and how other threads met and influenced their own. Finally he came to the pattern, running the picture through again for the purpose of explaining its meaning.

"This shows you what you should aim to accomplish during your incarnation. Though what you actually attain may be something quite different. You cannot escape your destiny, but you are master of the manner in which you handle that destiny and the time you take to accomplish it."

With breathless interest Michael watched the unfolding of the future. It was a tremendous moment in his life. When the picture was ended the professor ran it through a third time and now Michael was able to pick out the points where faults were indicated in the weaving of his suggested incarnation, indicating crises which would give him opportunities for overcoming obstacles and thus gaining a step in his evolution.

There was a final talk with the professor, who pointed out that his acceptance of this incarnation at this time was entirely voluntary. But Michael was definite in his acceptance and only too eager to commence his new experience.

The professor smiled understandingly. "They are mostly the same; they all want to get on with the business." He wished his visitor a happy visit to Earth and then rose to conduct him back to the hall where Tendor awaited him. Eager to acquaint Ann with all that had transpired, Michael was not sorry when Tendor aided him to make the transition back to his own realm. He was fast becoming overwhelmed by the intense light and high rate of vibration of a sphere in which he was not equipped to dwell.

Soon Michael and Ann were alone in their house where he

retold with infinite enjoyment the experience he had just undergone. Ann began to feel rather miserable as she realized from the recital that her beloved was to be taken from her for a period, into a dark tunnel which led to goodness knew what terrible experiences. But Michael knew not fear and revelled in the thought of what lay before him. Thrilled by what he had seen, he longed to get to grips with the substance of this queer world of matter, which could be fashioned into symbols of such portentous nature and such far-reaching results. When the recital was over, the two children, as if by common consent, stood for a moment in silent meditation and allowed themselves to be caught up in a blissful at-one-ment with the Great Spirit, an action so usual in the Spirit World and yet so vitally renewing on every occasion. Not only did Michael and Ann feel that they were individually at-one with their Father but were mutually drawn together into a state of complete unity. It seemed as if they had indeed melted their personalities into one. It is the purest form of attraction of male and female which we call love, manifesting in lower or higher degree according to the plane on which it is expressed. It will be realized that sexual attraction, as we understand the term, has no place in the realm of Spirit, being an attribute of physical expression manifested through the emotional body. In the higher realms the same urge manifests as a pure expression of love, which means unity with the object loved, just as loving God means unity or at-one-ment with Him. The realization of this fact throws a powerful light upon our understanding of that much abused word, love.

There is therefore a direct connexion between physical desire and the pure flame of love. But it varies in its mode of expression because of the emotional stimulus exerted by the soul-body which is avid for the deepest form of experience. If its influence is allowed to operate unchecked, it may drive the individual to depths of perversion. It has truly been said that love turns the wheels of the world, but the real power behind it is the eternal Spirit force which emanates from God.

Soon after this Michael began to experience what he called "funny fits". There being no illness on the Spirit plane and tiredness being easily corrected, it was something new to him.

He found that his thoughts would suddenly and without cause become accentuated in a certain direction, or he would lose control over himself. He found this most disconcerting. On one occasion he and Ann were visiting an exhibition of garments and materials in current use on Earth. Some of these they tried on and shook with laughter at the sights they presented, especially when the curator told them that they had got the male and female garments mixed up. Suddenly Michael's features became convulsed and he went a fiery red. Tearing off the garments he was wearing, he stamped on them. Then he turned blazing eyes on Ann and—vanished.

Sorely troubled, Ann fought back the sympathetic emotion she felt and sent out a thought ray to contact her beloved. Finding that he had gone home she swiftly followed. He was lying exhausted upon his couch, too depleted even to withdraw into the mists of oblivion. Anything less than radiant health was a stranger to Ann, and in her distress she summoned the being who never failed her. Tendor came on the instant and after a glance at Michael sensed the trouble. Bending over the couch he placed his hands upon his forehead. Ann, watching, could see the shafts of power and healing that passed into the body of her beloved, rekindling the radiance within him which had become dulled. At length the guide desisted and turned to her with a reassuring smile.

"You have no reason to worry over this event," he said; "in fact, I expected it. It is due to the fact that he is beginning to assume his new emotional body of which I told you. This ferment, which is merely uncontrolled emotion, is a sign that Michael's time is rapidly approaching." He turned again to the couch. "You, my dear son, will soon accustom yourself to this new garment so that it does not get stretched, as it were. Do not struggle or resist; you will only make it more difficult to assume. Just remain poised and calm and all will be well."

"I don't like it," complained Michael, still affected by the new and disturbing sensation.

Tendor's eyes twinkled. He did not offer any further aid. Ann supposed that he wished to make Michael use his own will to overcome his troubles. At length Michael made the effort and sat up. Very soon he was his old laughing self. Tendor was obviously pleased.

"If you go on like that," he said, "you will find no difficulty in controlling your emotions on Earth."

"It was a nasty experience," admitted Michael. "It just seemed to take hold of me and shake me; I was quite helpless."

Ann, recovering from her alarm, observed, "It does seem a dreadful place we are going to. I don't like this idea of not being able to control oneself."

Tendor said, "It is only dreadful to those who dread, to those who shut Spirit out of their lives. Fear is a greedy weed which entwines itself round the mind till the unfortunate victim comes to believe the bonds are real and cannot be loosened. Remember that there is a lovely side to physical life. The emotional mind which is developing in you now, together with the emotional body, will pull both ways. Just as you may savour the deep shadows so you will taste of the bright side of earthly life. There is family life, for instance; you have not yet experienced the joys of mother-love, the sweet love that a mother gives to the child she bears. The early years of parenthood can be a supreme joy. I trust that you will both be parents on Earth. Try and remember that you are custodians of those young lives even as I am your custodian. You must not be possessive of your children nor exact from them a loyalty you have not earned. You may win the love of your children, but you may not demand it. They will be a sacred trust given into your care by the Great Spirit and your treatment of them will be by way of a test of your progress. It will be for you to guard and guide them until they are as well equipped as you can make them to accept responsibility for themselves."

The words sent a thrill coursing through Michael's being. He had forgotten the storm which had passed. The thought that he was about to become a man, a begetter of men, filled his mind with longing for this new experience. Hitherto his love for Ann had been on such a high plane that he had accepted it as he accepted all other aspects of life. The idea of loving someone else gave him rather a shock. He looked across at his beloved and saw that she was regarding him thoughtfully. Afterwards she confessed that she had been entertaining similar thoughts.

"I just couldn't think of our loving anyone else but each other," she said simply, in the face of a great wonderment. She did not realize it but she was face to face with one of the first fundamental lessons of her young life. Love, to her, meant the great overwhelming at-one-ment she was conscious of in her relation to the Great Spirit she worshipped, and it meant the bond that held her and Michael together as one being. The thought of separation from him was as yet unreal because she had not experienced it. There was also a deep and abiding love she held for Tendor, the love of a child for a parent. To her friends she gave affection, but being in the same stage of spiritual development as herself, they made no demands upon her; they did not call forth love. She had yet to learn *how* to love, how to feel at-one with all the fellow-children of the Great Spirit, how to experience the unity of the human family in its larger sense. She pondered long over the problem but it seemed there was no answer here.

The boy, become man in embryo, now felt it incumbent on himself to study the manly pursuits of his sex. He spent long periods at the colleges reading up stories of the great deeds of human accomplishment, the age-old story of man's conquests over the elements and over his fellows. The morality of the tales rather bewildered him, but the theme of triumph over obstacles seemingly insuperable, filled him with a welling pride. The saga filled him with a new thirst for accomplishment and he could scarcely wait for the incarnation to begin but must needs plague Tendor to hurry it up. But the guide damped his ardour by explaining that the laws of God are not to be altered at the whim of one of His children. There could be no alteration from the destined course.

But by way of appeasement Tendor announced shortly after that he had arranged for both the twins to visit Earth. They were both immensely excited at the prospect, Michael especially so because of the difficulty he found in handling his new emotional contact. At the appointed time Tendor arrived and by means of his great power transported the three of them to a distant part of the Spirit World. When they had alighted they saw before them a building of severe design very unlike the beautiful buildings they were accustomed to seeing. Looking round, they saw that the surroundings too, were very different, being arid and devoid of vegetation. There was a subtle chill in the air and it was noticeably darker.

At the door of the building an assistant in a white tunic, suggestive of laboratory work, met them and invited them to enter. As they passed through the hall, Michael's questing eyes noted strange machinery and instruments that filled his mind with wonder and a desire to know of their use. The assistant saw his interest and explained that this was a laboratory devoted entirely to perfecting means of communication between the different planes of existence, in particular with that of the Earth. After a short conversation with Tendor, in which both used many queer technical terms that had no meaning for the twins, the assistant invited the party to enter a room. When they had done so he closed the door. Ann gave a gasp of fright, for it was pitch dark except for the glow given off by their own radiance. Michael had experienced gloom when he witnessed the unrolling of the scroll of his fate, but this was far more intense and occasioned him some uneasiness. But his interested mind noted how in this new element their bodies glowed far more brightly than ever they did in ordinary spirit light. The assistant now produced some robes of a dark material.

"I want you each to put on one of these robes, and I must warn you that we shall be in complete darkness, for these robes will almost entirely cover up our own light."

Obediently the twins put on their garments, Ann at least finding the operation distasteful. She exclaimed with dismay when she saw the bright form of her beloved disappear within the folds of the hateful robe. But he was seemingly enjoying the experience for she could hear him chuckling in the darkness.

"Do not be afraid," cautioned the assistant. "There is nothing to be afraid of, and any display of fear might affect the vibrations and spoil the experiment." He went on to give them some technical directions as to how to proceed in the new environment they were about to contact. Then he offered up a prayer to the Great Spirit to guide and guard this party which was actuated by no desire other than to labour in His service.

Soon Michael began to feel a queer sensation in his solar plexus. The tension increased until Tendor began to speak, when the sound of his beloved voice relieved the tension somewhat. Presently he became aware that the light was increasing, for he could distinguish the dim hooded figures of his companions. Slowly the grey dawn increased until he was able to see that the walls of the room no longer existed. He and his companions were standing in a garden.

As his eyes became accustomed to the new light Michael felt the assistant touch his arm. "Come with me," said the other. He led the way to where a figure was seated on a chair. Michael stood in wonder. Then he began to recognize the garments the figure was wearing and realized that he was beholding what he had so long desired to see, an incarnate soul.

"Will she mind if I go nearer?" he whispered.

The assistant laughed. "She can neither see nor hear you, though she may possibly sense your presence. Go close and look into her face, for that is your mother-to-be."

The words sent a thrill through Michael's heart. Before him was the object of all the secret longings of his heart. He was to be her son, born of her body; would he be the beloved of her heart? Unable to rid himself of the idea that he must be visible to the lady who already occupied such an important place in his mind, he crept forward and peered into the face of the woman who was sitting so quietly knitting. At first sight he had rather a shock, for she appeared to him as intensely ugly. Then he remembered that he had always found pictures of human beings to be crude and ugly to eyes which had only beheld beauty. For all spirits are intrinsically beautiful; they are not subject to the imperfections of the human form. Michael continued his inspection and noted that his destined mother had good colour in her aura, for he was knowledgeable in such matters. There appeared to be no unnatural colouring or uneven radiance, which indicated health and even temperament and the absence of evil or ultra-selfish thoughts.

His scrutiny ended, he looked up and round him with eager gaze. Without a doubt this was the house into which he was to be 'born', and this garden in which he stood would be his first playground. He would have liked to linger there absorbing this new and delightful sensation, but the assistant was at his elbow and he knew he would have to go.

"We may not linger here," said the assistant, "we are using up the power and we have another visit to make."

Michael found himself back in the dark room once more and the garden faded out of sight. While he was yet turning over in his mind what he had seen he noted that it was becoming light again. This time it was a room they were in and the assistant gave his attention to Ann. Michael stepped forward and found himself in a long room, furnished most strangely to his mind. There were so many things in it that he became lost in wonder as to what could be their possible use. In material fact it was a drawing-room over-furnished in Victorian style. It was apparently the home of a family which still clung to the old life and the old things.

As Michael's eyes roamed round the room they were arrested by the sight of a woman, little more than a girl, standing at the far end. Something in her attitude made him stare in growing astonishment. To his untutored mind her features were plain and homely, yet they were distinctly familiar to him. He recognized that the clothes she wore were of the kind affected by the Earth folk. Then the girl turned her head towards him and he realized with a shock that it was his own beloved Ann. Why, he wondered, had she chosen to dress herself up in those queer unsightly garments, and why was she wearing the mask of physical features?

The voice of Tendor broke in upon his thoughts. "That is your Ann as you will see her when you first meet her on Earth."

For a moment Michael was crestfallen. He didn't like his Ann dressed up in this way; it was unfair to him and to her. Then he recollected that his dear one was merely inhabiting that dull form; she had not really changed for the worse. He laughed, and the act seemed to break the vision, for first of all Ann disappeared and then he felt himself being drawn back into the darkness.

The return journey was similar to the outward one, but in reverse. After removing the dark cloaks, the party stepped out of the dark room into the brightness of the world they knew. Back in their own home Michael begged Tendor to explain the mystery of his vision of Ann in earthly guise.

"It was a little trick we played with this strange element called time," explained Tendor. "Ann was permitted, for a moment, to project herself into the future and show herself as she will be when you both meet for the first time in incarnate life."

"Then we are going to incarnate together," exclaimed Ann, an intense relief in her voice.

Tendor nodded gravely. "It is written that you shall. But when your turn comes it will rest with you whether you accept the incarnation."

"Oh, I shall, I shall," she averred. Then she turned mischievously twinkling eyes on Michael. "What did you think of me?"

Michael replied with youthful candour. "I thought you were terribly ugly. So was my mother."

Ann was rather taken aback, when Tendor broke in. "You, too, will be ugly, my son. All incarnating spirits have to inhabit bodies designed to cope with the conditions on Earth. To the mind of Spirit, which responds to something nearer perfection, those bodies are not beautiful, either in form or grace. But without them you could not deal with the climatic and other conditions of Earth."

"It seemed to me that I had become someone else," exclaimed Ann. "It was a most curious condition. I knew it was myself inside the body, but I seemed to be shut in and unable to do anything I wanted. I wanted to take a lot of notice of the things I saw around me, but my mind sort of took it all as natural and wouldn't show any interest."

Tendor explained. "That is because you were not fully in occupation of a human body, but only a thought-form of the

30

body that will some day be built for you. You saw the things around you clairvoyantly, but you couldn't express your thoughts about them because you were hemmed in by the mind of the body you were in. You haven't learned how to use that yet."

"I am not sure that I understand all that," laughed Ann. "I shall have to read it all up at the university."

Michael now became more than ever anxious for the great experiment to commence. Tendor had explained that he would have to enter a clinic for the final period before his physical birth. This period was to correspond to the period of human gestation and was made necessary by the strain imposed upon the incarnating spirit at this time. For himself he did not care, but he was still a little resentful that his beloved Ann was to appear so much less beautiful than she really was. As time went on Ann noticed that she was becoming depleted. She no longer had the happy thoughts which had made their joint lives so delightful, and her light was definitely becoming dim. In order to discover the reason, she went into meditative retreat in her room and on returning to consciousness found that she had been allowing herself to worry over the impending separation. With the aid of the ever-present spiritual power she made the effort and overcame the temptation to imagine herself to be upset, and thus gained her first victory over the self she was beginning to assume in preparation for her own incarnation.

There was one other puzzlement which she was not so successful in combating. Both she and Michael were aware of something new in their relations. She would sometimes find Michael looking at her with an expression that was odd and rather disturbing. There was something strange about him too, causing a new sensation to rise within her. As a result a gulf widened between them which promised to separate them even before the inevitable fact. Ann made an appeal to Tendor for an explanation. He readily gave it, pointing out that it was entirely illusory, for nothing could separate them in reality. It was part of the price to be paid for incarnation, being due to a fundamental difference between the sexes which had to be assumed with the emotional body.

31

It soon became time to make the final preparations for Michael's departure to the clinic, but just before the event Tendor appeared, to announce that he was able to take the twins on a visit to a higher sphere. He would not explain the object of the visit but gave instructions regarding certain purifying ceremonies and the preparation of special robes.

At the appointed time Tendor joined them and they sat together in the central room of the house. He explained that they were about to visit a very high plane of existence and would have to leave their present bodies in order to do so. He instructed them how to sit in meditation, concentrating on a certain vision he presented to their mind's eye.

Michael felt himself wonderfully uplifted and then slowly lost consciousness. He awoke to find himself standing on a lawn of velvety grass. He felt unusually light and volatile, and he noticed that his robes were of an unusual brightness. Beside him were Tendor and Ann, equally resplendent. As he looked round he saw that everything was of a brightness and vivid vitality he could not remember having seen before. Tendor led the way in the wake of other spirits as brightly arrayed as themselves. Finally they reached a temple of such splendour as to be quite incomprehensible to earthly minds. The temple was no stone structure, cold and impersonal, for it was composed of living trees planted in rows so that they arched majestically to form a vast arboreal nave greater than that of any earthly cathedral. At one end was a stone altar on which was a spirit light that glowed and radiated. The peace and beauty of the scene were such that Ann gave a little gasp of wonder.

"Oh, isn't it lovely," she exclaimed. Then her voice was hushed as a heavenly orchestra began to play and the tone-rays lit up the whole interior with their symphonic interplay. The party took their seats at the direction of one of the attendants. Presently the music ceased and Tendor explained what was about to take place.

"We are about to experience a great privilege. It is the custom, before spirits incarnate, for them to meet the Master in Person. Now that you two, and these others here, are acquiring stronger personalities, it is the Master's wish that you should meet Him in His Personality so that the memory may

32

abide with you and form a source of inspiration to you in times of trial and difficulty. It is a form of Initiation."

As he spoke the music began again and presently a great stillness and feeling of peace stole over the assembly, broken only by the soft strains of the music and the gently weaving colours. Presently the tempo changed and the colour theme became predominantly silver-blue.

"The Master's Ray," murmured Tendor.

The music was now vibrant with a new life, and its *motif* was the song of a bird that is pouring out its heart in joyous praise of the spring sunshine. It was a symphony of pure love that called forth a corresponding emotion from the spirits gathered there. Everyone felt instinctively that He was coming. The part of the temple near the altar glowed with silver-blue light and then He appeared. From the depths of the trees He came, alone and radiating the peculiar vibration of love that He alone can give out, lifting them all up into a wealth of joy and gladness they had not believed possible. He was smiling and it seemed to each one that His special regard reached out for that one individually.

Michael's heart leapt when he saw Him first. "Why I know Him," he cried exultingly to himself. He felt sure that he knew this radiant Being as one who had a part of his life. He had no conscious memory of having seen Him before; it was rather that the Master was familiar to him through the beauty of the landscape, through the scent of the flowers, through the very power that vitalized the atmosphere. Surely the Master had managed to weave His Personality into the very fabric of existence; it was impossible to regard Him as a stranger.

The Master began to address the assembly. There are no words in which to describe the wonder of that voice. It was rich and full and vibrated with such compelling power that its cadences carried the people away into a joy unspeakable.

"My children, soon you are going to fold your brightness and creep into the environment of birth, deep into the life of Earth which my Father has made my particular care."

He went on to tell them of His own visits to Earth from time to time and what He had accomplished there. He told them of the blindness and ignorance that had spread over the face of the Earth till the people were lost in illusions which had become so concrete that few were able to break out of their self-imprisonment. He explained how their selfish thoughts, generation after generation of them, had formed a mist so dense that it was difficult to make contact with them and generate the spiritual power needed for their awakening to a knowledge of the Truth. He pleaded with those about to incarnate to strive to carry with them a memory of their divine origin and their ability to spread the knowledge of the glorious and inevitable destiny of mankind among the needlessly suffering peoples of the Earth.

"The children of God walk in the darkness of their own ignorance," He said, with an intensity of feeling that affected all His listeners. "They are so immersed in the selfishness and greed accumulated down the years that they no longer look to my Father for help. They seek to solve their problems by the light of earthly wisdom, and in that they cannot hope to succeed. The evil of ignorance is too strong to be overcome without the aid of the Spirit. My Father did not create evil; it was His wish that Earth should be a place of happy experience in which His children might learn to know themselves. Evil is made by man when he uses his free will selfishly, producing that which will harm his fellow-men. And it can only be transmuted by good, by the good of the Great Spirit which is the Father of us all. Century by century man has accumulated evil till it mounts up into a great unsurmountable obstacle. Only by the power of God can that obstacle be removed, and only at the earnest desire of man can that power be unleashed. That is my Father's just law."

He paused. Then His voice rang out, full and deep and strong. "Remember the Divine Obligation of God. He gave you life, you are part of Him. Because that which is His cannot die, cannot become lost, therefore He must redeem you in the end. You can have no life apart from Him and He is incomplete without you. You and I and my Father are One!"

There was a silence, deep and overpowering; the very atmosphere was surcharged with dynamic power which swept in great waves over the assembly. There was not one present who did not feel that those words of living truth were stamped upon the core of his being.

"It is my Father's Will and Law," the Master continued, "that His children should learn their lesson of incarnation, and in the doing redeem that which has been wrongly created on Earth. Do not condemn these for their evil, their ignorance, for condemnation is my Father's work, not yours. A great period of Earthly manifestation is drawing to a close and a new and greater era opens out before you who are to incarnate at this time. Go forth now and you will find opportunity opening out before you as a flower opens to the sun. You take with you my Father's precious gift of free will. Use that gift to labour with me as I work to bring my Father's Light to the people of Earth. Take heed lest you find yourselves caught in the web of selfish desire, the sparkling tinsel illusions which lure my beloved ones from their quest of the real gems. Keep your eyes fixed on the jewels from my Father's casket, the jewels of love and service, of tolerance and sacrifice.

"Already you have begun to assume that cloak of protection in which my Father wraps His children that they may not be burned too severely by the fires of experience. Guard well this soul body for it is vulnerable and its brightness is easily dimmed. Yet remember that without it you could not fulfil your destiny."

Now He allowed His gaze to travel round the assembly and it seemed to everyone there that He had a special regard for each. "I shall be with you always. I shall never leave you. Take you my hand and we will overcome together. Call to me and I will help you. Think not that you call to empty space when I cannot speak into those physical ears; My voice would shatter them. The eyes of Earth cannot behold Me as I am, for I should blind them. When you need My help come to Me by way of the Spirit, meet Me on the ground where I can and will help you over the obstacles that strew your path. But if we are to meet in this way the channel by which we can reach each other must be kept clear. Do not let it become blocked by foolish thoughts, by lack of faith in the reality of Spirit. Keep the channel clear that I may bring you the gifts of the

Great Spirit, the health, wealth and happiness for which you will crave. I shall bring with Me, too, fresh duties, new work for you to do, new opportunities for doing it. Keep, therefore, these three bodies of yours, spirit, soul and physical, in as perfect condition as you can, make them serve you as your feet serve you, but care for them as you care for the members that carry you step by step. Do not punish them for they are loyal workers of the Spirit, love them as you love those that serve you well. Then shall you be lighthouses in the darkness, beacons of power that nothing may harm, and every step that you take shall be a benediction. You shall be worthy tools for My Father to use that the land of Earth may be tilled and the seeds of knowledge and wisdom broadcast upon its surface.

"My children, I am conscious only of My Father's Will. Be you only conscious of that guiding star within you, that Light which must ever burn within your heart, part of the God who made you, an ever-living promise that must be redeemed."

When He had finished speaking He moved about among those present, and as He approached each one, he or she felt drawn by the power of those gentle yet commanding eyes into a feeling of at-one-ment with this glorious Being, who was so great and yet so humble, so inspiring and yet so approachable, so ready to help those who would let Him. When He came to Michael he gazed into the Master's eyes, so strange and penetrating that they seemed to look right into his heart, yet so loving and tender that they sent a thrill of joy and gladness through his whole being. In the intensity of that benediction he felt himself welded to this great Exemplar in service. He felt that there could be nothing he could not accomplish for His sake.

None could say that they saw Him go. It seemed to Michael that He had not gone at all. The memory of Him lingered when the silver-blue light had faded and the music increased in volume and then burst into such a pæan of praise and worship of the Great Spirit that the whole temple became one glorious crescendo of colour and sound.

They all prayed. That is to say, they stood, uplifted into

the consciousness of the Great Spirit, and Michael and Ann found the nearness of God to be even more imminent here than on their own plane. They did not utter words, they did not express themselves through the spirit language of thought, for God does not need such forms of address. They simply let their own consciousness open out so that the divine spark within them became One with its divine Parent. It was a moment of deepest ecstasy, beyond compare, for it was of the peace that truly passes understanding.

Michael and Ann came to in their own room. Tendor had disappeared. It took them some little time to recall all that had occurred.

At length Michael looked thoughtfully across at Ann. "Well, we cannot fail after that."

"I am not so sure," said Ann. "If the Master had not known how easy it is to fail I do not think He would have been so insistent on the necessity to strive with all one's might."

Michael sprang to his feet, charged with a sudden access of emotion. "We cannot fail," he cried; "oh, how could we possibly fail? Look at what He told us. Think of the power that we can summon to our aid. We have only to keep the channel clear, as He said."

But Ann could not rid herself of an uneasy doubt that a great test lay ahead of them. Yet she could not help basking in the warmth of that great love which still seemed to wrap her about. And she felt, too, that this bewilderingly happy event had drawn Michael and herself closer together. For did they not share a tremendous secret, did they not share a common task? And behind it all was that wondrous thought that some time, whatever happened, reunion with each other was inevitable, to be followed by a move forward into that eternal Love of which they had had but a glimpse through the eyes of the Master.

The final preparations for Michael's departure were soon made, and at length came the warning for which they had waited. Together Michael and Ann made a last tour of the garden in which they had toiled so hard. Michael gave a few last-moment instructions as to certain minor changes he had

had in mind. Ann agreed, trying to keep this strange new sense of emotion in hand. It was almost with relief that they became aware of the near approach of their guide.

They looked at each other helplessly, for they did not know how to say goodbye. This new and potent expression of their mutual love was proving difficult to handle. Then with a tender boyish smile Michael took her hands in his. "I have been learning how to say goodbye in the earthly way," he said, rather self-consciously. And clumsily, for it was a physical gesture alien to the Spirit World, he put his arms around her and drew her to him. Then he kissed her on the lips.

Wonderingly, Ann returned the greeting. Her eyes where shining, for she found the emotional stimulus exciting. Never had Michael paid her such a tribute as this, little though she understood the import of the symbol. She took hold of his hands and held them as if she would never let them go. Then, in a sudden and inexplicable desire to make a sacrifice she pushed his hands back to his breast and released them. At that moment Tendor appeared at her side. He took in the situation at a glance.

"Do not let this new emotion blind you to the truth," he said. "This separation is partly an illusion. You will not be really apart. When Michael has incarnated he will be able to come over here and rejoin you while his physical body sleeps."

The journey that Tendor and Michael took was soon accomplished, and the two found themselves in the same district whence they had paid their previous visit to Earth. But the building they now entered had a more homely appearance than the laboratory. The staff appeared to consist mainly of women who wore the garb of spirit nurses. But presently a doctor appeared and to him Tendor gave Michael in charge. Then he took his leave.

"Here we must part, my son," he said. "I know that you will be in excellent hands and you will find it easier to accomplish your mission successfully if you remain undistracted by thoughts of your old environment." He regarded Michael gravely, giving no hint of his feelings. But he was well aware that the work of countless years of striving was about to be put to the test. While incarnation is the lowest point on the arc of man's journey through the Universe, it is also the crowning achievement. It is here that the finest opportunity of forging character is presented, it is in the crucible of the material experience that the character is refined and the dross eliminated, providing only that the spirit is strong enough to face up to the task. At no other stage in the spiritual career is this longed-for victory over self so easy to attain, for the reason that nowhere else is it necessary to exert so much effort to overcome; and it is this expenditure of effort which gives the achievement its real value. It is this fact more than any other which impels a spirit to undergo incarnation more than once.

Tendor knew that, for the time being, his guardianship must be relaxed. His children must now learn to stand alone, this child of his heart must face his own destiny and encompass his own future without direct aid. By carrying the burden of personal responsibility he would find the key to progress. With a final blessing he left Michael with his new friends.

For a while Michael was afflicted with nostalgia owing to his separation from Ann. He knew that he had only to will himself back in the house with her and the desire would become fact. But he knew, too, that such a course would wreck his chance of assuming the incarnation he had selected. As time went on he found that resistance to the desire lessened its pull and he threw himself into a study of the problems that arose in connection with the clinic with a whole-hearted interest. He liked his doctor and found the nurses charming and helpful. He was allowed to wander at will through the wards and grounds, and he was surprised to find what a complicated business was this approach to physical birth. There were lectures to attend where much was explained to him. He learned that a successful culmination was dependent on several factors. Chief among these was the fact that it is a co-operative business between mother and child. It is essential for the expectant mother to keep in as fine a state of health as is possible and to care for her body at this time. He also found to his surprise that he himself could exercise a considerable effect on the embryo body which was being built for his use. He was required to concentrate at stated periods on this aspect alone, to direct his thought on the perfection of physique and the correct assimilation of atomic substance into the tiny form. Examples were shown of the difficulties encountered where the mother-to-be was careless of her role, or who resisted the idea of motherhood either through fear or lack of desire. Even worse was the situation to be dealt with where there was severe physical illness or a body whose etheric envelope was distorted by narcotics or other abuses. In these cases the incarnating spirit had a very trying experience, usually being prostrated throughout the period of gestation. Sometimes the attempt had to be abandoned because the mother-to-be so ill-used her mortal body. The unfortunate spirit struggled to the last to incarnate with the object of establishing even a brief acquaintanceship with physical life; in the event of failure it was forced to relinquish its hold upon the embryo body and slip back into Spirit life once more. The whole process of selection and preparation then had to be repeated.

It was usually the case, Michael found, where difficulties were most severe, that the spirit had deliberately accepted the risks, knowing that by overcoming them he would progress so much the faster.

As time went on he began to feel the magnetic pull of Earth. It began to manifest as a downward attraction from the feet, much the same as the pull of gravity, except that he was more conscious of it. It was hardly perceptible at first, but as time went on it increased to an uncomfortable extent. He realized that the use of such a clinic as this was was almost imperative if distress was to be avoided. He was relieved to hear from his doctor that in his case a perfectly normal birth was anticipated, for his mother was a spiritually minded woman and the thought of his coming was a source of delight to both parents. Michael thought sympathetically of the unfortunate spirits around him, many of whom were already aware that they were unwelcome visitors in the family circle awaiting them, that they had a poor chance of experiencing the love they so longed to feel.

"If only the people of Earth would realize," the doctor explained, "what depends on their attitude to parenthood, it would make the whole affair so much safer and easier in both worlds."

"What conditions would you consider the best for an ideal birth?" asked Michael.

"Why, I should say that physical health and a well cared-for body are the first essentials. Next comes the desire to have a child and lack of anxiety about the trials of physical birth. Without these there is bound to be sub-conscious resistance to the event which will hamper our efforts and react on the child. But transcending all these in ultimate importance is the desirability of the would-be parents having developed a spiritual outlook. If they view marriage as a supreme gift from God in that it gives them the opportunity to perpetuate themselves in accordance with His will, and if they approach Him with love in their hearts and a request that their bodies may be used in His service, then I am convinced that a happy birth is almost inevitable, and, moreover, the incarnating spirit will be one of high spiritual development with great ideals of service. But so deep is the ignorance on Earth that seldom is such a state of affairs obtainable."

Michael was allowed to be present at several cases where the birth was finally accomplished. Most of these were normal, successful affairs, but there were some where the dictates of destiny interfered. At first he was terribly distressed to see spirits depart into physical life with crippled limbs or lacking the use of one of the senses, such as sight. The doctor pointed out that in most cases it was pure destiny, though sometimes it was due to inherent causes which could have been prevented by the parents.

"These questions of ignorance and destiny are so bound up together," he said, "that it is difficult to see where the dividing line is. But we have to realize that the spirit has selected that condition and hopes to profit by the fact. That is all that we can concern ourselves with here, but we do know that it is the plan of all workers to foster a return to better conditions; that is the object in view. These bad conditions are certainly used by spirits who have elected to try and set right something of their own *karma* by this means, but that is no excuse for their

41

continuance. We must all work to improve the conditions, otherwise we are simply contributing to a vicious circle."

The Earth attraction was now becoming so strong that Michael found it better to keep to his couch. More and more his thoughts were bound down to the Earth level. His favourite nurse spent much time with him and promised that she would stay with him until the transition was complete.

The doctor made a final examination and expressed himself as satisfied. He gave Michael some final advice.

"You must remember that in the first stages of your Earthly life you will not be able to manifest very freely. Your growth into manhood will be in three stages. From birth to the age of seven years your spirit will only indirectly influence your mortal life; at the age of seven you will take a step forward and the etheric coalescence of your soul and physical bodies will become more marked. That will enable you to manifest more positively. At the age of fourteen you will take another step forward, into the difficult age of adolescence. At this stage your emotional body will become stronger and will require careful control. Finally, at the age of twenty-one, you will be able to draw fully upon Spirit power and commence to manifest to the highest spiritual degree that you are able."

Soon after the doctor's visit Michael began to lose some of his consciousness. He was only partially aware of what was going on around him except that from time to time his nurse would bend over him and smile confidently at him. Gradually the room got darker, the nurse took tight hold of his hand. The pull at his feet became almost intolerable, he felt he must be dragged off his couch. He heard the nurse telling him to let go mentally, not to cling to his present state. He felt himself slipping, there was a rushing sound in his ears, then complete darkness and swift oblivion. . . .

*　　*　　*　　*　　*

Somewhere in the house a door opened and shut. Footsteps began to descend the stairs slowly, terribly slowly to the man who was seated in the study below. The footsteps completed the descent and came to the door where they halted for what seemed, to the man who awaited their advent, an eternity. He

42

rose impatiently and was about to call out when the door handle turned and the doctor entered.

"Well, Mr. Blair," announced the doctor, a trifle pompously, "I have some very good news for you." He smiled benignly.

The man who faced him relaxed slightly. Then he burst out, "Well, what is it? Don't keep me in suspense."

But the doctor was not to be denied his moment. His smile, however, became a little more understanding and he bent his head to gaze at the other over his glasses.

"You are a proud father, Mr. Blair, and both your wife and the child are doing well."

Mr. Blair sank bank into his chair, overcome by the anticlimax to his weary vigil. His eyes asked one more question.

"A son, my friend, a fine boy," beamed the doctor. "Have you thought what you are going to call him?"

Mr. Blair was of that school which considers it to be tempting Providence to name a child as yet unborn. Now he searched his mind. He had no notion how the name came into his mind, but without a moment's hesitation he replied, "Michael, that shall be his name."

Chapter 2

INCARNATION

The Youth

Robert Blair was a miller at heart as well as in fact. He had been born in the shadow of the old mill, and the sound of its great throbbing heart was his first conscious memory. It had been built by his grandfather and carried on by his father, both of them men of acute business instinct and frugal habits. It was natural, therefore, that he should regard the business as a family affair with corresponding obligations.

When he married Mary Wontner, spinster of the same parish, he made it reasonably clear that he expected a son to carry on the business, perhaps two for good measure. He only got one, and then after some years of anxious expectation, but he was prepared to admit that Mary had clinched the deal in a satisfactory manner and left him no ground for complaint.

In all his life he had rarely left the little town of Belchester. He had at least a nodding acquaintance with most of its inhabitants and knew quite a deal of their family history, as is the way in these small communities. Mary, on the other hand, was counted a stranger in Belchester, for her family had come to the town when she was five. She had been brought up by a code which demands rigid obedience to certain rules of life, beyond which little is expected but a passive acquiescence in whatever fortune is doled out by fate. She knew that attendance at chapel admitted of few excuses; cleanliness of the home was as important as the wearing of the Sunday best; she respected the sanctity of the clothes line of a Sunday; and she brought to her husband unquestioning obedience in certain defined matters. Apart from these conventions she was free to drift along with her neighbours in the current of respectability.

Outwardly she did so. Inwardly she was sensitive under the

45

seeming placidity. There were intimate moments with her son, whom she adored and completely failed to understand, that revealed depths of spirituality which had never seen the light of external expression. One of the jewels that never leaves its case.

On this sunny morning in May, one of those mornings that seem to have slipped out of August by mistake, the Blair parents were awaiting the return of their son from the grand university in London where he had just completed his education. Blair himself was over in his office, pretending to be extra busy, but in reality having little better to do than whistle to himself and gaze out of the window down the road along which Nesbitt's noisy old car would presently bring his son. He glanced at his watch, got up and went over to the old mirror on the wall and studied his reflection. He was proud of his fifty odd years, though he was getting nearer to sixty than he liked to admit. He thrust out a determined chin as he glanced up at the greying hair. He turned to look through the window at the mill which made up his life and which, indirectly, had made him. The rhythm of its ancient machinery was in his blood, it regulated his thoughts, his ideas, which came and went in consonance with the thud thud of the great driving wheel and the relentless, ever-greedy maw of the hopper.

Not old yet, thudded his thoughts, not old yet. But it's time the youngster took a hand; there's a deal that can't be learned all at once about milling. A nice little business to take over, too, when the time came. He patted the pocket in which he kept his note-case as if to assure himself of the permanence of its integrity, then went out of the door and across the yard to the house.

Just as he rounded the building Nesbitt's car wheezed up to the gate. The front door opened and Mary appeared on the step, her face beaming and shining like a polished apple. A youthful figure leapt out of the car and began dragging an assortment of battered suitcases, sports gear and sundry parcels onto the pavement.

Born in a hurry was Michael, smiled Mary to herself proudly. She found herself almost swept off her feet as her tall son charged upon her and gathered her up in an armful of bag and baggage. Then it was father's turn. Dropping everything, Michael grasped his father's hands with his own, shooting breathless greetings at him, none of which made much sense. Michael was home.

The boy had come tumbling into Mary's life at a time when she was beginning to fear that she might be childless. And although she loved him intensely she had always been just a little afraid of this hectic creature who grew so rapidly, both in mind as well as body, so that she felt left behind early in the race. She had never caught up with him again. They loved each other, that was never in doubt. But apart from those lovely intimate moments which were becoming fewer as the years drew him from her, there seemed a gulf between them, a mental gulf which she felt incapable of bridging. She put it down to her own ignorance, for in her day there was little to inspire in the teaching that the little school in Timm's Road had to offer. And now he seemed further away than ever, for was he not a graduate of the grand big school they called a university? As she watched the boy empty the car of his possessions her thoughts went back to that bewildering day when Robert had taken her to London and to the great mass of buildings in which her son had acquired all this knowledge. She could remember little of it but the rooms where he lived and the woman who looked after him. These had met her critical scrutiny.

She turned to follow him as he went charging into the house sniffing into odd cupboards, like a dog that remembers the bones he has buried, and she found herself wondering whether he would ever settle down to the humdrum life that management of the mill had to offer.

"It's grand to be home, mother," he cried as he met her at the top of the stairs, his arms full of gear.

"It's fine to have you, boy," she gave him back, her eyes shining like a maiden's.

He bent over to kiss her and then staggered off to his room with his load, while she went blushingly down the stairs to get the meal she had planned for so long a while.

Alone in his room, Michael kicked the door to with his foot

and heaved his burden onto the bed. Then he went to the open window and leant out to survey the familiar scene. The mill, which had seemed so big and important and noisy when he was a little chap, had shrunk more than ever. The thud of its busy heart had assumed a minor key since his acquaintance with the great city and all the marvels it held.

Funny old-fashioned outfit, he reflected, and dad would like to tie me down to those wheels so that I would go round and around for ever and ever, amen. He turned in the other direction, towards London. It was the rhythm of that great heart that stirred his pulse rather than this familiar thud. From early youth he had been conscious of an insistent desire to get to grips with life. He felt that deep within its mysteries there was something for him, something he wanted to know. He knew that he would not find what he sought in Belchester. He began to hum some half-forgotten melody as he turned back into the room.

At supper that evening Michael found himself pressed to tell of his life at the university. Robert Blair had paid what he considered a mint of money for the privilege of sending his son to be educated there, and incidentally proudly telling his friends about it, and he felt that it was only due to him that he should share vicariously in his son's success. As he listened, his mind toyed with the idea of testing the boy's views on his future, here and now. But he put the notion aside resolutely. That question would have to be discussed in the sanctuary of the office, and perhaps, yet why not? celebrated in a glass of the old sherry he and his forebears had laid down for the sealing of important deals.

Mary Blair's mind was in a tumult. There was so much she wanted to ask Michael, all the intimate and domestic details that her motherly heart craved to know. But Michael had got on to industrial problems, a subject in which he had specialized. Dull and boring she thought them as the boy discoursed on technicalities that he rolled round his tongue with the relish of a connoisseur for his favourite wine. Robert Blair began to feel uneasy. Michael seemed to be getting away from familiar ground. All this talk of production technique made him acutely conscious of how small the family business must appear in Michael's eyes. He cleared his throat noisily, and that seemed to cut across his son's talk. For a while there was silence until a question from his mother roused Michael to laughter.

"Did you meet any nice ladies where you were?"

"Mother, you old dear, you are a marvel. They don't have nice ladies nowadays; they've all become beloved mothers like you or else they are sour old spins. The young 'uns would scream with laughter if you called them ladies."

Mary felt rather shocked and her eyes said so. Michael leaned forward and put his hand confidingly over hers. "I know what you want to know, mother mine. You want to know if some bold, bad creature has stolen my heart away and left none for you. Well, you needn't worry. I haven't met any girl I care two hoots for, so far."

And as that was the answer she wanted, Mary was satisfied and content to bask for the rest of the evening in the radiance of this her son, while he and his father went over local gossip.

For the first few days after his return Michael roamed the neighbourhood of his home, picking up old threads, greeting old friends, visiting old haunts, some of them with poignant memories of boyhood's joys and alarms. He went into the mill and tried to feel impressed with the minor improvements that his father pointed out. There was nothing here to satisfy his growing instinct for industrial problems; it was all too pitifully inadequate. He talked with Josh Clark, the grim, narrow old foreman, and asked after his daughter Vera. Vera and he had grown up together, played and quarrelled together. Then as adolescence approached they had drifted apart, following diverging interests. During recent brief homecomings he had seen little of the girl. He recollected that she must be nineteen now, for she was two years his junior.

As the days drifted by Michael felt a growing uneasiness at the prospect of the interview which was impending. There was no longer any doubt as to the wishes of Blair senior. He didn't want to hurt the old man's feelings but the thought of burying himself in this old backwater for life just couldn't be entertained. If only the old chap wouldn't make such a religion of the inheritance business. It would be so simple to get a decent manager in when his father was unable to do the work himself. Why, Josh could do it on his head.

One morning he swung out of the garden gate and almost bumped into a girl. "Oh, I'm . . .," he began, then, "why, if it isn't Vera! Well, how are you?"

The abruptness of their encounter robbed them of any shyness they might have displayed, and Vera curved her red lips in a dazzling smile.

"I heard you were back, Michael. Seems a long time you've been away."

They exchanged platitudes and discussed mutual friends in the way people do who come back fresh to an old friendship. Michael dropped into step beside the girl. He glanced now and again at her and wondered at the way in which the child had become the young woman. Vera was a pretty girl despite the cheap cosmetics and the too brazen curls and the cheap but colourful costume. But she wore these with an air which deceived Michael, to whom the veneer of assurance gave an impression of character.

He told her of his life in London and something of his ambitions, and the recital was obviously of absorbing interest to her. She questioned him shrewdly.

"I suppose you'll soon be off on your travels again, then," she queried. "I can't see you settling down at the mill." She had always known Michael to be headstrong, but she realized that his impetuosity was likely to run away with him. It would take a strong-minded woman to hold him.

Michael laughed, with the clean joy of a future flung out before him. "What do you think? I don't see myself being buried here." As an afterthought he added, "Don't you ever want to get out of this place?"

She turned a dazzling pair of eyes on him as she replied, "Guess it depends on where I was going." With which enigmatical remark she smiled a good-bye to him and turned in at her own gate.

They saw a good deal of each other after that. It seemed that Vera had frequent messages for her father at the mill. Robert Blair used to watch her trotting in at the gate and he would smile understandingly. Nothing would have delighted him more than to see Michael married to the daughter of his foreman. Mary was more farseeing. She knew that there was little room in Michael's mind for thoughts of matrimony at the present time.

In the end it was Michael who brought the interview with his father to a head. He had met Vera in the yard and they had stood talking for a considerable time. When she went, Michael entered his father's office. Robert Blair smiled a genial greeting at him. "Well, my lad, 'tis a pretty lass the girl has become. You might do a deal worse." He chuckled and rubbed his hands together.

Michael gave a half laugh. "Why, dad, I'm not going to marry Vera, or anyone. I can't keep myself yet, much less a wife."

His father laughed heartily and rubbed his hands the more. "Oh, no, of course not. Plenty of time for that, plenty of time for that." Then his features grew grave. "I've been wanting a talk with you, my boy. About time we settled your future. You'll be wanting to come into the business, of course." He glanced keenly at his son as he spoke.

Michael bit his lip. So it had come. Well, it had to come some time, best get it over. He looked up at his father. "Why, dad, you've no cause to think of getting out of the business for a good many years yet, and there isn't work for two of us. And besides, I have it in mind to go into business with a friend in North London. It's a new patent for using plastics. I believe there is a great future in it."

Robert Blair frowned and looked down at the blotter in front of him. The disappointment had been a shock to him.

"I'm not so young as I was, Michael. And I don't think you realize how much there is to be learned in a business like this. It took a long time to build it up and it isn't all plain sailing. There's three of us been in it now and none of us found it other than a man's full labour and more. Besides," he went on hesitatingly, "I have ideas for improving the mill, expanding it, bringing it more up-to-date like. I thought that you and I . . ."

"I'm sorry, dad. I know it'll be a disappointment to you.

51

But I've got my own life to live and I think it's up to all of us to try and live our lives as we feel we were meant to. I could never do justice to my training here. I feel that I must strike out on my own."

There was a silence for a while. Then Robert Blair replied, mouthing his words to keep back his feelings. "I'm sorry you should find the old mill isn't good enough for you."

"It isn't that, dad. How can I make you understand? I've got ideas in my head that I think will be a success. I feel I must try them out. I'm sure they are worth trying."

"H'm." There was a wealth of meaning behind the expression. "And who is to put up the money for this business?"

"The man I hope to go into partnership with has got most of it already. I am to contribute these ideas of mine and . . . and to put in five hundred pounds." He smiled disarmingly and his father was conscious of a jab of memory and the picture of a little boy asking for sixpences.

"Tell me about this business," he demanded. And Michael plunged into technical detail. He spoke well and convincingly, though to the simple mind of the older man all these intricacies of production curves and overheads conveyed an impression of unwarranted interference with methods made holy by age-old tradition. He pinned his faith to rule-of-thumb himself.

When the boy had finished the father asked a number of shrewd questions. He thought for a while before he went on.

"I am not saying but what I am disappointed that you are not prepared to come into the business that your grandfather and great-grandfather spent their lives in building up. But I will put it to you like this. I will look into this concern you are so interested in and find out if it promises all you say. If I am satisfied I will advance the five hundred pounds. If the business succeeds, well and good. It it doesn't . . . you come into the mill." He leant back in his chair, eyeing his son shrewdly as he had eyed many a tricky customer sitting in that same seat which his son now occupied. He had made up his mind in a hurry, a thing he seldom did. But he felt somehow that the matter was urgent, and he felt, too, that he was on a good wicket. He had heard of ventures like this one; very few survive the first two years of their existence, while others no more than pay their wage bill with nothing coming in on the capital. Only the lucky few turn into the gold mines that the owners always anticipate. It might prove cheap at the price to let the boy buy his experience and then come more willingly into the business. And anyway, it was always possible to find something in the preliminary investigation. . . .

But Michael had not the guile to follow such tortuous reasoning. His heart leapt at his father's words. Success! and so easily! Really the old chap was being awfully decent. He had scarcely hoped to get the money at all. He stammered his agreement and thanks and staggered out into the sunshine, a little drunk with the unbelievableness of it all. He looked round at a world that suddenly seemed to be almost too good to live in. He wanted to shout and yell. Pulling out his pipe he strode off in the direction of the open country, resolved to work off his rising emotions.

The mill was on the edge of the small town and soon Michael was climbing the hill that lay behind it, his long legs making light of the slope and his thoughts milling round as the scroll of his ambition unrolled before him. Independence, freedom to try out his new ideas, lashings of work, obstacles, things to be overcome, beaten, then success. Life was grand! As he topped the hill and stood for a moment surveying the landscape, his eye caught a tiny moving patch of colour below. Presently he made out that it was Vera, out for a walk. Vera was a good listener; she had a sympathetic mind. It would be grand to tell her all about it. He plunged down the hill, his legs carrying him over the ground at a great rate. As he drew nearer he let out a hail. Vera gazed all round her except in his direction. Michael hailed again. He had no thought of why the girl happened to be here, for she had said nothing of a walk when they parted so recently. It did not cross his mind that she might have seen him start out up the hill and cut across at its foot so as to meet him. The minx spotted him the second time and with a look of complete surprise exclaimed:

"Why, Michael, whatever were you doing up there?"

"Hullo, Vera, glad I spotted you. I say, I've got something to tell you."

They set off together, she trying to keep pace with his long steps. He began to tell her of the momentous interview and its results. He fired her with his imagination till she realized, with a start, that she was fitting herself into a niche in his life which there was no possible hope of her occupying. She knew her Michael. Nevertheless she loved the intimacy of it all. That he should need even this of her, that she should be a sounding board for his ecstatic hopes. If she couldn't find a place in his heart, well that was just too bad. But there was no reason why she shouldn't pretend. Her face was flushed under the rouge with the exertion of the pace he was setting and with the warmth of her feelings. A convenient spot offered in a deeply shaded coppice and she sank to the ground with a sigh and refused to go any further without a rest.

Michael was penitent. But the need to pour out all that filled his mind was uppermost and he finished what he had to say as he strode up and down the little glade in front of her.

"Don't you think that sounds pretty good?" he asked, when he had finished.

Vera tossed her golden curls as if to suggest that it would be a better idea if he admired them. "I think you are wonderful, Michael," she said gracefully.

Michael gave a little laugh of deprecation. "Oh, no, it's only what every chap wants to do, if he can get the chance. I'm lucky to get the chance." He was smiling at her, his enthusiasm bubbling over. Then he caught sight of something smouldering beneath the level gaze of her eyes and it upset his equilibrium. Something called to him as it had never done before. He'd never had much to do with girls except in the mass, at college parties. He'd always found them rather an unknown quantity underneath the veneer of sophistication. His mind was not attuned to reactions of this sort. There was something urgent and compelling about the way in which Vera was looking at him. After all, she was a jolly pretty girl, you couldn't get away from that. He hadn't properly realized it before. Not quite like . . .

Michael's thoughts took a jerk backwards away from the present. Somewhere in the recesses of his mind there had always been a vague, indeterminate picture of a woman. Rather an ephemeral sort of picture which he had never quite succeeded in featuring objectively. It was an ideal, an abstraction which nevertheless had become very dear to him. He used to think of her in quiet moments and tell her his most intimate thoughts. Then he would come to and chide himself for being sentimental. Queer that he should think of her at this moment.

"A penny for your thoughts, Michael."

The voice jerked him back to the insistent demands of the moment, and the dream picture vanished. In its place were Vera's eyes, still regarding him, still smouldering. And all the time she smiled at him, the slow provocative smile of the Mona Lisa. He dropped down beside her. Her eyes widened and what he saw there sent his thoughts racing in a tumult. He put his hand on her arm and the contact thrilled him. He gripped her arm more tightly and drew the girl towards him. She made no effort to resist. The pulses in his head were beating, thudding far faster than the old wheel at the mill had ever done. Something inside him was holding him back, something important, commanding. And this compelling allurement drew him onwards. He was conscious of the tension. Then Vera lifted her face to his, her lips invitingly open. Something snapped in his head and he crushed the lips against his own in overwhelming emotion.

Vera snuggled into his arms with a little sigh of satisfaction.

*   *   *   *   *

It was some hours later when they made their way home over the fields. Michael felt rather ashamed of his surrender to his feelings and yet, in a way, rather pleased with himself. They said little during that walk home, though Michael felt there was a good deal that he ought to say. They came to her turning. He stopped and faced her.

"I'll be seeing you," he said, with a half smile.

Vera opened her mouth as if about to speak, then she changed her mind and her mouth curved to a smile. She waggled two fingers at him and turned away towards her home.

The next two weeks were full ones for Michael. There were interviews to arrange between his father and Davis, his prospective partner and owner of the patent. There were financial matters to be examined, too, and these all entailed journeys to London. Then there were empty factories to be inspected, machinery catalogues to be studied, labour problems to be considered. Thus it was that his meetings with Vera became somewhat infrequent. Much to his relief, she did not seem to resent this and accepted his plea of being hopelessly involved in his plans. Sometimes he wondered why she did not demand more of his attention during the first fine flights of the affair. But he was thankful that she did not make things difficult, for he wanted no difficulties while the question of the loan from his father was still unsettled.

Robert Blair, to his surprise and a little to his chagrin, could find no possible flaw in the proposals set before him. The whole thing appeared to be honest and above-board and the patent certainly seemed to have possibilities. Only time could prove whether the concern would be a success or not. So he decided, not without pangs, to cut his losses and give in with a good grace. He had no illusions now as to his own inability to direct his son's steps where he wished, and he was not going to have it said that Robert Blair did not do the right thing by his only son. No, sir!

So the cheque was signed and Michael Blair was firmly launched on his business career. The time came for him to leave Belchester and seek quarters near the scene of his work.

He went for a last walk with Vera. It wasn't a very satisfactory walk, for they were beginning to find that they hadn't really very much in common except his need for her as a sounding board for his thoughts. She was beginning to find that a dull sort of game. Presently they found themselves back by the old mill. It was after working hours and the great thudding heart of it was still. A chill wind made it unpleasant to tarry.

"Suppose we ought to be saying good night," he said.

Vera answered with a quick little sweep of her lashes.

"I'll be coming back soon and then we must see more of each other. I'll often be home."

Vera nodded. "Of course," she observed to a tight little ball of linen in her hand. Then she looked up. "I hope you'll meet some nice people where you are going."

He smiled down at her. "Expect so. But I'll be too busy for a long time to be able to do much socializing."

"Well, good-bye, Michael. Take care of yourself." Her eyelashes swept him a little curtsey and she turned towards the gate. Michael stood, and waved to her as she paused at the gate. Then she was gone.

In the sitting-room he found his own father and Vera's engaged in a business discussion over a defaulting customer. A grim old man, Josh Clark, thought Michael as he dropped into a chair. He had always regarded him as a bogey man in his youthful days, who was always chasing him out of the places he wanted to explore. Taciturn, he never had much to say, though Blair swore by him as a workman and he was good at handling men. Presently Clark got up to go, and turning to the young man, wished him success. He offered his hand in a grip that made Michael wince.

"Gosh!" he exclaimed to his mother when the two elder men had gone out of the room, "the old fellow has got a grip."

"Aye," agreed his mother, "a hard grip and a hard man." She was relieved at Clark's departure, for this was Michael's last night at home and she wanted him to herself. It had been bad enough when he went off to the university, but this time, she felt, he was breaking the old ties for good. He would only return to her roof as an occasional visitor. She gave a plaintive little sigh.

It was not a very happy evening for Michael. Despite his father's attempts at heavy humour there was a touch of gloom in the atmosphere. He had a very genuine love for these parents of his, and it hurt him to feel that he was a cause of distress to them. But he consoled himself with the thought that he would visit them frequently, and he looked forward to the proud moment when he could announce to them the success of his venture. The day of his leaving Belchester was wet and cold, and there was a small excuse for standing about prolonging farewells. Soon he was off, in the wheezy old car, to the station.

It was not in a few weeks or a few months that he returned. He was to find the establishment of a new business a matter sufficiently absorbing to the most prolific energy. It became almost impossible for either him or his partner Davis to get away. The many problems demanded persistent application in order to avert disaster. It was nearly a year after he had left Belchester that he was walking towards the factory when he met an old man whom he recognized as having been employed by this father.

"Hullo, Amos," he cried in greeting. "What are you doing up in London?"

"Eh, Oi've left the old mill," explained the old fellow, "along o' the rheumatics in me back won't let me lift they sacks no more. So Oi've come up to Lunnon to be with me son, seeing as me darter 'as married and gone way up north."

"And how did you leave things at Belchester? I hear from my home but they never told me you had left."

The old man gave him the latest news from the market town. Then he paused, uncertainly. "Ye'll have heard about Josh Clark's darter, seemingly?"

"No," said Michael, with quickening interest. "How is she?"

Amos shook his head dolefully. "A bad business indeed. 'Pears she was going to 'ave a baby, and Josh 'e found out about it—we know the like o' man 'e is. Well, there was a fine flare up and a to-do. She wouldn't say who the father was, and Josh, 'e turned she out."

"What happened to her? Where did she go?" It seemed to Michael as if a stranger's voice was asking the questions.

Amos peered up the road, as if seeking for someone. "They found 'er 'bout three miles down the mill stream. Drownded she was."

The Man

It is eight years later and Michael is now twenty-nine. He still bears the mark of the shock that Amos unwittingly gave him. There are lines on his face that are alien to a man who has scarcely taken his leave of youth. There is a trace of

58

cynicism in his make-up that was engendered by the tragic ending to a young life for which he felt himself to be directly responsible. Life for Michael had been bitter-sweet during these passing years, for the business had prospered beyond the most sanguine hopes of the two partners. Michael himself had contributed some novel developments of the original patent and there was a steadily rising demand for the products. But with the death of Vera a door had slammed upon his capacity for enjoyment. Success he met with the same grim reception he gave to difficulties. It seemed as if he had allowed the channel of inspiration to become choked. He worked with a kind of spiritless endeavour, driving himself along with nervous energy. Eventually this excess of expenditure over receipts had demanded stimulants, to which he had more and more recourse.

Michael could now afford to sit back, for money was accumulating in a most satisfactory manner. Occasionally he made an effort to consider life from a new angle: he joined an expensive club, bought a new car, learned to play golf, gathering a new set of friends in the process. But that was only a background; it did not animate his life to any extent. In each new addition he made to his list of proficiencies he found some disappointment, failed to find the distraction he had hoped. From time to time he went home and tried to recapture some of the carefree impetuosity of his youth. But he was not successful. There was a canker locked up inside him and he did not know how to let it out.

Willing tongues among his acquaintances whispered darkly of a broken love affair which spurred on some of his female pursuers to make unmistakable offers of consolation, either temporary or permanent. But, somehow, Michael seemed to to slide past these embarrassments. One of his would-be distractors murmured to a confidant as he passed, "All that money and no one to love it, my dear, isn't it tragic?" Which probably accounts for Michael's free passage through his difficulties.

It happened one day that a business call took him to a district not far from the factory. The firm needed some adjacent land for development and he wished to interview the owner, a Mr. Bainbridge. At the time agreed for the appointment, he appeared on the steps of a grim old Georgian house that must have been a gentleman's residence when this suburb was a village well out of the metropolis. A maid opened the door and on learning his business showed him into the drawing room to await her employer's arrival.

Preoccupied with the problems connected with his visit, Michael scarcely noticed the room at his first entry. It seemed to him much like any other room of the kind. Then he realized with a start that he was not alone. It was a long room, over-furnished in the late Victorian style, with a multitude of ornamentation and the peculiar air of everything being screwed in its place which this kind of room seems to acquire. As his glance swept round he was suddenly and acutely conscious of having seen it all before. Yes, of course, he had stood on this very spot and seen . . . why, great heavens! It is she! His heart missed a beat as he stared unashamedly at the girl by the window. The very posture, the colour of her hair, and the DRESS! His dream woman, come to life. Silly, his mind told him; that sort of thing only happens in old-fashioned novels. Yet here she was, alive and, yes, actually smiling. He was conscious that he was staring at her in a manner that would have been rude if it had not been ludicrous. What he did not know was that the girl was just as astonished, just as tongue-tied as himself.

She was the first to answer. Composing her features into a conventional smile, she said: "I think you must be Mr. Blair. My uncle is expecting you, he will not be long. Won't you sit down?"

Michael sank obediently into a chair, he wasn't able to speak yet. Mad thoughts were still racing through his mind and he was probing the chaos in an endeavour to extract a certain memory, one of those 'tip of the tongue' thoughts that are so elusively near the surface and yet so tantalizingly hidden. If only he could get some association of ideas to work on, some incident, trivial in itself but which would make this provoking whirl of his thoughts resolve itself into some well-remembered shape. At length he obtained control and managed to formulate his thanks.

They began to talk, though Michael retained little recollec-

60

tion of what they talked about. His mind was still busy taking in the piquant situation. Presently Mr. Bainbridge came bustling in, full of apologies for being late.

Apologies, ye gods! thought Michael as he rose to shake hands. Why couldn't the old chap have stayed away for the whole afternoon. The girl rose and came across the room. "I'll leave you two together to talk business," she smiled at him as she passed.

"Oh, I'm sorry," exclaimed Bainbridge. "I see you have introduced yourselves. Ann, this is Mr. Blair. Mr. Blair, this is my niece, Miss Rochester. So now you know each other."

"Indeed we do," said Michael feelingly. Then he added, "I hope we shall meet again." Ann had reached the door. As she opened it she smiled back at him. It might have meant anything.

When Ann had gone Michael came to the point and put his proposal concerning the land. He found the older man a ready seller and the transaction could easily have been settled that afternoon leaving only the conveyance to be carried out by the lawyers. But now he had an incentive to protract matters. He made a point about getting his partner's agreement to the details they agreed upon and emphasized several clauses which might require later discussion. He made a further appointment for a subsequent afternoon. There was no sign of Ann as his host showed him to the door.

Still with a feeling of amazement he made his way home on foot. This girl whom he had just met, no, whom he had always known, filled his thoughts to the exclusion of all else. He knew her, knew all her moods, she was the embodiment of so much that was in the back of his mind. In a moment he knew that he loved her. That rather shocked him who had held that love should be approached with due deference and sincerity.

He made a point of arriving early for his second appointment and was rewarded by finding Ann in the drawing room again. She looked charming and fresh as she stood to receive him by the window she affected. Michael noted with a thrill that there was a chair drawn up near her own. It had not been there the last time.

"I've been looking forward to seeing you again," he said, as he seated himself at her request.

"Thank you, that is very nice of you," smiled Ann. "Uncle will be here in a moment."

Michael devoutly hoped that Uncle would forget the appointment entirely. There was a book lying at Ann's elbow.

"May I ask what you are reading?"

She told him and they found they had at least this interest in common. They went on to other subjects. As they talked, his busy mind photographed her appearance. This Ann of his, curious how he could not help regarding her possessively, she was so exactly as she ought to be. That lovely fair hair, so finely spun that it might be made of silk, those grey-blue eyes that held so much merriment yet which seemed to conceal something deep and sincere that lay behind them. Her voice was charmingly modulated and she expressed herself well. Michael found her a trifle confused after a while and then he realized that he had been staring at her hungrily and cursed himself for his lack of self-control. Something prompted him to ask her if she painted. "I am sure you do," he said, "I feel it in my bones."

"Then your bones must ache intolerably," she retorted. "I play with water colours sometimes but wild horses wouldn't make me display my efforts. Now it is my turn to ask questions. What about you, what do you do to amuse yourself?"

Michael thought for a moment. "Work, I suppose. I can't really say that I make much of a showing at golf or bridge. I have never given them the time to become more than a mere rabbit."

"You ought to have a hobby, you know," she observed, gazing reflectively at him. "It is such a nice way of working off the petty annoyances that one collects during the day. When I feel cross I work it off on my sketching block and paint box. You've no idea how satisfying it can be to daub lurid sketches into which all one's inhibitions can be worked off. At least it saves one working them out on the family. But perhaps you are not married."

Michael shook his head emphatically. "No I am not married."

Ann couldn't help laughing. "You seem so positive about it one feels you must have been running away from marriage. Doesn't the idea attract you at all?"

"Why—yes it does. For the first time in my life I do want to get married."

Ann's eyes lighted up with interest. "But this is splendid. I am sure she is very charming."

"She?" echoed Michael.

"The girl you are going to marry."

"But there isn't any girl, I—er—mean, I . . ."

"What a shame to tease you, too bad. All right, we will let you off the inquisition."

"But you've got it all wrong. There isn't any she."

Ann regarded him with a puzzled expression. "What do you mean? You say that for the first time in your life you want to get married and then you say there isn't anyone you want to get married to." Then suddenly she coloured. "I say, I am awfully sorry, I am being terribly impertinent. I really don't know how I got on to this subject. Let's talk about something else."

"But please, there is nothing—at least there isn't any—oh, what a muddle we are getting into."

They both burst into laughter at this and it was Michael who changed the subject by asking her to meet him the following day at an exhibition of water colours where a friend of his was exhibiting. Ann had just time to murmur a quick acceptance when the door opened and Bainbridge entered, profuse with apologies as usual. Michael blessed him for his habit of being late.

It was at this stage of his friendship with Ann that Michael began to take stock of himself. For the first time he saw his own position from a viewpoint external to himself. He told himself that it was his love for Ann that enabled him to do this. He saw himself as he really was: eager, headstrong, yet failing to use his driving force, drifting with the current instead of steering his own course. He had let the old inspiration die of inanition because of that tragic event at the opening of his career. In an attempt to shut out that memory he had shut himself up in his shell like a clam. And he had tried to replace the expenditure of nervous energy with alcohol as a fuel.

It wasn't a very imposing picture that his mind conjured up. He had succeeded in business it is true, succeeded beyond his most sanguine expectations. But what had that brought him? The chance to use work as a sort of dope, something into which he could throw his whole interest and energies. And that bottle, he would have to get the better of that before he asked Ann to marry him. He vowed that he would set about that task at once. A thousand times he set himself wondering whether Ann in any way felt about him as he did about her. The doubt fidgeted him and made him morose and optimistic by turns.

He made the proposal even sooner than he had intended. And it was Ann who, unwittingly, brought it about. He took her for a run in his car one fine Sunday. They stopped for a picnic at the foot of a long sloping hill. When they had finished Ann proposed a climb. Arrived at the top they stood for a while and gazed at that wonderful vision of checker-board England which a hilltop gives and which never fails to attract. It was a clear day after recent rain, and the fields looked so tiny yet so compact and clear cut. Michael felt a sudden dismay as he likened the scene to that other hilltop near his home whence he had descended to meet Vera, an incident he would have given years of his life to eradicate. Driving the thought from his mind he turned to Ann. Flushed from the exertion of climbing she looked lovely. There was a strong wind blowing and her fair hair was drawn out from her head like golden flames. She turned shining eyes to his.

"Race you down the hill," she cried to him above the roar of the wind.

"Let's go," he answered, meeting her enthusiasm with a boyish zest he had not felt for years.

Together they tore down the hill but soon his long legs gave him the lead. Breathless, they pulled up at the bottom where

Ann subsided on to the grass. Michael sat down too, facing her. He thought she had never looked so beautiful.

They talked for a while and then Ann indicated where the red roofs of a house peeped out of the trees that surrounded it.

"Doesn't that glimpse of a house look delightful," she observed. "Those chimneys are Elizabethan; I am sure it must be a lovely place."

Michael rolled over to look. "Yes, it does." After a long look he rolled back again. "You know, I have always had a desire to build my own house, to plan it all from the beginning."

Ann, hugging her knees, glanced quickly down at him. "Have you really? How funny, so have I. I used to draw pictures of a little house when I was so high. It was always the same house."

Michael sat up suddenly. "Good lord, so did I. I've just remembered it. My mother was always chaffing me about my little house. And I was always rubbing it out and doing it again."

Michael's face suddenly became tense. "Ann, I am going to call you Ann whether you like it or not. Do you know that I had the most extraordinary sensation when I first saw you, in that room. I felt that I had done it all before. That I had met you before, in that very room."

The flushed look fled from Ann's cheeks, and she went pale as ivory. "Michael, what does it mean? I had exactly the same feeling," she whispered, scarcely heeding that she had used his Christian name.

"Ann, I can't keep it to myself any longer, I must tell you. I love you, I have loved you ever since I can remember. When I first saw you I knew at once that it was you who had been in my heart for always. Ann darling, I don't know what it all means but I do know that I need you, you are part of my life."

Ann recovered her composure with the instinctive defence of a woman. "But Michael, I . . . you . . . we have only known each other, almost a matter of days. We mustn't take this strange experience to mean more than just something in our minds."

"Ann darling, it does mean much more than that, to me at any rate. I don't know anything about these things, but I do know I want you, I want you to marry me." He possessed himself of one of her hands. To their sharpened sensibilities the contact sent an electric shock through them both. It seemed to quicken their extra-sensory perception for, as they afterwards agreed on comparing notes, they suddenly became aware of some deep and intangible feeling between them. An age-old memory it seemed, but it was real to both of them; formless, ephemeral, it yet held meaning for it held them together with links that neither could sever if they would. It gave them both a sense of at-one-ment with each other. For a while neither of them spoke; words would have been an anti-climax to that satisfying experience.

"Ann," Michael breathed the word presently. She turned to face him and he saw her eyes widen and the heavenly blue of the sky was reflected in them. There was something else there, too, something for which his heart had longed. A little cry escaped from him as he drew her to him, a cry in which all the pent-up emotion of the years seemed to be freed. Her face came up to meet his. Strangely enough, while his senses were dancing as their lips met, he could not resist the thought that sometime, somewhere, he had kissed her before.

Presently, when the first ecstasy was over, he held her back, the better to devour her with his eyes. Her eyes were laughing now, shining with merriment. There were tears there, too, tears of happiness. He saw them and insisted on kissing them away. A new life filled him. He told himself ecstatically that here was the point where he would start life afresh. He would, he must. With this dear responsibility he would challenge the fates themselves.

They settled down to exchange those dear confidences which lovers adore. Treading upon air they explored each other's minds with that deliciously intimate freedom that lovers know in the first rapture of the new relationship. Happily they began to unearth those treasures which a kindly fate buries anew for each pair of customers to discover and claim as unique. Always they came back to the queer circumstances of their first meeting.

"It sounds awfully silly, I know," confessed Ann, "but I have always had a queer feeling that I should meet the man I was to marry just like that. I have lived in that house for years because my parents both died while I was still at school, and that funny old drawing room that Uncle won't have altered has always been bound up in that thought of mine."

"I have heard that it is due to split personality or something," Michael remarked.

She laughed out at that and he caught the infection. "Oh, Michael," she bubbled, "don't go and spoil it all. Here we have a lovely dream about our love being made in heaven and you go and say it is a split something or other."

His arm went about her again. "Darling, I apologize. Let's call it dual personality, that sounds much better. When shall we get married?"

"But this is so sudden," laughed Ann. She began to pat her hair into place. With a glance at the slanting sun she made some remark about getting home.

"I suppose we must," observed Michael regretfully. "There always seems to be an end to lovely things like today."

They came to the car. As Michael closed the door on her he leant forward. "Let's build that house, shall we? Our dream house?"

Ann's eyes lit up. "Oh, Michael," she breathed, "what a heavenly idea. I never thought it could possibly come true."

Michael smiled happily. "Lots of things are going to come true. I wonder whether my wish to kiss you again will come true?"

It came true.

Events in the lives of Michael and Ann now began to move rapidly. Once more he felt himself impelled by an abundant energy. Ann's uncle made no demur at losing his niece, who was also his housekeeper, and soon the two of them were swept into the preparations for the wedding. Michael scarcely ever glanced at the whisky bottle. There was so much to do, not a little of it 'buying things' for Ann. Never had she known such an orgy of spending. She protested but it had no effect. Michael was wound up and she realized that she would have to let him run down or bust. There was a house to be found until the dream house could be built and to add to Michael's burdens Davis announced that he was going into a new line of business and that in the future he would be only a sleeping partner, leaving all the work to Michael. This of course meant an increase in his income at a time when he most needed it, but it also meant longer hours and greater strain.

He took Ann down to Belchester and was happy to see how his parents both fell in love with her. She loved the old mill and insisted on visiting all the haunts of his childhood. Robert Blair was filled with pride at his son's success and was reconciled to his absence from the family business. The thought of his marriage to this charming girl made him more expansive than ever. Mary Blair was a little overcome at the prospect of a grand wedding but managed to conceal her apprehensions.

The marriage took place from the Bainbridge home and there was only one dark moment. It was while father and son were waiting for Ann to come down in her going-away dress that Robert Blair put his foot in it.

"You mind old Josh Clark's daughter?" he asked his son, "you and she were a bit friendly like at one time, ye did well by waiting."

Michael's face grew dark. Like a wave recoiling out of the past the old phantoms rose into his consciousness from the depths of his subconscious mind. He had managed to subdue them one way and another till he had almost forgotten their existence. Now the old moodiness sat brooding on his brow again and he muttered something unintelligible. Fortunately Ann's arrival and the consequent stir put an end to any more of the older man's confidences, and Michael took advantage of the general excitement to get a grip of himself. Nevertheless, for him, the sun shone a little less brightly as the pair emerged out onto the drive.

* * * * *

Here we must leave this second glimpse of Michael's earthly life and slip forward once more into the future. We see the two again, sitting on a lawn. It is the garden of the dream house and if you would know what manner of house it was you may let your imagination take you over it. It was as you would like to find it. It had been a glorious experience, engendered by a delightful fusion of ideas and carried out regardless of anything but the notions of its designers. Some of the designs came from Ann's own hand and she spent many happy hours searching for the best that eager markets could provide. As the two bent together over the plans they would laugh with sheer happiness in their task and their joy would be spiced ever and ever again by the queer feeling of having done it all before. Ann used to assert that they had lived before as man and wife and built just such a house as this, while Michael pointed out that unless they had reincarnated as rapidly as the Dalai Lama they could hardly have lived in such a modern dwelling as this.

The harmony of the garden scene is heightened by the sound of children's voices, for Michael and Ann have been married nine years now. The children come running across the lawn. First there is Stephanie, she is seven and like her father. Then there is Peter, aged five, and in every way a little Ann. There is a prodigious noise and much laughter from mother and children. Father is buried behind a newspaper and Stephanie cannot resist the temptation to hurl herself at that vast expanse of inviting scrunchy paper. She does so and there is a deathly silence, surmounted with a heavy scowl. The huge joke has fallen flat, quite flat. Frowning slightly Ann gave a quick look at Michael, then gathered up her children and with an admonition that 'Daddy is tired,' shepherded them back to the house.

Yes, there is no doubt about it, daddy is tired. One glance at the lines round the eyes that we haven't noticed before, and the fact that he has just behaved like a sulky child in front of his children, shows us that something is definitely wrong. For some reason or other he has slid back into that choked-up condition he was in before he got married. It began to come back when things went wrong in the business. The novelty of the plastic goods which the firm manufactured was wearing off, while opposition firms had managed to produce similar goods at cut rates without infringing the patent. The money market was flighty and that affected sales. Michael had rashly invested reserve capital in new machinery in an endeavour to cope with lower prices and there was little available for a rainy day. The golden stream of profits that had promised never to run dry was now a mere unsatisfactory trickle.

With an impatient exclamation Michael got up from his chair, shook off the depression that held him and went in to change for dinner. When the meal was over he retired with Ann to his study, a delightfully informal little room where they each had a comfortable easy chair in front of the fire. Parker, efficient as always, served the coffee, and having placed the decanter within Michael's reach, bade them good-night.

"Good-night Parker," Michael looked at the decanter with a hint of desperation in his eyes. He knew that he was one of those unfortunate individuals who cannot hold liquor, and the old craving was getting hold of him again. He knew he ought to tell Parker not to put the decanter so tantalizingly within his reach. But he had always loved to display his manliness before Ann and the thought of such an admission as the order would entail, defeated that intention. He made a determined effort to keep his mind off it. He tried to carry on a cheerful conversation with her but without much success. Ann seemed to have retired within herself tonight. He knew that she was growing aloof from him owing to his tantrums, and the thought increased his irritation. He had read all of the paper that he wanted to and his novel bored him. He smoked hard for a while.

"We shall have to get that bathroom leak seen to," remarked Ann in a flat voice, without looking up from the small garment she was mending. "It has soaked through the plaster in the hall ceiling."

"I'll ring up Foster's tomorrow," said Michael. "You know, I am sure we made a mistake putting it over on that side."

"I expect you are right," murmured Ann absent-mindedly, "what a pity we cannot rub out bits of our house and do them again. Like the children do with theirs."

Michael looked up wearily. Time was when he would have responded to that queer mind-memory they shared. But now somehow it had ceased to enliven and he relegated the thought of it to the limbo of things forgotten. There were so many other things to occupy his mind, unpleasant things. There was silence for a while and then he twisted in his chair and took hold of the decanter. He had been feeling foul all day, he told himself after Ann had gone to bed. It was late when he followed her.

Ann was full of a dream she had had when she came down to breakfast the next morning. "I dreamt that I was floating down the banisters, my feet scarcely touching the ground. Then I floated out of the door and into the most amazing garden, much larger and with much finer flowers than ours. There was someone with me, not you, but an older man, I think, I couldn't see him because he always seemed to stand just behind my shoulder." She looked at Michael over her coffee cup. Michael grunted.

But Ann was not to be put off. "Then this man took me to the most wonderful places you can possibly imagine. The colouring was beautiful . . . you don't seem interested, darling."

Michael managed a sort of a smile. "I'm not much taken with dreams myself."

"Oh, but darling, this was a super dream. I do wish I could tell you how really lovely it was. I sometimes wonder whether we don't travel about on the other side when we are alseep."

Michael hooted. "The other side of what?"

"Oh, you know. There must be some place you go to when you die."

"A damp cloud perhaps," scoffed Michael. He had never thought much about such faraway things. Then he put down the paper and got up to leave the table. He was feeling pretty grim. Digestion all wrong. He felt he must really see a doctor. But he didn't.

It soon became evident that Ann was noticing things. His hand would shake and he sometimes knocked things over with undue carelessness. And the thought of it, his Ann, drove him madder still. She had begged him to see a doctor about his indigestion but he refused, saying that he had got some pills from the chemist which were doing him good. He began to drink away from home, at his club or in the company of friends. Ann insisted on a change and got a cousin to come and look after the children while they went to the East Coast. That made things a little better and the worn look left his face.

71

Besides, the decanter wasn't so get-at-able as it had been. They seemed to get back nearer to the intimacy of the old days. But they had to come home some time.

Back at his office Michael discovered that things had become more serious than ever. If something were not done the firm might have to close down. In desperation he wrote Davis to come and see him.

Davis came, and was typically blunt. The two men had words. In the end they decided there would have to be a complete reorganization. Cut profits meant cut staff, cut wages, cut salaries, cut everything except his own office hours. It almost meant starting again. Michael looked at his bankbook when Davis had gone. He was shocked to see how low his total resources were; all his savings were in the business. And there were bills, and the house wanted so much doing to it. He might have to give up the house; the thought gave him a horrid feeling. So much had gone into that house, it stood for so much. He gave a sigh as he made up his mind to go home and tell Ann the truth and take her advice about it. He drove his car into the garage and then walked across to the house where Parker had a note for him. In it Ann told him that her uncle had had a stroke and she was going to spend the night there. The note ended with some instructions about Peter's cough mixture.

With a gesture of annoyance Michael went into the study and called for a drink. It was too bad that this had to happen on this night of all nights, just when he needed Ann more than ever before. He glanced uncertainly at the telephone. But he realized that he could give no cogent reason for Ann's immediate return. He refilled his glass. Then he sank moodily into his chair. By dinner time he was feeling better and had an exciting half-hour with the children. Dinner sobered him up a bit, then he settled down for the evening. He tried to concentrate on a new novel but his head was aching. He took some aspirin and that made it worse. Parker came in and said good-night, leaving the decanter in its usual place. He had another drink and that made him feel a bit better. Somewhere in the back of his mind there was an idea, a novel method of using plastics. If only he could get at it, there might be money in it. Dash it all, it was on the tip of his tongue. Perhaps

72

another drink would clear his head. He had several and before long was in a hazed condition, half irritably conscious, half pleasantly dreamy. Presently he slept.

He awoke suddenly, startlingly aware that something was wrong. There was a queer background of sound that had no part in his normal life, a smell . . . But the movement of his head upset his precariously balanced equilibrium, and a wave of nausea swept over him. He struggled to his feet, groping uncertainly, aware of a terrible urgency for action but quite incapable of steering any sort of course. Movement became a hazard, uncontrollable, with the damnable thought that he could not convey his desires to his errant limbs; he was helpless. He saw a thin wisp of smoke curling under the door and knew what it meant. "Oh God, let me get to that door," he cried, and knew that his lips could only stutter at the words. He lurched towards the door but a french window swayed stupidly in his path. He wrenched at the catch, cursing under his breath because his fingers were all thumbs. At last it opened and a rush of cold air swept over his hot face, driving the last ounce of sense from his head.

When he came to he was in bed. He realized that it was in a hospital for he could see a trailer in a corner of the room laden with surgical equipment. Presently a nurse tiptoed into the room and bent over him. She smiled when she saw that he was awake. "Feeling better?" she asked.

Michael shook his head feebly. He was feeling anything but better. The nurse gave him some medicine which tasted foul but pulled him together a bit. He knew there was something wrong because there was more than a hangover on his mind. He tried to arrange his thoughts but the bemused mind refused to cooperate. If he so much as moved his head it gave him a swimming sensation that was unbearable, so he lay very still. "Tell me," he murmured to the nurse when she came near him again.

She looked steadily at him for a moment before replying. "You were found lying by the side of the road last night and so you were brought here."

Michael struggled to remember. "Was there a fire somewhere . . . ?"

The nurse hesitated. She had no orders to tell him the truth.

"Yes I believe there was. But don't you worry about that. Try and get to sleep again, it will do you good." She busied herself with his pillows.

But Michael would not be denied. There was a note of urgency in his voice as he demanded further details. The nurse persisted in her efforts to put him off but he threatened to get out of bed if she did not answer his questions. At length she went off to call the house physician. In a few moments she returned with a small man in glasses who peered keenly at him. "Well, what is it?" he asked.

"I want to know what happened last night. I am Michael Blair. Why am I here?"

"What can you recollect of last night?" parried the doctor.

Michael frowned in his effort to recall some coherent picture of the events of the night. "I—I had a good deal to drink, I think. I had had a very worrying day at the office. Then I fell asleep and . . . after that it's all hazy. I think there was a fire somewhere, something burning. I can remember opening a window and feeling the cold air rush in." He gazed anxiously up at the doctor. "Tell me, was there a fire? My house . . . ?"

The doctor nodded. "Yes." Then he added, "It was burnt down." Michael's eyes widened. His brain reeling, he struggled into a sitting position. The uncompromising face of the doctor told him there was more to come, the worst.

"The children . . . ?" he managed to whisper.

The doctor's eyes flickered uncertainly for a moment. "You must be brave, Mr. Blair. From what I hear I do not think they suffered at all. The servants managed to get out at the back of the house but the children must have been overcome by the smoke while they were still asleep."

Michael collapsed upon the pillow. The doctor's voice receded into the distance while a great black cloud of horror swept in upon him. Everything seemed to be falling away from him. The news was too awful, too stunning for him to contemplate. He felt a prick in his arm and merciful oblivion overcame him.

*　　*　　*　　*　　*

We must leave Michael and Ann to face the shock and horror of that tragic time alone. Ann, too, collapsed, and

74

nearly three weeks elapsed till they met again. She made no recriminations against him, and the children were never discussed. But something vital was gone out of her; there was no longer any light in her eyes. There seemed to be nothing left between them, and they lived separate lives, having nothing in common with that other existence. The children were gone, the old home was gone, both felt that they had been cut adrift. Michael's eyes were haunted by the memory of what had occurred. The lines deepened on his features showing the extent of the suffering he was enduring. But to the outside world he maintained a cold hard exterior, seemingly devoid of feeling.

Meeting only on the plane of conventional existence, the two made some attempt, as time went on, to pick up the threads of life where they could find them. They took a house far from the old one and Ann engaged in some welfare work while Michael threw himself, with a fierce despairing energy, into the reorganization of the business. They both received a surprising measure of kindness from their friends who seemed genuinely anxious to help them to forget the past and start life afresh. Some of these spoke earnestly of possible reunion with the children in some future life. Michael's reaction was negative for he held no assurance of the continuity of existence. Ann clung to a belief that her darlings must be alive somewhere. She put the matter to the vicar when he called to condole. His attitude was not very helpful. It did nothing to assuage that terrible ache which tore her heart like a cancer. A lukewarm admonition to have faith was a poor solace for a heart that yearned to know the truth. But she thought it would be wrong to try and get in touch with them. In the end she relied on those precious memories tight locked in her heart. Over these she stood guard like a stricken beast at bay.

Ann's uncle died at this time and she made that an excuse for not accompanying Michael down to Belchester. But when the matter was settled she agreed to accompany him for the weekend. On a wild wet morning they set out in the car. Michael was driving while she sat beside him, a still, lifeless figure. Occasionally he gave a sidelong glance in her direction, wondering how he could set about the task of breaking down the wall that had arisen between them. They had left the

75

crowded streets and were speeding along a broad empty ribbon of road. As the hedge-bordered highway widened its arms to engulf the onrushing car, Michael's senses became lulled by the rhythm, and it seemed to him that they were rushing away from the past into a future where reunion with his beloved might become possible. Once at the old mill. . . .

A blurr of brown and yellow swept out of a hidden turning. Michael wrenched at the wheel as he had a glimpse of an enormous coach leaping at his hood. There was a crash and the front of the car seemed to concertina. He gazed at it foolishly, then felt himself sinking back into an abyss of noise and darkness.

Chapter 3

TRANSITION

When Michael came to he found himself lying at the side of the road on the grass verge. Cautiously he raised himself to a sitting position, felt himself carefully over and was surprised to find he had escaped without broken bones or bruises. He struggled to his feet and swayed a little, for he felt rather giddy. Only to be expected, he told himself, after a shock like that. Lucky to be no worse. Then suddenly he gave a gasp as he thought of Ann. Where was Ann? He looked round and saw a number of people gathered by the wreckage. He was about to approach them when to his intense joy Ann detached herself from the crowd and came towards him. She looked shaken, but in spite of that the set look was gone from her features and there was a vestige of a smile on her lips.

"Oh, my darling, thank God you are safe!" he cried as he seized her hands and drew her to him.

Presently he remembered the accident. "I say," he ejaculated, smitten with dismay at the thought, "I ought to go and see if I can help."

"You need not worry, sir," said a voice at his elbow. They both turned to see a man in rough dark clothes who had the appearance of being a gardener. His voice had a rough country burr to it.

"The injured are all being looked after," the stranger continued. "The ambulances will be here any minute now. In the meantime perhaps you'd like to sit down a while in my cottage." He jerked his head across the road.

Michael followed his glance and saw what in the hectic moments following the accident had escaped his notice: a neat little cottage with a little gem of a front garden, ablaze with flowers. It was strange to find such a picture bordering an arterial road, still within the confines of Greater London. Michael presumed that its natural beauty had saved it from the greedy maw of the development companies. He turned to Ann, who was obviously impressed.

"It certainly looks most inviting," he remarked, "but I expect that policeman there will want to question us at any moment and see my licence and so on."

"You needn't worry about that, sir," said the gardener, "he's a friend of mine and I'll see he sends word over to the cottage when he's ready for you. You can see he's got his hands full."

And indeed it was clear that the constable had no leisure for the moment, for he was busy superintending the extrication of the injured from the wreckage.

The gardener looked enquiringly at Ann. "I would be so grateful," she said, with a wan little smile. "I feel that I simply can't stand up much longer."

That settled it. With his arm about her Michael started across the road, intending to come back when he had seen her comfortably settled. The gardener led the way up the path of the minute front garden. Ann gave a little sniff of delight as the mingled scents of the flowers assailed her.

"How lovely," she exclaimed. "I am feeling better already."

The gardener opened the door and stood, respectfully, waiting for them to enter.

"'Tis but a poor little place, ma'am," he ventured. But Ann cut him short.

"Oh, no, it is a gem of a place. I think it is the dearest little cottage I have ever seen. I am sure happy people must live in it." Michael looked at her as if he could hardly believe his ears. The old note of happiness was in her voice, something he had not heard since . . .

"To be sure, ma'am, they be all happy people that does come here, but like most on us they don't always know it."

As Ann passed into the cottage she gave a little cry of joy and called over her shoulder. "Oh, Michael darling, look, how perfect it is."

Looking past her, Michael could see, framed in the open back doorway of the cottage, an exquisite glimpse of another flower garden even more colourful than the front. Evidently, he thought, this gardener was an expert as well as a flower lover. He followed Ann through into the back garden and the gardener came after, shutting the door softly behind him. Then he went forward to point out some of the prize blooms.

"You must win a lot of prizes at the shows with these gorgeous specimens," said Ann.

"Nay, ma'am, I have no time for they flower shows. I just grow them because I like flowers, and besides, they have their uses."

Ann wondered, from the way he spoke, whether he had some private sorrow and did not pursue the subject. The owner of the cottage indicated two garden chairs set in a shady corner of the tiny lawn, and then suggested a cup of tea. Ann smiled gratefully. "I can't think of anything I should like better," she replied, "if it won't be putting you to a great deal of trouble."

The gardener made a little gesture of dissent. "'Tis no trouble, and after all you have been through you'll be needing it." He started off to the cottage door, pausing at the entrance. "It won't take but a minute, the kettle is on the hob."

"Isn't he a perfect dear!" exclaimed Ann, when he had gone. Then she added, thoughtfully, "I can't help thinking I have seen him somewhere before. I suppose he must be a type."

"How do you feel now, darling?" asked Michael. He was still at a loss to account for the change in Ann and feared at any moment the old moodiness might return.

Ann gave a hesitating little laugh. "Well, I must say I did feel a bit rotten when I first got out of the car. The bodywork was all scrunched up and it was rather a business getting out. But as soon as I got into this dear little garden I began to feel better. In fact, I feel all right now." She smiled confidently at him.

"It's the reaction," he commented. "I would take it easy for a bit. It must have shaken our nerves up a lot."

"And you, darling? Are you all right?"

Michael gave a little laugh. "I'm the luckiest chap alive to escape from behind the wheel of that car with not even a bruise." Then he got to his feet. "I am going back to see what has happened. You'll be all right here." He turned to find the gardener barring the way with a tea tray.

"I would have just a cup before you go sir. Set you up, like. I had just a look before I brought the tea, and the injured is all away. There is no need for hurry." The man almost edged Michael back to his seat. Then he set a wooden tray down on the rough garden table. It was covered with a snowy cloth and held a brown china teapot with cups and saucers bearing a considerable load of gilt and floral decoration. Also there was a plate of delicious looking scones and a homemade cake.

"I guess that's proper, that is," said the man, smiling with justifiable pride as he straightened himself. "Lady friend of mine next door fixed it up when she heard what had happened."

"That really is marvellous," said Ann. "Perfectly sweet of her. I must go and thank her presently."

"What about the policeman?" asked Michael as he helped himself to a scone.

"He had all your particulars," said the gardener, "you left your pocketbook in the car. He is taking down the details now."

Michael slapped his empty pocket. "By jove, so I have. Must have dropped out in the accident, and no wonder."

"He'll keep it safe for you, sir. No need to worry about that." Then he added, "You'll excuse me if I leave you to your teas. I have a few things to attend to and then I'll be back."

"Of course," smiled Ann. "I am afraid we must have interrupted your work."

The gardener gave a little shake of his head as he started off up the path towards the back of the garden. He walked with the calm purpose and lack of haste that is characteristic of the true rustic. Ann smiled gratefully after him. Perhaps it was the tea but she began to feel more mentally at ease than at any time since the loss of her children.

"Michael," she said presently, "I feel there is something I

80

must get off my chest. I am afraid I wasn't very considerate of you since . . . you know."

"Ann dear, I deserved it all," he protested. "I just can't bear even to think about it. I don't expect you to forgive me."

She put her hand over his. "Perhaps I do know now, what you have suffered. I was wrong to shut myself up like that; it did neither of us any good. Let us face up to it, now, before we leave this garden. We can't go on living like we are."

There was a catch in Michael's voice as he answered. "Ann dearest, you give me new heart. Perhaps if I tried all the rest of my life I might begin to make restitution to you. I will try. But to them. . . ." He buried his face in his hands.

"We have both of us got debts to pay, Michael dear. God will help us to pay them."

"If I only knew the way," sighed Michael.

"Let's leave the working out of things to Him. Let's just do the Christian thing by each other and leave the rest to God."

"And that means. . . . ?"

She gripped his hand a little tighter. "We start again where we left off before. . . ."

He nodded, his heart too full for words. The emotion passed, to be succeeded by a deep calm. There was something peaceful about this garden which sublimated all thoughts of struggle.

Michael looked at his wrist. "Dash it," he exclaimed, "lost my watch too." Then he looked up to see the gardener returning. "Afraid we shall have to tear ourselves away," he explained, "we have promised to be at Belchester by lunch time. Can you tell me the time?"

"I don't rightly know, sir, but I reckon you have plenty of time."

Ann rose to her feet. "But we have already trespassed too much on your kindness."

The man smiled with pleasure.

"Is there a telephone anywhere near here?" asked Michael, becoming business-like; "we must have a taxi sent."

"I don't think you'll find one around here," said the man slowly.

"What do you mean?" exclaimed Michael, turning towards

the cottage. Then he gave a gasp of wonder. The cottage had vanished. Slowly he turned his face towards the gardener, his face turning pale with a sudden fear.

"What has happened?" he demanded.

As the man made no answer Michael, exasperated, took a pace forward. "But I must go. There is nothing wrong with me. I don't know what conjuring trick you have done with that cottage but I tell you I must go, and my wife too."

The gardener's features did not change but he made the tiniest gesture of acquiescence.

Michael turned to Ann for support. Then he saw that she was staring intently at the gardener, and there was a look of horror in her eyes. She put her hand to her mouth as if to stifle a scream.

"My God!" cried Michael roughly, "what is the matter? Tell me, Ann. Who is this man?" He put his hand arrestingly on her shoulder.

But Ann seemed unaware of the movement. Instead she found herself staring at the gardener with a great question in her eyes.

Very gravely he bent his head to her.

When he looked up again there was another, more eager question hovering for expression. He gave a little smile of understanding and his eyes gave the slightest directional movement. A glad light shone from Ann's face. They understood one another.

Michael glared desperately from one to the other. "What is it?" he cried, "why are you two . . . ?"

Ann faced her husband, her features transfigured with a new joy. The gardener walked away once more.

"Don't you understand, Michael?" He shook his head irritably.

"Darling." Ann took his arm confidently in hers. "You must prepare yourself for a shock. But a nice one this time."

"I don't understand you," he said angrily, shaking his arm free. "What is all this tomfoolery about?"

"Darling, we have . . . passed over . . . died."

Alarm, wonder, dismay, fear, incredulity chased each other

across Michael's features as he gazed at his wife. Despite a growing sense of uneasiness he forced a laugh.

"Ann, my dear, that is not a nice thing to joke about, especially at a time like this when we ought to be thanking God we have escaped."

Ann shook her head in determined fashion. "Michael dear, we haven't escaped. You have got to realize what has happened. I have just remembered who that gardener is."

"Well, who?"

"Someone we, that is you and I, knew long ago. I just had a glimpse . . . oh darling, I am not crazy. You must believe me."

"My very dearest. I wouldn't disbelieve you for the world. But I understand. This accident has shaken you and no wonder."

"Michael. Where is the cottage?"

He looked round him. "We must have wandered away from it. This is the next door garden. I expect the old chap plays this trick on lots of people. He is probably hidden in those bushes now, laughing at us."

Ann shook her head sadly. Once more she took possession of her beloved's arm. "Supposing it were true, would it worry you very much?"

He gave a rueful little laugh. "Well, I don't know. I suppose it wouldn't matter when it was all over. But there is a lot of unpleasantness to get over first. Dying isn't a nice business." Then he gave himself a little shake as if to free himself from unpleasant thoughts. "Let's think of something cheerful. Where's that old chap got to?"

Suddenly Ann's body stiffened. "Hark," she cried, and there was a great exultation in her voice. From far, far in the distance there came the sound of children's voices, echoing in happy laughter through the woods. Presently a man came into sight, tall and good-looking, but dressed in some queer outlandish clothes that puzzled Michael. In each hand he led a child, who, as soon as they caught sight of Ann, let go and raced towards her with loud cries of "Mummy, Mummy!"

Michael stood watching the children, his eyes staring. Then

he uttered a great cry of desolation and stared round him like a hunted animal. Without another glance at the reunion he plunged into the bushes and was gone.

By this time Ann had her arms full of a confused mass of arms and legs, and her voice, hovering between laughter and tears, was murmuring the lovely intimate things that bind baby hearts with a great mother-love. The stranger stood by looking on with the proud and happy smile of one who has accomplished his heart's desire.

The first fine rapture over, Ann stood to face the man who had brought the children. She answered his smile with her own. "You are . . . the gardener?"

He bowed, with an old-world grace. "A mere garment that I put on and off, as need dictates. My name is Tendor, at your service."

Ann's face lit up momentarily at the mention of the name. "It is all at the back of my mind but I just can't get it clear. We know each other, don't we?"

"We are well acquainted. Memory of that time, that other life, is overclouded by more recent events. Do not let that distress you, the mists will clear in time."

"And you have been looking after my babes?" she asked him softly.

"It has been my joy and privilege to watch over them since they came here. Nay, do not let yourself be distressed any longer over that tragic occurrence. All recollection of it has been smoothed away from their little minds. They have come on a visit to the seaside. The place where they live is in a beautiful bay and presently you shall join them there. But first there is the dust and stain of travel to remove, and your loved one, he will need your help for a little while."

"Michael!" exclaimed Ann, glancing anxiously about her. "Where is he? In my selfish joy I had forgotten him. I thought I . . ."

"Have no fear," put in Tendor reassuringly. "He has gone off to face himself. It is sometimes better so. When we have injured ourselves we cannot bear to look at the self-inflicted wounds. But they are healthy wounds and will heal in time; presently he will realize that."

84

"Poor Michael," murmured Ann. She was watching the children who, with the inconsequence of childhood, had begun to play among the flowers. "If you are satisfied that my darlings are well looked after, I would like to stay and help Michael. I feel that he needs me."

"He does need you. He needs the help that you alone can give. It will be an errand of mercy if you will stay with him for awhile; it will mean much to him."

"Look, Peter is sleepy. Do you think I ought to take him home?"

Tendor looked compassionately at her. "Not if you are going to stay with Michael. They live on a plane which he cannot reach at the moment; their real home is not here. And if you accompany them it will be difficult for you to return to your Michael. It is not sleep that overcomes Peter and makes him yawn: it is the heaviness of this region. It will vanish when he gets back to the atmosphere he is accustomed to. You will have to choose—now."

Ann's heart smote her as she looked longingly at the children. With all her heart she longed to go with them; the agony of separation had been so acute she felt she could never face a second parting. She wanted to see where they lived, to put them to bed and tuck them up once more, to fill her mind with all the little worries that once had made her life.

Tendor seemed to sense the drift of her thoughts, for he said: "The time will not be long and you will be able to visit the children after a little while. It will be good for them if you decide not to accompany them yet awhile. You will be inclined to influence them with the earthly point of view and you will have brought over certain psychic effects which it would be well to rid yourself of before you enter fully into their lives."

With a little sigh Ann shut out the entrancing vision. Besides, Michael needed her; she could not desert him now. She looked anxiously round but there was no sign of him. When the moment came she had to make all sorts of promises to the children, promises which she could not comprehend the meaning of or have any notion how to fulfil. But as Tendor stood approvingly by she supposed that it was all right. She stood and watched the little trio as they wound their way out of sight and it seemed to her that they pulled the heart out of her body, so intense was the desire to fly after them. With a little sob she turned to see that Michael had emerged onto the garden path, where he stood in the shadow of a tree, an expression of such bitterness on his features that she ran to him with a little cry of sympathy. He took her in his arms and for a while they stood, mutually comforting each other.

Presently they began to stroll through the woods that lay at the back of the garden. From these they emerged into a valley that was bathed in bright light, yet was not excessively hot. There was a peace and stillness everywhere that gave them rest, and a quality in the air that infused new vitality into their bodies. Already the wounds in their souls began to heal. They did not know that this valley was created especially for the reception of such as themselves and that the atmosphere was adjusted to heal and strengthen those who had just made the transition. It was purposely located near the Earth plane so that the spirits in flight from mortal life could easily attain it and endure the light which they found there. Obeying a common impulse they sought a place in the long soft grass and there for a while they slept.

Ann was the first to awake. When she had assured herself of the reality of the events which had preceded her sleep, she awoke Michael. He woke easily and naturally, feeling immensely refreshed. He was more inclined to treat their adventure as a dream until Ann indicated the absence of his watch and note case. For a long while he sat, absorbing anew the terrific fact of his survival. Presently, responding to the inflow of vitality, he got up and suggested exploring the valley. There was much to see for it was broad and contained streams and meadows, small woods and outcrops of rock. There were innumerable wild flowers of a sort they had not seen before. They found the going easy and experienced no sense of tiredness while, owing to the absence of sun, there was no night or day, no sense of time. Occasionally they saw other people in the distance but no one came near to disturb them. During this period they were both conscious of a new orientation of their relationship. No longer were they two individuals united by marriage, but two halves of one self and the new unity was one which transcended anything they had experienced on Earth. They learned much about each other that they had not known before and the new knowledge threw a revealing light upon themselves. Added to these experiences were scraps of an old memory that obtruded at intervals, building up a picture of some far-off existence which they could not yet recall in full.

Michael still held a lively memory of his earthly existence though the details of his passing were beginning to grow rather dim. Sometimes he would look a little wistfully at his wrist, feeling it strange to be no longer a slave to the ticking of a watch. At other times he would pinch himself or study his skin closely just to reassure himself that he still had a body that was tangible and alive.

"I really don't know what I expected when I died," he said. "But I certainly never anticipated anything like this. Just look at that pastureland, those rolling downs, why it might be Hampshire on a lovely summer's day."

"Oh, Michael, no, not even dear old England could be so beautiful as this. Look at that colouring, look at the texture of the grass. You never saw anything like that on Earth."

"I suppose not," admitted Michael. "Look at those birds, aren't they brilliant. I wonder what they are."

"And there's a different feeling in the air, a lightness. I never felt so well on Earth."

Michael paused to gaze up at the high tops of the long ranges of hills that enclosed the valley. "I say, I wish we could climb up those hills, then we could really see what this place is like."

"Do you think we ought to?" Ann demurred. "Somehow I feel that we ought to stay down here till someone fetches us."

"Do you think anybody will? Who was that chap who came with the children?"

Ann faced her husband. "It was the gardener, Michael."

Michael frowned. "The gardener? Why he was a different sort of chap altogether."

"Yes, I know. But I guessed that he had only put on that

disguise in order to meet us. We would never have gone with him into the cottage if he had appeared like something out of a Grecian history book. Michael dear, he is part of this queer back-memory we are recovering. I don't quite understand it all yet, but he confirmed that we had known him long ago. He said that it would all come back gradually, as the Earth influence faded out of our minds."

"Curious. I should like to meet him again. I wonder why he is interested in us."

"We are indebted to him for looking after the children anyway."

Michael looked longingly up at the hilltops again. They were bathed in even more generous light than this radiant valley. "I do wish we could get up there. I am no climber but I've a good mind to have a try." He turned to her, the old excitement glinting in his eyes. "Coming with me?"

After a dubious look round Ann followed him. His long legs made light of the ground and soon they were mounting the lower slopes. Ann found it difficult to keep up with him; he had always been able to beat her at climbing. She struggled up and up and at length was on the point of crying to him to wait for her when a sudden thought struck her. Throughout their exploration neither of them had felt the slightest sensation of tiredness, why should she find this sudden difficulty? Was there not some way of overcoming it? Again came that haunting memory. Surely the answer was on the tip of her tongue? She looked up at Michael away above her and still going strong. She set her teeth. "I won't let him beat me," she muttered to herself. Using all her efforts she set out once more. To her astonishment she found herself moving through the air in a gentle graceful leap that carried her some twenty yards.

"Gracious!" she exclaimed, astonished. Then she gathered her strength and leaped again. This time she was carried on beyond Michael, exceeding his distance by about fifteen yards. She heard his gasp of astonishment as she passed him.

"Hey there! What are you playing at? How did you manage to leap that far?" His voice was imperious.

Ann's laugh came echoing back to him. "Watch me," she

called to him. Like a bird poised for flight she took off in another gliding leap. Now she was fifty yards from him.

Michael's eyes flashed with excitement. "I say, that's grand. How do you do it?" he yelled up to her.

"Try it," she called back. "Just take a jump as if you were going to do a long-jump and set your mind to where you want to land."

Eagerly as a schoolboy trying a new stunt, Michael did as she told him. After a few stumbling leaps he became as proficient as she though he swore that he could not emulate her grace. Ann could alight as gently as a bird.

"I say, there are points about this place. Come on, let's leap to the top. It is still a devil of a long way off."

Together they leaped onwards in the novel manner, covering tremendous distances at each effort. But the summit seemed as far off as ever. This time it was Michael who showed signs of exhaustion while Ann seemed to be gaining vigour at each leap. Now it was Michael's turn to set his teeth. He was determined to gain his objective. Ann slowed her pace to suit his leaps which were growing less in vigour and distance. She watched him with growing alarm.

With a final effort he shot forward another hundred yards. Then he stumbled and fell, and began to roll down the hill, striving helplessly to stem his rapid descent. Ann screamed as she saw him bumping downward, like a leaf blown by the wind. Then she thought suddenly of her friend Tendor. Scarcely was his name on her lips when he stood, urbane and smiling, at her side. "Michael!" she gasped, then as she noted the confidence in his smile she relaxed.

"There is no need to be alarmed," he remarked. "Our young-friend-in-a-hurry had to be taught a lesson in a way that would sink into his impetuous nature. He will come to no harm. Elemental spirits, invisible to your eyes, have borne him up and will prevent him from hurting himself."

Taking Ann's hand in his he travelled with her down to the bottom of the hill, accomplishing the journey in less time than it takes to tell. There they found a rueful Michael sitting by the side of the path. He looked accusingly at Tendor as if that kindly soul had been responsible for his downfall, "I don't know what has happened," he said, "it seemed as if some bruiser landed me one on the chin. I just went down like a ninepin."

Tendor nodded sympathetically. "You became a victim of the forces of nature. You challenged them by insisting on continuing your climb when your instinct should have told you that it was unwise. That is one way in which lessons are taught over here. But you will find that you are not hurt."

Michael got up and brushed the dust off his clothes. He seemed to be none the worse; only his pride had been hurt. He looked up as Tendor began to speak again.

"I have come to show you the way to a temporary residence we have prepared for you. Come, give me your hands."

Taking each by the hand Tendor caused the three of them to move through the air as if in a flash, so swiftly that neither Michael nor Ann was aware of the route they took. But when they alighted both gave a gasp of surprise. For there in front of them was their own house as they had built it on Earth. With exclamations of pleased surprise they entered and commenced to examine it in detail. It was in wonderful order; evidently someone had cared for it in their absence. At length, their inspection over, they joined Tendor in the drawing room. Here they shot so many questions at him that he held up his hand in laughing protest.

"We can do many things over here," he said, "but we have not yet mastered the art of answering a dozen questions in one sentence. Now sit down and I will explain. First of all you must realize that everything that you create on Earth, of whatever its nature, has its counterpart in this world. The more strength of mind and the more care you lavish, the greater the love you pour out on your work, the finer will be the etheric result. This house is the exact counterpart of your earthly home and because you lavished so much affection on that task you will find that you have an enduring result over here."

Michael looked puzzled. "But," he protested, "our house was burned down. How can it still be here?"

"If every destructive effort on the part of spirits in human bodies were to have its effect over here we should indeed be at your mercy. No effort on the part of incarnate spirits could destroy this house. It is built of more enduring material than physical matter."

Michael turned interested eyes upon this strange being who spoke so convincingly. He saw a man of apparently the early thirties, yet he wore the air of a man full in years and experience. He was good-looking but with a classical turn to his features which gave him an aspect of more than mere comeliness. The eyes were strange and compelling yet held tenderness and compassion. Michael felt he would trust this man anywhere.

"Why did you say this was a temporary home?" asked Ann.

Tendor made a slightly evasive gesture. "I will not try and explain at the moment why it is so, but you built this house on more than one spiritual plane. There is a prototype of this house on a still higher plane than this. You two built it and lived in it many, many years ago. It is the original which inspired the construction of your earthly home and therefore of this one. Someday you will both return to it to dwell there in happiness with your children."

There was a silence as the two thought tensely of the joy that awaited them. Presently Ann gave a little exclamation and bent to examine the skirt of her dress. "What dreadful material," she murmured with a vexed note in her voice.

Tendor followed her glance, then he smiled understandingly. "I told you everything on Earth has its counterpart over here. That dress you are wearing is a copy of the one you wore at the time of your transition, the etheric counterpart. But such materials are not designed for spiritual needs and soon it will fall to pieces."

Ann gave a little cry of dismay. "But look, it is falling to pieces already. And my wardrobe upstairs is empty."

"We removed the etheric copies of your earthly dresses as they will be of no use to you. We ventured to provide some robes for you both which may serve until you can design your own. You will find them now in your own rooms."

Excited, Ann ran off to inspect her new garments, Michael following more slowly.

"Oh!" exclaimed Ann when she saw what lay upon the bed, "what pretty material." She held up the robe, surveyed it, draped it upon her person, then surveyed herself critically in the glass. Like a pleased child she hurried after Michael into his dressing room where she pounced upon the garments that lay upon the little bed there.

Michael dear," she cooed, "you are going to look as lovely as one of the Wise Men from the East."

"What do you mean?" he demanded, taking the robe from her and glaring at it distastefully. "I refuse to wear fancy dress. . . ."

"Michael dear, do look what is happening to your old suit." She took hold of his sleeve and the material gave way as if it had been rotted by acid. Michael looked disgustedly at his coat, then he glanced at Ann's dress, and crowed at her.

"First remove the beam from your own eye," he quoted, "look at your own frock."

And truly Ann's dress was disintegrating before her eyes. With an exclamation she seized her new robe and flew off to the bathroom whence there soon came the sound of running water and sundry splashings.

Presently she reappeared and Michael had to admit that the robe suited her to perfection. It seemed to him to shine as if it reflected a light. The colouring was that of pale rose and the texture of the material that of the bloom of a peach. She had never looked so lovely and he told her so. Giving him a pleased smile and a kiss as a reward she sat down at her glass to complete her toilet while Michael scurried into the bathroom to gain cover before the complete dissolution of his suit.

Being ready first, Ann rejoined Tendor in the drawing room to receive his compliments on her appearance.

"Thank you for studying my taste so well," she observed with a pleased smile.

"I am glad you like our efforts."

"The robe is lovely and terribly flattering. I shall never want to wear any other sort of clothes again."

"Earth clothes are certainly unbecoming. But then you have to consider climatic and atmospheric conditions which do not trouble us here. You will not find that your robe flatters you; that is not an effect of spirit robes. They have rather the effect of showing people up in their true colours, they show you as you really are."

"I believe you mean that," observed Ann solemnly. Then with a quick glance at the door, she added, "I want to know something, before Michael comes back. Why did Michael fall down that hill? And why did he feel so distressed when climbing while I never felt fitter?"

Tendor looked at her thoughtfully. He seemed to be gauging her capacity to receive a confidence. "My child," he began, "I call you that with reason, for I have stood in the place of parent to you and Michael since longer than you will ever remember. God has made certain plans for the advancement of each one of us, He has given us the opportunity to learn how to live, how to discover certain things about ourselves. To enable us to accomplish this He has given us the priceless gift of free will. If we use it right, good and well, we gain our reward without undue effort. But if we are foolish enough to let its attraction blind us to its reality, if we are foolish enough to ignore the call of the Spirit within us and submit to the demands of the outer self, then we find that we have lost our way and have to retrace our steps and set right that which we have upset. Pain and suffering come from pandering to the outer self; the pathway that would injure the spirit is hedged with thorns in order to give both warning and guidance. The Great Spirit ordains the way we shall go by means of His law of Cause and Effect, 'As ye sow so shall ye reap.' Michael has not yet learned to control that turbulent self of his; it is more apt to control *him*. In his incarnation he ignored the warnings, he walked away from Perfection instead of towards it. And those who break the laws of Spirit on Earth and are unable to restore the balance within the span of their incarnation, have to balance the account over here, else they can advance no further. But the opportunities here are not so profound as on Earth; the process is more lengthy and more difficult.

"Once Michael learns not to cramp his spirit with the thought of self and begins to open his consciousness to the abundant flow of riches, to the power and love and wisdom which God is waiting to pour into him, then he will advance rapidly, for he is a powerful spirit and potentially able to accomplish much. But he cannot be allowed to have recourse to that power until he has learned how to direct it.

93

"Had he reached the top of that hill with you he would have seen something of the glory of a world into which, at the moment, he may not enter. And because his condition is not yet such as will allow him to remain there, he would suffer through discontent at having to remain outside its borders. Through his mistakes on Earth he has caused his etheric body to harden and become denser than yours. That is why he felt the strain of the rarer atmosphere as you approached the top of the hill. First the lesson to learn, then comes the reward."

"Then you mean that we . . . ?"

"You, my child, have not the same debts to pay, your *karma,* or indebtedness, will not take long to repay. But Michael will have to enter a sphere of action where he can learn the lessons he needs. The keynote of this world of Spirit is service, and it is through service that he will find his feet again."

"Poor darling, I am beginning to think I might have helped him more."

Tendor shook his head. "Some day you will understand more fully why these things have happened. You helped him a great deal; your love for him and the restraint you exercised during a time of great stress, have smoothed over some of his difficulties already. They have enabled him to come here with you instead of making his entry into this world at a lower level than this."

"Has he got to go to a lower place then?"

"Every wrong that a spirit does has to be righted, to the last fraction, before he can rise to a higher state of consciousness. That is the law. And as the rectification is made through service it is only natural that the place of the greatest opportunity will be on a lower standard of life."

"And he has got to go . . . alone?" she whispered, with agony in her eyes.

Tendor bent his head gravely. "He will make his way better alone. He will return to you all the sooner."

The door opened and Michael entered, slightly self-conscious in his new robes. Ann noted that he did not shine very brightly; there was as much difference between her robes and his as between her own and those of Tendor. But they became him and he looked more handsome than she had ever seen him before.

"Are all the men over here dressed like this?" he asked.

"Nearly all," said Tendor. "But I know of a few die-hards who insist on having their old earth clothes, so we have to oblige them and help them to patch them up. One old gentleman insisted on going about in patched earth clothes until his own tailor came over and was prevailed upon to make the old chap a suit. But you will find that you are quite in the fashion."

"You don't seem to be very populated just round here," remarked Michael, looking out of the window.

"There is a reason for that," explained Tendor, "it is usual not to crowd round those who have just come over. You will have plenty of visitors when you wish to receive them."

"How will they know we want visitors?" asked Ann, with a view to possible social obligations in front of her.

"They will find out for themselves. We have no conventions of the earthly kind over here. Visitors just tune in to your wavelength and thus they find whether you would like to see them or not. But it is seldom that people do refuse visitors, so you see there is no difficulty about entertaining."

Michael had been looking curiously at Tendor while he was speaking. "I say, excuse me, but I seem to be getting your thoughts at the same time as you speak. They seem to explain a great deal more than you say in words. Is it so or is it my imagination? I never thought I could thought-read."

Tendor smiled. "Oh yes you can. That is the way we communicate with each other over here, but to newcomers we usually speak in the language they are accustomed to until they learn to do as we do. It comes easily enough."

"I'll say it does. Why I get your meaning absolutely and much quicker than if I had to think what you were saying."

Here Tendor rose to go. "I have other work to do," he explained. "Enjoy yourselves and be happy together." His eyes twinkled as he added, "The nature spirits will prevent you from coming to any harm. But should you want any service of me just will me to be here, and I will come." With a parting smile he walked a few steps and then faded into thin air.

Michael watched in amazement. "I say, that's clever. I must learn to do that. I wonder how it's done." He turned back into the house. "Ann, isn't this all rather wonderful? This chap Tendor who has attached himself to us is just like the Genie from Aladdin. Rub the lamp and he appears. I wonder who he is?"

"I expect most fairy stories are memories of this life," observed Ann.

"By Jove, yes, I suppose they are." He laughed heartily. "Fancy fairy stories being true. Fancy going into the club and talking about what we have found here. I should be asked to resign and dubbed a lunatic. What a mess it all is."

Ann went upstairs to her room and Michael wandered about the lower floor making a further inspection. He stood and gazed reflectively at the study from the doorway. Here it was that he had made that terrible blunder. He felt grateful that he had shed much of his emotional capacity with his mortal body. He could stand detached from the event and appraise it in its true light now. He began to see how the events of his life led up to that happening. A sudden thought struck him and he went across to the dining room. There in a cupboard sure enough, was the whisky decanter. Going to the window he hurled the bottle as far as he could. It shivered into a thousand fragments. He felt better after that.

Michael and Ann spent happy times together in their old home. They explored the neighbourhood, bathed in the lake or read again some of their books, copies of which were arranged in the study just as they were in the material house. Once or twice visitors called and they had long and interesting discussions concerning their new environment. It was instructive, they found, to get viewpoints other than their own. Some of these visits they returned, finding much to interest them in the variety of the dwellings these people built for themselves or which they occupied as communities. Ann was delighted to discover that her ability to paint had increased beyond all her hopes while Michael too, began to sketch and tried to transfer some semblance of the brilliant colouring of their surroundings onto paper. In common with their new friends they attended art schools where the technique necessary for the altered conditions of the Spirit World was taught to newcomers. Going further afield they discovered that in this new life all the unfulfilled longings of earth life can be fulfilled in the widest sense. Those who longed in vain for children are given the care of them here; those whose lives have kept them apart from the animals they love can have charge of them here; those who desire to express themselves through art can find endless opportunities to develop such talents in the many planes of the Spirit World. There are hobbies and pursuits in abundance. But Michael and Ann noticed that eventually most people respond to the urge to devote their labours and their talents to some form of service. It is generally accepted that this is the quickest way to progress and to assuage that constant urge to fulfil oneself which animates the whole Spirit life.

Presently Ann began to realize that the time must soon come for Michael to start his new work. She viewed the approaching separation with mixed feelings. With all her heart she longed to accompany him and aid him to overcome the difficulties that apparently awaited his conquest, but equally was she drawn in that other direction, to the side of her children. She longed to accomplish the impossible and cut herself in two.

But first occurred an event which had a profound influence upon their outlook. Spirits released from mortal life must, at a certain stage in their career, face the record of their progress. Michael and Ann had learned from their friends about this experience which some of them had already undergone. After discussing the matter with Tendor they expressed their readiness to go and face their own records.

Tendor expressed his pleasure at this. "I must warn you," he said, "that it is not a matter to be lightly undertaken. Much will depend upon how you view what you see and how you respond to the lessons that you will find you have already learned. But if you can face it and endure to witness the actions of your real self, then you will have made a great stride forward."

At the appointed time Tendor appeared and using his great power, transported the three of them to the grounds of a building which, on closer inspection, had some semblance to the type of small cinema used on Earth as a news theatre. There was a piece of sculpture over the entrance representing Justice bearing her scales in one hand and a flaming torch in the other. There was a small entrance hall where an attendant showed Michael and Ann into the dim interior. Here, in the semi-darkness, Tendor bade them a temporary farewell.

"It will be better," he observed, "if you face yourselves alone." The two younger spirits were fully conscious by now of the place that Tendor occupied in their lives, but never till this moment had they been so aware of the deep love that he held for them. As he stood there his whole being seemed to radiate love and power which conveyed anew his selfless devotion to them. With his going out of that somewhat depressing atmosphere some of the light and warmth of their lives seemed to go with him.

Here the attendant intimated that their ways lay apart. He showed each of them into a separate compartment. Michael exchanged one last glance of apprehension with Ann before the door of her compartment closed upon her, then he followed the attendant into the one reserved for him. He took his place in the single seat the room contained and settled down to await that which he must see and endure. He scarcely knew what to expect and his mind was filled with trepidation as he thought back along the eventful lines of his career as far as he could remember it. He was beginning to remember vaguely that he had lived before his earthly incarnation but the details were indistinct. He knew too that Tendor was closely bound up in that pre-existence.

In this gloomy interior the temperature was decidedly lower than outside, or so it seemed to Michael. The room was quite empty, he was alone with his thoughts, ranging along the past. He began to pray for strength to face its revelations. It seemed to him as he waited there that he was cut off from all life except that of himself, and . . . something else he did not know what. The loneliness of it was appalling. It was a relief when a light ray shone out and illumined a screen at one end of the long room. The picture assumed movement and resolved itself into a form of symbolism quite impossible to translate into words. The mind of Spirit however found it easier to attach a meaning to the symbols and Michael began to comprehend that he was witnessing the early life he had led prior to his incarnation. Deeply interested, he watched what he knew to be the unfoldment of his and Ann's entry into the realm of experience. He watched the course of their lives until he came to the time where they embarked upon the construction of their Spirit house. From then onwards he grasped the inner meaning of all the major events which built up the sequence of their existence. Little events of seemingly small importance now assumed a larger character by reason of their effect on himself or others. He became aware of a voice that provided a running commentary on the portrayal. At first he thought it must be part of the picture, an accompanying sound track, giving in thought-language the symbology of the events. The voice was critical beyond measure; he began to wonder who this person was who took it upon himself to judge him in such forthright terms. No one had warned him of this. His heart smote him suddenly. The awesome thought came to him that this might be some manifestation of God's anger with him. All the old doubts and fears of orthodoxy which he had imbibed in his youth sprang up once more to point an accusing finger at him. Was this the day of judgment? he asked himself. Was this portrayal of his life, which had now embarked upon his incarnate existence, a prelude to a judgment which would determine his future existence? Orthodoxy dies hard.

Then he remembered that others had faced this inquisition and they seemed none the worse for it. He summoned his courage and faced the picturization of his past in a spirit of determination. To his astonishment he discovered that the voice was not external to himself but was coming from within his own being. As if following his train of thought the voice broke in, "It is the voice of Conscience, your Conscience." The thought stunned him. It was not God who spoke, not some superior accusing Being judging him from the lofty seat of omnipotence. It was his own Self, his own Spirit speaking from the highest pinnacle of its consciousness, from the pure essence of his being. He shrank into his seat as the terrible significance of the fact burst into his mind. Never in his wildest dreams had he visioned his ultimate judge as himself. Not the easy-going, self-excusing mind of the human makeup, but the most implacable part of his being, the all-knowing Centre of his own super-consciousness. How could he excuse himself before the terrible indictment of his own Spirit?

In no uncertain terms the voice went on to emphasize his weaknesses and to mark the points in his career where his foolishness or ignorance or lack of effort had influenced other lives to their detriment. Again it would indicate where his failure to seize an opportunity had resulted in some unhappy consequence to others, which he might have aided them to avoid had he been less wrapped up in himself. The voice was fair; it gave him credit for what he had accomplished. But there was no doubt which way the scales of justice were balanced. As he watched, fascinated by the logic of it all, he was swept by the first waves of a remorse that was to hold his Spirit in subjection until it was redeemed by his own effort. He witnessed the crossing of the threads of Vera's life and his own; he saw the tragic effect of their foolishness; he experienced, vicariously, the full horror of what she went through consequent on the most tragic mistake of all. He witnessed the effects of the shock received by his own emotional and mental makeup on the news of her death. He saw how the light of his own Spirit tried to burn through into his outer consciousness, striving to bring spiritual wisdom and enlightenment into his outer mind. But the outer mind was too wrapped up in the clamorous needs of self; the light could not pierce the fog of self induced by his attitude of pride and resentment. The wretchedness that influenced his whole outlook was a cloak of self-accusation woven from injury to his own ego rather than regret born of altruism. So the surface of his mind was grimed and the light of the Spirit shut out. He lived solely in his outer mind. He viewed life entirely from the material aspect, not with the clarifying vision of Spirit. The toxin of alcohol took further effect, coarsening the film over his mind. Excess of alcohol engendered fungoid growths in his etheric body, throwing off a mental poison that affected all but his strongest thoughts. He saw his relations with his beloved Ann strained to the breaking point. He saw himself, while retaining

100

the outer semblance of gentility, gradually sink into a condition bordering on bestiality. His very soul cried out as he watched the creeping tongues of flame weaving ever nearer to the sleeping forms of his children. . . .

*   *   *   *   *

He came to with Tendor bending over him. It was a warm bright light that met his opening eyes and the scene around him was one of quiet beauty. He was in the open air beside a path that wound along a hillside. Behind Tendor was Ann, wearing a look of deep concern. She came to his side.

"Did you see what I saw?" he asked her. He gave her the chief events of the portrayal he had just witnessed.

She nodded. "Yes, it was something like that. Only I saw my faults emphasized, I saw where I might have helped you and did not. Oh, Michael, forgive me."

"I didn't deserve your help, my dear. Heavens, what a showing up. I'll never be able to live all that down."

"Oh yes you will," broke in Tendor. "You stood up to it very well."

Michael sat up and gazed at him in wonder. "I couldn't see much in my picture to be congratulated about."

"Do not be too concerned about that. What matters is that you stood it far longer than most people do. You will reap the benefit for your stoicism."

Michael looked puzzled. "How is that?"

"The scroll of life is allowed to unfold and to display the full *karma* of the individual, that is to say the aggregate of the debit balance which the individual has built up. Some spirits are of course unable to endure a tenth of the vision of their *karma* at one sitting. When they can endure no more they cry 'enough.' Then they set to work and start redressing the adverse balance through service. When they are sufficiently advanced they come back and see the rest of the portrayal. You were fortunate, you managed to endure nearly to the end."

"How can I set all that right? There is so much of it."

"On that you must enquire within. I have no mandate to

ordain what will suffice to wipe the slate clean for you. You must enquire within, of that voice you heard which is the manifestation of God within you."

Michael dropped his face into his hands, bowed down with the thought of what had confronted him. "How can I ever efface all that. Oh the misery of that poor girl, the sufferings that she endured. And oh Tendor! She is enduring still, she is paying the price still for taking her own life. That part of the picture had no ending, it stopped abruptly. I feel that somewhere, somehow, she is suffering still."

An arm stole round his shoulder and a voice whispered in his ear. "My darling, my love will shield and help you. Let us face this together. I am so filled with remorse. I see now how I could have helped you, but I was so filled with thoughts of myself, so horrified by the terrible temptation that was assailing you, that I failed you, I shut you out of my life when I ought to have loved you all the more. Something tells me that you will have a chance to help Vera. Let us keep our minds on that thought."

Tendor left the two to a truer and deeper reconciliation than either had dreamed possible. Out of the chaos of disaster was born the shining promise of wisdom, as is the way with suffering. The knowledge gave each of them new courage and new confidence.

Conscious that Michael had recovered his vitality, Tendor drew him near again and said: "It will be well if we walk home the short way, over the hill. It is not far."

So they set out and as they went Tendor discoursed on the ramifications of this great law of Cause and Effect which is the way of education of the individual. The path wound along the side of the hill and as they drew near the top of the ridge a stranger came in sight. He was a handsome man with a fine quality of expression. Ann thought his eyes the most wonderful she had ever seen. As he came close he stopped and greeted them. It was noticeable that Tendor greeted him with great respect.

The stranger turned to Michael and Ann; he had a beautiful voice. "I gather that you have both been witnessing the scroll of your lives and that you have accepted the implications of what you have seen."

Michael and Ann were rather nonplussed as no mention had been made of their recent experience. Michael gathered that he must be some person of importance who had means of ascertaining these things. As his eyes met the gaze of that other he felt the flow of love coming from him in which all his own misery and heartache seemed to be dissolved. The flame in his heart was kindled anew till it glowed in a glorious response.

"Many have made mistakes," continued the Stranger, "it is from those mistakes that you learn to use your birthright. Never forget that you are children of God. You have learned now never to judge others, for to judge others is to judge God. How shall you judge a spirit whose life is hidden in God? Thus no one shall judge you, but yourself. You have learned now that it is foolish to identify your being with the body instead of the Spirit. Let your mind dwell now on the importance of your relationship to God rather than on the importance of yourself as a unit. Creep back to the Father and say that you have erred, and feel once more the arms of Love that enfold your atom in His Greatness where it belongs, and again go out to learn to be great instead of small, to be powerful instead of weak, to be generous instead of selfish, to think in terms of the Oneness of mankind and not from your own little point of view. Go forward stronger and stronger in the Consciousness of God in you and spurn the old great lie of Self. Be at peace, all is well."

Michael and Ann saw Him raise His hand in benediction and felt the flow of power that streamed from it. They bowed their heads in reverence. When they looked up the Stranger had gone. Conscious that something of unusual nature had occurred, they looked to Tendor for an explanation.

"Do you know who that was?" he asked.

They shook their heads.

"It was the Master Himself."

Incredulity showed in two pairs of eyes. "How can that be? The Master must be a very Glorious Being."

"The Master is indeed a very Glorious Being, but He is also a very humble Being. He is your elder brother for both you and He are children of the Great Spirit. You must realize that He loves to manifest in many planes of existence in such a way as to be seen clearly on that plane. So He showed Himself now as you are, that you may know Him as someone very near to you. He does not wish to be regarded as a distant Deity. You will find that He manifests in many guises and in many places. He does not always declare Himself for it is the message that counts, not the messenger; that has always been His theme."

Overcome by the wonder of that contact Michael and Ann walked slowly on to their home. As they neared the house Michael stopped suddenly and faced Tendor.

"Tendor!" he cried, his eyes ablaze. "I will dare anything now. I have seen His face and He asked me to work for Him. The wonder of that will see me through anything. Tell me when and where I can start."

"I am glad you feel that," said Tendor quietly. "Let that light burn steadfastly, my son, for there is much for you to accomplish. Have no fear, the way will open for you."

With his usual impetuosity Michael could scarcely wait to commence his self-imposed task. He felt bursting with the desire to serve, to make restitution for all the mistakes he had made. But time and time again Tendor would impose restraint.

"The time is not yet come," he would say, "there is a time for all things and nowhere is that truer than in these realms."

To add to Michael's impatience was the fact that he found himself more and more unable to face the bright light and so was forced to remain indoors. Tendor explained that he was growing a new body, and with it a new pair of eyes, that would enable him to function and experience more efficiently on the lower plane whither he was bound on his errand of service. Ann noted that his robes were growing less effulgent, less able to reflect the light within. It was because his makeup was being reduced in vibration that he found it hurtful to expose himself for any length of time to the full effect of the Cosmic rays which lit up this sphere.

Presently they had a visitor whom they had not met before.

He was a young man, extremely good-looking, with the gentle reflective eyes of the thinker. He gave the name of John. Ann puzzled her mind to account for a strange likeness to Michael in his features. Michael had no brothers that she knew of. She mentioned the resemblance to Tendor at his next visit.

"So you noticed that," he remarked. "I sent that young man to you. He certainly has a resemblance to Michael for he is Michael's son."

Michael gave a gasp of astonishment while Ann's eyes opened in wonder.

"She whom you knew as Vera on the Earth plane came over to this side carrying your child, Michael."

"Yes, but the child was never born," said Michael.

"Oh yes it was," insisted Tendor. "You remember my telling you that everything in your Earth life has its counterpart over here. You cannot destroy Spirit. The young life that could not accomplish a physical birth, was born into this world instead. Vera took her own life and in doing so destroyed the physical body she was building for your child. But she could not destroy the spirit which was already in possession."

"B-but I don't understand," put in Ann, "that was a baby. This is a man."

"You must not think that we have no sort of time over here," said the guide. "We are not bound by clocks but we too have a cycle of events. Babies who pass into this realm at an early age go on growing until they reach the age of about thirty of your Earth years. Then they stop, they do not grow old. Old people who make the transition grow younger until they reach the same age, the ideal age. But they do not necessarily rejuvenate at once. That is one of the rewards for the acquisition of the necessary wisdom.

An exclamation from Michael caused the other two to turn in his direction. "If only we had known some of this on Earth," he cried, with resentment in his voice. "If only people realized what the consequences of their actions were, they would be more careful, they just wouldn't do these things. If I could only go back and shout these truths from the housetops."

There was a wistful smile on Tendor's face as he replied. "We all say that when we first come back from Earth. You can see now in what depths of ignorance they are living. But if you retain that desire to go back and try to get the truth through, then an opportunity will assuredly open up for you to do so. But remember that things are not so bad as they appear at first; everything is in the hands of a wise and all-loving Father who does not make mistakes. It is we who make the mistakes. No suffering is in vain, no one can lose through suffering."

"How can that be?" cried Michael. "Are we then to sit like a lot of prigs and watch our friends suffering and make little or no attempt to help them?" Then, ashamed of his outburst, he added, "But I expect you are right, you always are."

"Do not mistake my meaning," said Tendor patiently. "You must never forget that God is all-love and all-sympathy and He would not have you other than like Him. With the Earth in its present state of ignorance, incarnating souls have to take it as they find it; they have to plunge into the depths to learn its lessons. But remember that the deeper you plunge, the greater the experience, the greater the gain as a result of that experience. God does not wish the Earth to remain in such a condition, and when the World becomes lifted up in consciousness and realizes the state it is in, then its inhabitants will learn to live in harmony and mutual service as we do here. When the present fear and acquisitiveness have been overcome, the experiences will be far less painful, suffering will be far less acute, and incarnating spirits will be able to learn their lessons vicariously to a large extent. Take your own case. Had you passed through life like a butterfly, tasting here and there the little sweetnesses, would you be able to hold the depth of sympathy that you do now? Would you have benefited if someone had cut short your incarnation so that you did not experience your share of suffering?"

"No, I am beginning to see what you mean now. But if the world gives better opportunities for experience in its present state of ignorance, why alter it?"

"God does not wish His children to suffer for the sake of suffering. It is they who establish the causes and therefore have to endure the results. God's wish is to wipe out the ignorance on Earth so that mortals can gain experience without plunging so deeply into suffering. But he would not help mankind by doing that as a single act of His Will. It was the cruelty of man to man, the greediness of man to acquire, born of his inherent desire to experience, that has closed down the channels of inspiration in so many human bodies, and made the earthly mind responsive only to material and intellectual considerations. But Earth will not always be the dense material realm you found it. The redemptive process is going on through the efforts of spirits who incarnate and suffer, and thereby learn the needs of Earth, from which springs a desire to help it. Earth is changing its condition; at present it is at the bottom bend in its curve, but soon it will begin to rise on the ever upward cycle. It is the work of such as you, who have realized its need, to help it to rise and even in some cases to incarnate once more in order the more effectively to bring it aid."

"You speak as if Earth were a living creature," said Michael.

"Of course Earth is alive, it is indeed a living entity. You must get rid of that idea that man, in his conceit, has proclaimed, that only man has a soul. Remember that every atom in the Universe, whether it be rock or gas or human flesh, is animated by God's power, without which it would disintegrate. Every planet, every star, is a huge reservoir for God's power which holds it together and gives it life. And in the millions of years of its existence that living, animating power acquires characteristics which are implanted by the spirits which incarnate upon that planet. The civilization which man has built up on Earth is reflected upon its atmosphere, and has given it certain characteristics, the chief of which is suffering. And as it is man who has imprinted that character so only man can redeem that imprint."

"Shall we incarnate again?" asked Ann.

"I have no authority to answer that question. It will be for you to decide, in communion with your inner selves." He rose to depart, and soon Michael and Ann were alone.

Hardly had Tendor left than a visitor arrived. In the sensitive way of the Spirit World they became aware in their minds of the near approach of a stranger and sent out instant thoughts of welcome. A moment later John entered the door and gave them greeting in his quaint reserved way. "May the Great Spirit bless all in this house," he murmured as he crossed the threshold. "It is good of you to receive me," he added, his face lighting up in a smile for Ann.

Michael got up and went to the boy and put his hands upon his shoulders. "I have just learned the truth about our relationship. You are aware that you are my son?"

John bowed his head slightly. "Tendor, the learned, has told me."

"This is wonderful," said Ann, impulsively, "why didn't you tell us before?"

"I do not quite know what it means to be a son," he said, simply, "you see I have not experienced Earth life."

Michael was having a little struggle with himself as he observed: "I am sorry, that was my fault to a large extent. I have learned since I came over what it means to cut short an incarnation."

John's eyes lit up. "That is kind of you to say that. You see I know so little, I haven't much experience. But I have reached Earth through you, and I am grateful for that. It is nice to think that I have accomplished that much."

Michael made a despairing gesture. "That madness which Vera and I gave way to, it seems to follow one everywhere."

"Please do not distress yourself on my account," begged John. "I am really very happy. I am able to study a lot and so remedy my ignorance about incarnation on Earth. Perhaps it is for the best. If I had stayed there I might have made many mistakes and acquired a lot of *karma*. Then I might not have been able to do the work I love so much."

"What is that?" enquired Ann.

"I am entrusted with the reception and care of some of the animals who come over here from Earth, especially those who are hastened out of their incarnations by mankind. My particular areas are set apart for animals slaughtered for food; I have a sort of hospital for them. Poor creatures, they are so terrified that sometimes we can do nothing with them, and they tear madly round our fields trying to escape from a fate which no longer threatens them."

108

Ann gave a cry of dismay. "Poor darlings, how they must suffer. What terrible things we humans did on Earth without knowing what we were doing."

"I have been studying in the colleges here about the effect of eating meat as the earth people do. Fear nearly always fills the minds of the animals about to die and it has a direct effect on the flesh of their bodies; it creates poisonous toxins which permeate the flesh and are so subtle that the human system has difficulty in eliminating them. So they accumulate until they find expression in the form of disease. I find it all very interesting. I am told that having only touched the fringe of human existence I have established a link that animals understand, yet I have not acquired the subconscious fear that divides animals from men. So we get on very well together."

"Well, that's another lesson I have learned," commented Michael. "By the way . . . have you . . . er . . . contacted your mother?"

A pathetic little smile hovered on John's lips as he shook his head. "No, I have tried, but I cannot get there. I am told that she is learning new lessons and must not be disturbed. But we are to meet again some day. Oh how I long for that time. There is so much that I long to learn from her about incarnate life. Perhaps you could teach me?" he asked wistfully, addressing Michael.

Michael's eyes dropped. It wasn't easy to confess failure to his own son. "I am afraid I cannot teach you. I, too, have much to learn and I must go to the place where lessons are easiest to learn. But should I happen to meet your mother I shall have some wonderful news to give her."

"Oh if you would." There was a passionate note in John's voice that spoke of intense frustration and a deep longing to taste of that mother-love so tragically denied him.

"John." It was Ann who spoke and her eyes were shining with a soft light that found an echo in John's heart. "Will you let me help you in the meantime? When Michael goes to his new work I am to go home to my children. Perhaps you could visit us there, and I would so love to help you to understand some of the problems and perhaps . . . some of the joys, too, of Earth life."

109

John's eyes lit up with a sudden hope. "Oh that would be wonderful. I know so little, I have so much to learn. And I would love to show you and your children my animals. Even the fiercest become tame in time and they are lovely to watch."

"The children will love that," said Ann, "and so shall I." She did not add that the notion gave her a new hope. Not only did the mother in her long to comfort this youth who had been denied so much, but she clung to this new interest in the hope that it would assuage the ache of parting from Michael.

It was soon after this that warning came from Tendor that Michael should prepare himself for his new venture. The opportunity had come. Ann and he drew closer together in the time of waiting, comforting themselves with the knowledge that he had chosen right and would meet and overcome his *karma*. Nevertheless it was with beating heart that Ann saw the form of their beloved guide approaching, and noted with dismay that he wore a robe of some rough material so unlike his usual bright array, which dimmed his iridescence. In his hand he carried a stout staff.

A tender look came into his eyes as he saw the misery in Ann's face. "Fear not, my child; this is an occasion for rejoicing, not for lamentation. Your dear one sets out on an errand of healing and rescue. I hope for great results from this venture." He turned to Michael. "And now, my son, are you ready? It is not too late to change your mind."

"I have made up my mind," affirmed Michael stoutly. "I see that this is the way out for me."

Tendor nodded his head sagely. "Well spoken, my boy. It would only be delaying your progress to let this opportunity go. Come, let us be on our way." He started off down the path, leaving Michael and Ann to make their final farewells.

These two had learned to improve on the straining embraces of Earth life. They just allowed their consciousness to merge into one another, a far more satisfying and ecstatic at-one-ment than any fondling could emulate. Then with one final deep look of understanding and love, they parted. Michael followed Tendor down the path that led into the valley below while Ann stood at its head watching as long as she could see them. At a bend in the path Michael turned to wave his hand to his beloved, perched high above him.

"God bless you, my darling," he cried to her.

Soft as the whisper of the wind came the answer, floating down into the valley of the shadows, "I am always with you, beloved."

Chapter 4

DESCENT

As Michael and Tendor strode onwards a change in the natural surroundings began to be noticeable. The green grass and graceful foliage of the upper slopes gave place to rocky outcrop and stunted undergrowth. The atmosphere was getting cooler and Michael found a strange heaviness assailing his legs as if he were wading through shallow water. Tendor gave him his hand and the feeling lessened.

"You will soon get used to it," he said. "It is due to the sudden transition from the rarer atmosphere. It is for that reason we are walking instead of using a more rapid form of transit. You will find the sudden change difficult to cope with as you are going to remain down here for some time."

Nevertheless they covered the ground at a surprising rate and soon the valley began to widen into open country. Here they came upon the first signs of habitation. Varying from shacks to large farmhouses, there were signs of attempts to re-create the environment of Earth life. Many of the dwellings had been commenced and then for some reason left incomplete, while in most cases there were indications of lack of skill, some of them pathetic. Usually the dwellings were surrounded by some sort of garden but only rarely could any attempt at cultivation be discerned.

Tendor described these abodes as the homes of people who on Earth were restricted in their views and stunted in spiritual development. Those who are naturally lazy and unwilling to think for themselves make the transition with a complete lack of the equipment which makes for spiritual progress. Thus they naturally drift towards congenial influences in the new world so unexpectedly presented to them. Inertia cannot find

113

a place in the busy realms of the higher spheres and so it is to the lower planes that these people come. There is nothing evil about them; they are merely unawakened spiritually. Presently passers-by began to be more frequent, some of them in earthly dress still, though most of them wore spirit robes of dull hue and inartistic design. They all appeared to be intent on their own business and paid little attention to other travellers.

Michael gave a little shiver, due not so much to cold as to the lack of the life-giving rays to which he had become accustomed. He realized that it was due to this lack of vital life-forces that the inhabitants of this plane seemed to be so lifeless and uninterested. Also he was beginning to be troubled by earthly memories which were assuming a sharper outline than he could remember since he passed over. Little events connected with his business came floating back into his consciousness like old familiar acquaintances.

He explained his experience to Tendor. "Is it owing to association of ideas because we are seeing habitations and people more like the earthly ones?"

"Not entirely that," said Tendor. "The nearer you get to earthly vibrations the more earthly your thoughts. You are always surrounded by your thoughts wherever you are, but in the higher realms thoughts of a lower vibration are less able to impinge upon your receptiveness. When you come down here your vibrations are lowered and such thoughts have easier access to your mind."

"Is that what is wrong with these people whom we are passing? One can see the difference in them to those you meet further up the valley."

"To some extent these people have brought their own environment over with them and you can see the effects of it in the dwellings and other attempts to adapt themselves to their surroundings. You managed to break away from your environment very quickly, largely as a result of Ann's love for you. That enabled you to go to a higher plane, temporarily, until you had found your feet and mapped out your future progress. You can see there the power of love: it is not mere sentiment, as many seem to think."

They were now entering the suburbs of a large town and Michael noted with astonishment the signs of earthly civilization carried over into this new dimension. There were even shops with a display of goods and he was about to question Tendor concerning these when he saw a familiar figure coming towards them, a man short in stature, with a little wisp of a moustache, clad in a dark city suit.

As he drew near Michael pulled up with a jerk. "Why, Smith, how did you get here?"

The man looked Michael up and down, then his face lit up. "Why, if it isn't Mr. Blair." Rather shyly he took hold of the outstretched hand. "Well I never, fancy meeting you down here, sir. Doing a bit of helping work, I expect."

Michael shook his head. "No. I have to stay here for a while. If you understand me?"

"Well, wonders will never cease. To think of our meeting like this. Many is the time you've come into my little shop for some baccy and then found you hadn't the price of it. That was in the old days. Then you got rich and you insisted on dealing with me for your cigars and such like. That was fine, that was. And may I enquire for the lady, sir?"

"She and I came over together, I have just left her. Where do you live?"

"I've got rooms not far from here. And you?"

"I've only just arrived. . . ."

"Perhaps you would like to take rooms in the same house as your friend," put in Tendor.

Michael looked enquiringly at his late tobacconist. But the little man smiled deprecatingly. "It wouldn't suit you. Not what you are accustomed to. You'd best try one of the big hotels, not that I think very much of them myself, a pretty rotten crowd uses them."

"I'd much rather stay in the house where you are, Smith."

Smith looked delighted. "Oh, would you sir? Well I must say that is very nice of you. But you know, Mrs. Bean is not all one could desire, although the place is clean as you could expect. I'm always getting it for not wiping my boots."

"Come," exclaimed Michael, "let us go and interview the worthy Mrs. Bean."

A few minutes later Smith halted outside a five-storied house which displayed a notice 'Apartments' in a ground floor window. While they waited for someone to answer Smith's ring at the bell, Michael looked up and down the road. It was strangely like any road in a European city, and yet there was a difference which he could not at the time recollect. Here in the town the air was thicker than in the country, as if there was some smoke haze about. He turned as Tendor came to his side.

"I shall leave you here," the guide announced. "Your friend Smith will look after you; that has all been arranged. I know this house and the woman who owns it will look after you if you treat her right."

Michael nodded. "You will be seeing Ann?" he asked.

Tendor smiled understandingly. "You do not need me as an intermediary, but I will give Ann full details of your welfare and whereabouts. Call on me if you need help but it will be better if you try and deal with your troubles entirely on your own. That is the surest way to overcome them." With a tender smile of farewell he turned away and was soon lost among the crowds that thronged the street.

"Here you are, Mr. Blair, Mrs. Bean can give you a room." Michael swung round to where Smith was interviewing the landlady. He saw a tall angular woman of a regular type. She looked him over appraisingly.

"I am a respectable woman, Mr. Blair," she said, "always have been. And I expect my gentlemen to be respectable too. No late hours, no coming in the worse for a drop, no lady visitors, them's my rules. Take 'em or leave 'em." She retailed the list with an ease born of practice.

"I should like to come and stay here and I promise to abide by your rules," said Michael with an ingratiating smile. He and Smith followed her up the stairs while she continued to talk.

"Not but what I've had much trouble in this place. Quite a well-behaved lot I've had, I must say. It was different in London, but once having made rules I believe in keeping to them. This will be your room, Mr. Blair. First floor front, my best room. You will have to excuse the shabbiness. It's the

116

atmosphere of this place, gets into the material and even the woodwork, something shocking, just rots everything it does. It's the same everywhere. I am always replacing things but they fall to bits almost as fast as you replace them."

"All right, Mrs. Bean," put in Smith with a decisive air. "I will show my friend round, we won't trouble you anymore."

Mrs. Bean blinked, as if she would have liked to be troubled a good deal more provided she was allowed to continue talking. Then a cunning look came over her face. "You'll excuse me, Mr. Blair. But seeing as how you've no luggage, it would be best to have no misunderstanding. Pay in advance is the best way."

Michael's hand flew to his breast where the notecase should have reposed. Then he realized that he was wearing robes. He had neither cash nor notecase. Smith came to the rescue. Diving into his pocket he produced a golden sovereign, then another and another. Into Mrs. Bean's eager hands he dropped them with a little smile. A glint of avarice in her eye, the woman pocketed the coins and withdrew, leaving the two men alone.

"I say," exclaimed Michael, "that was awkward. So sorry to have to sponge on you, I don't quite know how I can repay you."

An amused smile spread over Smith's face. "Sit down," he said, motioning to a chair. "Now hold out your hand, palm upwards." Michael did so.

"Now concentrate your thoughts as hard as you can and 'will' that a sovereign shall lie upon your palm."

Michael did as he was told and to his amazement a golden sovereign began to materialize in his hand. Just a semblance at first, then it grew more and more solid. He picked it up and felt it. It was perfectly hard and correctly marked. A slow grin spread over his features. "What wouldn't they give to be able to do that on Earth." Still smiling at his achievement he added, "But why sovereigns, and why does she want them from us, why can't she make them herself?"

"She hasn't got the hang of it yet; she still believes material things to be all-important and until she has learned that it is unnecessary, she must be dependent upon others for money.

117

We still keep to the gold standard because paper notes are even more perishable than metal down here. Nothing lasts very long in this atmosphere. You will notice that workmen are constantly repairing the buildings. Even this gold will disintegrate in a few days. It is one of the ways of teaching people to desire something more lasting than mere material objects. But the money has its uses; they will accept it in the shops."

"Shops?" echoed Michael. "Do you mean to tell me that those were real shops I passed coming here, with real things to sell?"

Smith smiled. "You have a lot to learn. You must remember that we are very near Earth here in every way. To this plane come those who are so wrapped up in the material life that they cannot comprehend existence without many of the objects to which they are accustomed. You see, many of these people here were Atheists, or rigid sectarians who expected to sleep till the Judgment Day or to find God waiting to meet them and carry them off into the clouds. Of course these things didn't happen and instead they find an existence not very different from the earthly one and themselves with the same old longings and prejudices and habits. They would be miserable if they could not fulfil them, even in an illusory way, so gradually this City of Illusion has been built up, with some means of gratifying many of the wants of its inhabitants. In this way copies of earthly prototypes have come into existence. Take Mrs. Bean, for instance: the only life she knew of was that of the rather narrow-minded landlady. So as she could not throw off that life, she has re-created it here. She has been helped, of course, because through that experience she will eventually find release. Some of these people need almost a tin-opener to release their inhibitions. For the same reason we have shops here. People who cannot rid themselves of their dependency upon shops have caused their creation."

Suddenly Michael gave a little shiver. He laughed apologetically. "I suppose I must be cold."

Smith got up. "No, it is not cold, it is depletion, due to the sudden change from the plane on which you have been living."

He went over to a cupboard in a corner of the room. "I'll turn on the gas fire," he added.

"Wonders will never cease," laughed Michael, getting up and crossing the room to look into the cupboard. Sure enough, there was a meter similar to the gas meters used on Earth. Smith produced a shilling by his usual process and inserted it into a slot. Then he turned a tap and a gentle glow came from the fire grate. "Of course it isn't really coal gas," he observed as they resumed their seats. "It is really the Cosmic rays that light up the Spirit World conducted here in a condensed form. They have a wonderful revitalizing effect, just like a fire did on a cold night on Earth. So this fire serves the purpose for the people here and does them good spiritually as well."

Relaxing in his chair Michael began to recognize, in the rays that came from the grate, some of the heartening influence of the life-giving vitality that characterized the realm he had just left. The thought led him to wonder what Ann and the children were doing. Presently he turned to the little tobacconist and said:

"Tell me, if it will not distress you, how you came to be here."

For a moment the other gazed thoughtfully into the fire. "You knew my shop in London. But you didn't know my home that lay behind it. I lived there with my wife, my dear Kate." He spoke softly, as one who treads on delicate ground. "She was a lovely girl when I married her, pretty as a picture. We were so happy. But we had no children, perhaps that was the trouble. Kate was highly strung, very nervous. She took to drink, at first. Oh you can guess what happened. . . ." He spread out his hands in a pathetic little gesture. "Then when it wasn't enough for her, she took to drugs. I didn't guess the difference till too late. I tried, oh, how I tried. But it wasn't any use. They took her off to a home; she used to rave at times. She didn't know me anymore. My poor little beautiful Kate. . . ."

Michael said nothing. There seemed no words in which he could express what he felt. He had a vision of a poor raddled creature whom Smith insisted on regarding as beautiful, holding only the thought of what she had once been. These quiet little men, what tragedies are hidden behind their trim front-ages.

With a little sigh, Smith brought his thoughts back out of the past and continued. "Then, when she had gone, there didn't seem to be much to live for. I got ill and . . . came over here. I went to the Lowlands first and spent a long time studying things. But I wasn't happy, I wanted my Kate, I couldn't get on without her. Then one day I met . . . the Master. Such a wonderful face He had, such a lovely voice, yet dressed so simply, like any traveller."

"Yes, I know," put in Michael, "I too have seen Him."

Smith nodded. "Aye, once you have seen Him He binds you to Him with ropes of love. You don't want ever to be loosed from those bonds. He asked me to work for Him, down here, while I was waiting for my dear Kate to come over. He said I could help her that way. And He was right. In spite of the circumstances here I have been happier than since I came over. You see, I know that my Kate will come over soon, and they are going to put her in a hospital in the country here where she will start getting rid of the effects of the drugs, for she will still have the craving even here. I've seen the place; it's not bad. She wouldn't be able to stand the pressure any higher up. The doctors told me my love would help her a lot. I hope it will. I am trying to save up all the love I can."

Michael's heart warmed to this little man, so faithful to his true love, in spite of all he must have endured. "How do you mean," he asked, "save up love?"

"Quite simple. There is a law in the world of Spirit called the law of Cause and Effect, and another called the law of Compensation. When you do someone a good turn, whether on Earth or over here, the act has a result on your etheric condition, lightens it as it were. Money in the bank, so to speak. And when you do the opposite, well, you lose something from your condition, you pay out and eventually you may have an overdraft. Most of the folk round here have overdrafts and they cannot move on till they have earned enough to pay them off. And so I am saving up love so that

I can give it to others who need help, my dear Kate among them."

"Tell me, you have become quite different since we came in here. Were you playing a part when you met me in the street?"

Smith smiled deprecatingly. "Well you see, when I came down here I thought it best to remain what I was, just an unknown tobacconist. I don't usually mention that I came here of my own free will. I find it easier to help people if I meet them on level terms. I knew you were coming but I didn't know how you would be taking it. So I put on my old suit, just in case. Don't if you would rather not, but perhaps you would like to tell me your story."

Michael told him, revealing everything, hiding nothing.

When the recital was over Smith leaned back in his chair. "Yes," he murmured, "it is always the same. We would give all the wealth in the world to go back and undo what we have done. But that is the way of it. That is the way we have to learn, and the more wrong things we learn the harder it becomes to unlearn." He got up and went over to the window. "Come here," he said.

Michael got up and joined him. He looked out to see a familiar vista of chimney pots, backyards and washing, and in the distance, a vision of crowded streets. Suddenly a row of lights came on in the streets, then another and another. Although it was broad daylight the city was lit up.

"Goodness," cried Michael, "you don't mean to tell me that you have night and day here?"

"No, even the desires of the materially minded cannot accomplish that. But, you see, these people are so accustomed to being ruled by time that they hit upon this idea to mark the passage of what they call a day. It is now officially night and the shops and businesses will close and the people will go home. I shut my shop early today."

Michael frowned. "Your shop? You don't mean to tell me that you sell baccy here? Do people smoke?"

"Oh yes, some do. But remember that what we have here is only a counterpart of what you had on Earth; there is not much flavour about my cigarettes." He brought a case out of his pocket. "Have one," he invited. Michael took one and lit it from Smith's proferred lighter. He puffed and puffed. A little vapour came out of the paper tube but there was no taste, no satisfaction in the act. He turned a puzzled face to Smith. "Do you mean to say people buy these?"

"Oh yes. When they come over here most of them lose their taste for food or smokes because the spirit body does not need these things for its sustenance. But in some there is the incessant craving which, if it were not assuaged in some way, would obsess the mind to the exclusion of all else. That wouldn't help them to get on so we provide these cigarettes which give their stunted minds an illusion of smoking. I sell quite a lot. And if they haven't the price, well, that doesn't matter." He laughed. "It's like running a nursery, isn't it." He turned back into the room. "Well I think I will leave you now to have some rest on your first night in our City of Illusion. You can sleep here if you want to. It isn't necessary but most people do. Just lie on your bed and most likely you'll drop off."

"I don't know how to thank you for all you've done to help me."

But the little man would have none of it. "Don't thank me. It has been a pleasure. You see, you made a link down there on Earth, and that made it easy." With which parting shot he closed the door.

Left to himself, Michael sat and gazed into his fire and pondered over the strange events that had occurred since he left the Lowlands. How long ago that seemed already, or was it? Dash it, he was getting entangled in the meshes of time again. Then the fire went out and he had to conjure up another shilling for the slot. Scarcely had he got it going again when there came a knock at the door. At his invitation it opened and the landlady glided in. With a murmured apology Mrs. Bean went over to the meter and with a master key unlocked it and abstracted the two shillings. Holding them tightly, she carefully locked the meter again, and made for the door.

"They makes the money of such rotten stuff," she confided as she passed him, "that if you don't get rid of it quick it may melt away before you can spend it. I shall go round to the shops first thing in the morning and turn this into something more durable." Then she bade him goodnight and closed the door.

The incident gave Michael a sickening sense of unreality. It all seemed so different to what he had thought. And yet, as he reflected on the causes, he began to wonder if that would not, after all, be the quickest way of working on the mind of such as this woman. It was clear that no amount of talking would cause her to alter her fixed ideas. Gradually the transient nature of money and material things would sink in and she would begin to look for something more lasting. Perhaps after all this City of Illusion was a merciful dispensation. He became conscious of a feeling of sleepiness. He got up and lay down on the bed. He thought of Ann and with the thought she seemed to draw near him. With a delightful feeling of happiness he felt himself being drawn out of the dense body he was occupying. . . .

Michael awoke to find Smith bending over him. "Wake up," he said with a chuckle, "it is morning. At least, the lights are off." Michael got up and went over to the window. Sure enough the lights had gone out. In the City of Illusion it was officially daytime. With a little laugh he turned back into the room. He noted that Smith had abandoned his suit and was wearing a robe like his own.

Smith announced that it was time to set out for his shop so Michael said he would accompany him. There were few folk about as the two went down the street, Smith explaining that the crowds did not appear until the shops were open and the general activities of the city were in full swing. As they approached the corner of the block Michael stopped and began to sniff the air.

"That's a familiar smell," he declared, looking enquiringly at his companion.

"Fish," replied Smith laconically, "fried fish."

Michael shrugged his shoulders. "I give it up. I believe I am back on Earth and I have only been dreaming."

Smith laughed. "You have got a lot to learn, as I said before. Fundamental things."

At the corner of the street stood a shop replete with all the equipment of a fried fish shop, including the fish. Smith led the way in.

"Good morning, Mary," he said familiarly to a girl behind the counter. "I have brought in a friend of mine I should like you to meet."

The girl, she was a blonde, glanced curiously at Michael. "A friend of yours is a friend of mine, Mr. Smith. Feeling hungry, sir?"

"Why no," said Michael, "I don't think I am."

"It wasn't for that reason I brought him in, Mary. He has been over some time and has no need for food like your newly arrived customers. You see," he addressed Michael, "it is like the cigarettes. People coming here suddenly, without warning, find it difficult to get used to the new conditions; they feel they ought to be hungry and eat something. So we give them what they want till they learn to do without it. Try some of Mary's fish."

With a smile, and Michael thought her face full of kindness, she placed a small piece of fish on a plate and offered it to him. He tasted it. It didn't seem to taste of anything much though it gave an impression of being hot. Mary laughed heartily at his puzzled expression. "You don't like my fish, do you? Well that is a compliment really, though it may sound a bit Irish. And how do you like it over here?"

"Well, to tell you the truth I only got to this . . . er . . . city, yesterday. And since then my friend here has been showing me wonder after wonder."

"You haven't seen some of our high spots yet? Down by the river?" There was a bitter ring in her voice.

"Oh, come now, Mary," Smith protested, "I wouldn't take a gentleman like Mr. Blair to places like that."

"Depends on what Mr. Blair wants," observed Mary, regarding Michael thoughtfully. "What is your line, slumming?"

"I wouldn't call it that," responded Michael. "I have got some debts to pay and I am looking for a chance to pay them."

The girl tossed her head. "Oh, those. The more you pay the more you find. That's what most of them say here." Just then a customer came in and the two friends bade Mary a hurried farewell.

"Friend of yours?" asked Michael as they made their way along the pavement.

"Yes, very much so, in fact one of my best friends down here. She is a fine spirit. But do you know that when she was incarnated she was a prostitute in London. Now she spends her time serving fish to those who cannot restrain their appetite. Curious, isn't it? But she has long ago worked off her debts. She could go on easily if she wished but her experiences aroused such a deep compassion for her fellow creatures that she stays down here voluntarily. She is a grand worker."

"How did you meet her?"

Smith hesitated for a minute. "It was down by the river she referred to. That is a pretty nasty neighbourhood, especially on the far side. Don't ever be tempted to cross any of the bridges unless you have proper protection. I'll tell you about that another time. But I found Mary in a dreadful state of exhaustion, having just come over rather suddenly. She was in appalling conditions. But because her heart was good she radiated some light and I was able to find her and show myself to her. That isn't easy in some of those dark houses down there. I brought her back and got her on her feet again. Then after a bit she met the Master."

Abruptly Michael clutched his companion's arm. "The Master here?"

"Why not? Do you think He dwells only in marble palaces? This is where some of God's children are so this is His place. Of course He does not come in the full glory of His shining Reality, that would be too much for these folk, it wouldn't help them to help themselves. He usually comes as a mere traveller, quite simply dressed. He just talks to the people He meets, usually individually. He asked Mary to work for Him and not knowing who He was, she said she would. She liked the look of Him, she said. She had a fit when I told her who He was. Wouldn't believe it for a long time. Here we are, this is my little shop." He paused at the door of a small tobacconist's, the windows filled with attractive goods and advertisements. Unlocking the door he invited Michael to enter.

The inside was equally brightly displayed, while at the back of the shop was a well-stocked warehouse.

"Where do you get your supplies?" asked Michael.

Smith smiled mysteriously. "We don't say much about that. I draw my supplies from my warehouse and they are always replaced. They come, shall we say, in the same manner as the shillings. You see they are needed, so they are provided."

A young dandy came in with a swagger and demanded some cigarettes for his girlfriend. Smith asked some shrewd questions and then helped the youth to select a suitable box. When they were alone again he smiled knowingly at Michael.

"There is no end of opportunities here. By asking that fellow a few questions about his girl I was able to sense her state of awareness. Those cigarettes are medicated with a herb that grows here and is helpful in cleansing the aura of unpleasant influences. It is a sort of incense. They'll do no harm and may do some good." He grinned boyishly.

After a while Michael decided to go out and explore, so he bade his friend a temporary farewell. Out in the street once more he paused and looked about him. Smith had been quite right when he said that everything deteriorated rapidly here. Most of the buildings were in bad need of repairs, and on every side were ladders and other signs of repairs in progress. The whole place seemed to be crumbling. He asked a passerby the nature of some large buildings on the opposite corner. He was a fussy little man with an unrolled umbrella.

"Why, sir," he jerked out, obviously ready to talk, "that is the Town Hall over there, a fine building, you will agree. I helped to design it.

"Oh yes," responded Michael, "you must have been over here some time then."

"Over here? What do you mean, sir? I live here." Then, as if annoyed at the interruption, he went on to describe the other buildings as the College of Allied Arts, the General Hospital, the Free Library and the Masonic Hall. Then he turned to Michael to ask: "You do not live here, sir? I presume you live in the country."

"Oh no, I . . . er . . . that is . . . I have only just left Earth."

A dark shadow came over the elder man's face. "You are joking, sir."

"I assure you I am not. I lived in London."

The little man became livid with rage. Poking a finger into Michael's chest, he cried: "Don't you believe that sort of nonsense; it is the Devil's work. There are no real people on Earth, it is uninhabited. If you have been listening to those spiritists I strongly advise you to have nothing to do with them; they are evil, evil, evil!" Crying the last words in a rising crescendo, the man turned and scurried away, seemingly afraid Michael might develop horns and a tail. If it had not been pathetic Michael would have laughed.

Hardly had he progressed a hundred yards down the street when he had another queer experience. A man, well-dressed and cultured-looking, stopped him and asked in a matter-of-fact sort of voice: "Have you been saved?"

"Saved?" Michael reiterated. "Saved from what?"

For answer the man thrust a tract into his hand and hurried on. Michael could hardly repress a smile as he read the familiar quotations: 'The wages of sin is death,' 'Repent, for the Kingdom of Heaven is at hand.' Beneath was printed an exhortation to grovel before a revengeful Deity lest He cast you into a fiery furnace in an access of fury. "Even here," muttered Michael as he scrunched the tract up and threw it into the gutter. To his surprise the paper crumbled into powder and finally disintegrated.

Presently he came to a building that was obviously a theatre. Deeply interested, he crossed the road and studied the play-bills. To his astonishment the play advertised was "THE SIGN OF THE CROSS," and the principal part was to be taken by an actor whose name was famous on Earth nearly a century ago. A little further on he came upon a cinema and gasped when he found that the picture being shown was one that attracted much attention in London a few years before his transition. Filled with a desire to question Smith about these

127

discoveries, he retraced his steps towards the shop. On the way he saw a London General omnibus, *circa* 1920. But the destination board was marked 'Private' and it was obviously carrying a social party, for the occupants all wore buttonholes and appeared to be well acquainted with each other.

Smith was amused at his experiences. "There are lots of people here who still think they are mortals," he explained, "they won't believe they have passed over and they regard Earth people as spooks. The town is full of religious maniacs. But the theatrical show is real enough; we must go sometime."

"What about the cinema show? How do they get the latest British pictures?" asked Michael.

"That is easily explained. Everything on Earth has its material counterpart over here. When they make a new film in England the etheric counterpart is available over here. It merely requires the equivalent of an earthly projector to display the films in an objective way. We find it a useful way of keeping in touch with the trend of earthly progress. We do not make films over here but we do write plays and you will see many that have never been presented on Earth. The stage is used a great deal as a means of educating these people and bringing out their spiritual qualities."

"I suppose it does. Now what about the tracts, do you mean to say that they have printing presses here?"

Smith shook his head. "There is no need for anything so cumbersome as that. If you possess the necessary power you can materialize anything you wish, at least anything that you can visualize strongly enough. You can materialize a copy of Shakespeare if you want one, though there are other ways of studying classics like that. But I should imagine your tract was a product of that man's own mind because it disintegrated so quickly. I expect he used to distribute them on Earth and when he got here he found that he missed them and thought about them so much that they reappeared in his hand. As for old Joe and his bus, he is a local character; he won't be parted from his bus." He started to get busy with some packages. "While you were out," he went on, "I got a call to deliver some cigarettes to the troops in the line."

Michael clutched the counter, feeling dizzy. "This is too

much. You are not going to tell me there is a war on here?"

Smith looked pityingly at him. "Why wouldn't there be a war? This is not heaven. War is what largely occupies the minds of men these days. Didn't most of us say on Earth that wars are inevitable?"

"Yes I suppose most of us thought that."

"Well then. The same men come over here, and they don't alter their views much. Most of us bring the same hates and loves and prejudices and hide-bound ideas; our characters do not change. So you see we bring our wars over too. You can see for yourself if you would like to."

Michael having agreed to accompany his friend, Smith opened the door into the warehouse. At the back door was standing a lorry which Michael recognized as one of a type used in France in 1918. The driver was in khaki with a red cross on his arm. He was busy loading cases into the lorry.

"Can we come with you, Bill? My friend here would like to see the front."

Bill glanced round the back of the lorry at Michael. Then he shrugged his shoulders and replied: "Yes, if he fancies the idea." Whistling a few bars of 'Tipperary,' Bill loaded the last of the cases and then swung himself up into the driver's seat.

"There's room for both of you up here if you don't mind a squash," he invited.

Scrambling up into the lofty perch, Michael and Smith made themselves comfortable. Then they started. Traversing the main street of the city they had a good view of the cafés, the shops, large and small, the large residences and hotels, and the endless rows of small houses, some of them mere hovels, that made up this strange town. Overall was the atmosphere of decay, of crumbling, despite energetic repairs. Everywhere there were ladders and scaffolds, plasterers and painters. Gradually the dwellings were left behind and the lorry emerged into the countryside where it gathered speed in a surprising way. Then the scene began to change. From country dwellings and cottages, from hedgerows and woods, the scenery changed to rolling downs bereft of vegetation, to stunted woods that seemed to have passed through the scourge of bombardment, to ruins and broken implements of warfare.

"Are there many casualties?" asked Michael wonderingly.

"Not in the sense that you mean," replied Smith. "Remember that this is the Land of Illusion, to everyone except the unfortunates who are the victims of illusion. No one's country is conquered, this is No Man's Land, uninhabited except by the warring parties. No one really gets wounded or killed."

Presently they became aware of the thunder of guns on the horizon and then came the unmistakable tang of explosives in the air. Drifts of smoke spread over the battlefield and the wreckage of war became more and more evident. Away to a flank, a flight of aeroplanes swept across the sky.

Suddenly Michael exclaimed: "Look, there are some tanks. I never thought to see such things here."

"Why not?" said Smith, with a touch of bitterness. "You see there is an endless struggle going on here between the forces of Light and those of Darkness, the prize being these poor devils who come over fighting mad and cannot be persuaded that they are not still at war. The Devil and his tribe are very real people and they are immensely powerful in an atmosphere such as this. They have a great deal of knowledge and they use their powers to create weapons of warfare for the soldiers to use."

"Tell me," asked Michael, "surely all soldiers who die fighting don't have to come to this hell of a place?"

"Oh, of course not, no more than you came to a place of this sort. It is the evil-minded men whose passions were aroused by war and who liked killing, who drift into an environment such as this. A decent-minded soldier would be met by workers and conducted safely through all this sort of thing. Remember that it is all illusion; there is nothing here to harm anyone who refuses to let it influence them. But to the soldiers fighting still it is very real."

Presently a bunch of weary-looking men came into view, marching stolidly along at the side of the road. Their uniforms were covered with mud and they had the clay-coloured complexions of men to whom health and happiness are strangers. Bill stopped the lorry and jumped out.

"Watch this," said Smith. "We will try and get in touch

with these fellows. But if they are in the hands of bad officers we shan't be successful."

Bill reappeared with several packets of cigarettes which he offered to the approaching men. It was pathetic to see their worn faces light up as they saw the cigarettes. Just then a man came out from the back of the party wearing the uniform of an officer. He barked out an order in a language Michael could not understand. Without hesitation the men slumped their shoulders and trudged on, indifferent to the offer of Bill's gifts.

"You see," commented Smith, with a helpless gesture, "that is what usually happens. A few cigarettes and a little chat and we might have persuaded some of those fellows to come with us. But they are men without much intelligence or initiative and they have become so accustomed to obeying their officers that they do so unquestioningly. I don't mean that all the officers are bad. But the worst among the men often dress themselves up as officers and they are so full of their power over their men that they will do anything to stop them being taken away from them."

The lorry drove off again. The soil was getting wetter as they proceeded, giving the impression of recent rain. There were what appeared to be puddles here and there, among the shell holes.

"Is there no way of getting these poor chaps away?" asked Michael.

"We cannot influence a man without his consent; we cannot force a man to come away. We can sometimes put him to sleep if we think that will help him, but he usually wakes up just the same man as he was. Sometimes a soldier who has just been killed sees us and takes us for ghosts and hurries off to find some of his companions. He gradually learns to distinguish between those who are still incarnate and those who have made the transition, and the spirits then get together in bands or companies. Then the struggle begins. The evil forces influence their own victims to try and get the newcomers to join them while the spiritual workers try and persuade them to leave the battlefield."

As the lorry bumped along the uneven roadway the sounds

of gunfire grew louder and presently they drew abreast of a line of guns. A man in khaki came rushing out of one of the gun-pits towards the lorry. Bill drew up once more.

"Ammunition, ammunition," bawled the soldier, "have you brought the ammunition?" He stood panting by the side of the bonnet, gazing eagerly up at the driver. But Bill shook his head wearily. "No mate, it's comforts this time."

At this, the man, he was a sergeant, gave a bellow of fury. Michael noticed that he had a brutal face. He swore at Bill in no uncertain terms, claiming that no one ever brought up ammunition when it was most needed.. "Them blue pencil blanks will be round our flanks in a moment," he concluded.

Bill shook his head again. "You know you don't need that stuff, mate, why don't you quit this business? Here, have a packet of fags, you look all in."

The sergeant took the cigarettes and lit one. Then he screwed his ugly features up at Bill. "You're a good sort, Bill, you've been bringing us fags since longer than I can remember. Now if you'd only hurry up and bring them ammunition chaps. What's wrong? Another munitions scandal at home?" An ugly scowl spread over his face, "cos if there is me and my mates are goin' to give some of them chaps hell, d'yer hear?"

Bill refused to be impressed. "There isn't any ammunition because you don't need any. There isn't any enemy."

The sergeant looked astounded for a moment. Then he burst out into a loud guffaw. "Lumme that's a good 'un, that is. No enemy! If you had to keep the b . . . s back you wouldn't crack them jokes."

"Tell me mate, have you seen a single enemy since you came into this sector?" Bill's voice was earnest this time.

"Of course I . . . that is I . . . why they're all around us."

"And yet you haven't seen one."

"Well I can't say as I . . . 'ere what are you getting at? Are you a perishing Hun in disguise? No enemy . . . gurr! Listen to them guns, do you think they are firing at nothin'? Get out with yer." With a wave of his hand he consigned Bill and his friends to perdition and stalked off back to the gun-pits.

Bill chuckled as he went, "Got him under the skin, that did.

He'll turn that over in his mind and perhaps he'll see sense before long."

"But, good heavens," put in Michael, "do you mean to tell me that all these chaps are fighting an imaginary enemy?"

Bill looked steadily at him. "Didn't Freddie Smith tell you this is a land of illusion? There's no enemy here as I've ever seen. But you can't persuade these chaps that way. They are all convinced they are fighting for their lives, except perhaps for some of the worst of them who have learned after a long time here that the enemy only existed in their imagination. And those are the ones who get in our way. They're playing their own game." Suddenly he glanced up the road. "Here's our party," he exclaimed.

Michael looked up to see a strange little procession approaching. In the lead was a weary-looking figure in khaki wearing the dog-collar of a padre. Following him were two stretcher bearers carrying a pallid-faced youth on a stretcher. All three wore red crosses on their armbands.

"Hullo, Bill," greeted the chaplain heartily. "Got another one, thanks be. I see you've brought the fags. The chaps were all running short, they'll be glad to have this lot. Will you take this fellow into hospital, then we can load the stretcher with the fags. Hullo, some strangers here?"

Bill made the introductions, then he and Smith hurried off to superintend the transfer of the loads.

"Well, what do you think of this lot?" asked the padre with a grin.

Michael explained his recent arrival and consequent lack of knowledge of local conditions. "But tell me," he went on, "are you doing rescue work here?"

The padre nodded vigorously. "Yes, that's our job. Been at it some time now."

"It must be terrible work trying to turn these men's thoughts away from war."

"Terrible isn't the word for it. Many of them are so dashed obstinate you just can't knock any sense into them. I have to keep reminding myself that God knows His own business best. Lots of these chaps have got big lessons to learn and no doubt staying down here is the best way for some of them to learn.

These fellows only knew how to live on Earth through their bodily senses and they try and live here through the etheric senses, with much the same result."

"Then you mean to say that you stay down here in this awful mess, just waiting for a chance to influence one of these chaps?"

The padre grinned a little self-consciously. "That's the sort of idea. But when there is a war on, and there usually is somewhere or other, we are too busy to think much about it. We are only one step here from actual Earth conditions so we can easily manifest on the battlefield. We know when there are going to be casualties and we just wait around and help the chaps as they wake up in Spirit life. Most of them are easy to deal with and workers take them away up above. But some of us have to stay and deal with the bad cases. If we didn't there would be such a crowd of them here that they would get too powerful and we shouldn't be able to get onto the battlefields. There is no question but that the work has got to be done. Besides," he made an expressive little gesture with his hand, "many of these men are victims of environment, they are not all bad."

"Are they all British?"

"Good heavens, no. They are all nationalities. They are not organized in armies, you understand, but they get together in groups mostly of pals or of men with similar tastes. The groups seldom get together, which is a mercy. There is too much jealousy between them."

"Don't you ever get away, get any leave, I mean?"

"Oh, yes, we have to get away sometimes to recuperate. This place takes it out of you. My mother has got a little house up in the hills and I go up there and join her once in a while. But I don't care to go too often because the chaps don't like it. They want to know why the padre should get Blighty leave when they can't." He stopped speaking and inclined his head slightly. From far in the distance there came the clear call of a bugle. "The General!" he exclaimed, and turned to walk quickly up a small hill at the edge of the road, and Michael followed. "He'll come this way, you'll see him in a minute," added the parson.

134

"I think all this is fine," said Michael as they waited, "I have never heard of such altruism."

"Oh no it isn't, it is just our job and we happen to be the people who are best fitted for that job at the moment. Besides," the padre's chin went up and he eyed Michael resolutely, "it is the Master's work."

"I know," said Michael quietly, "I have seen Him."

The padre nodded. "Ah, then you understand."

Soon there came the sound of horses' hooves and into sight swept a cavalcade of horsemen. First came an officer in general's uniform whom Michael recognized with a thrill as a famous victor of the last war. Following him were two staff officers and, bringing up the rear, was a trumpeter carrying a small Union Jack at his lance head.

The padre drew himself up and saluted as the cortege went by and the general returned his salutation with a smile that conveyed the impression of a powerful personality. "There he goes," said the padre, "he's never far away from the chaps who fought for him, and he'll keep on coming as long as there are any left here. His real home is far away in the Uplands but that doesn't stop his coming down here. He's a grand chap and has a way with the men. They see the truth of things through his example quicker than any other way. He makes them think he is preparing for the final battle to end the war, but really he is lifting their minds above the level of their surroundings." He turned to bid Michael farewell. "I must go and meet him at the rendezvous. Goodbye, I've enjoyed our little chat." With a wave of his hand he hurried off down the hill, calling to his stretcher bearers as he went.

Deeply moved at all he had seen and heard Michael made his way back to where his companions were loading the stretcher containing the rescued soldier into the lorry. Soon they were bumping their way back to the city.

From now on Michael made his way alone about his new environment. He thoroughly explored the city and then made excursions into the countryside. He was astonished to find to what extent the inhabitants had brought over from their Earth life their own old surroundings as part of their mental equipment, losing no time in re-creating them as far as possible in

135

this new sphere. Many were quite prepared to settle down without a thought for the inadequacy of their conditions or a desire for something better. Inertia seemed to be as much a curse to these people as it is to the human race. Any attempt to instil an idea of progress into their minds brought only suspicion and aversion.

Here in this City of Illusion was enough to give an impression of solid comfort, hard cash, solidly built houses, household goods, and that appearance of outer respectability which is the shield and buckler of unthinking man. It seemed that these things were necessary so that spiritually unawakened souls might find surroundings that would not provide too great a shock to their mentality. But through the obvious impermanence of these things was gradually taught the lesson that material things are of no lasting importance. Thus the minds of the evolving spirits were driven to seek some alternative and immediately met with the ever-ready response of Spirit. Thus were their feet set gently upon the path of progress.

Once or twice Michael visited the theatre or cinema, sometimes with Mary, with whom he was becoming fast friends. The theatre specialized in drama, this being the medium which the spirit workers found most useful in teaching some spiritual verity to their audiences. Often the author, and sometimes the principal artists, were men and women who had earned high earthly repute. The cinema confined itself to the presentation of films which had already been shown on Earth. The machinery used was quite unlike any that he had seen before, being some method of bending and concentrating the Cosmic rays that illumined this plane. With the aid of this form of light the etheric counterpart of the film was displayed while from the Akashic Record was drawn the sound.

Altogether Michael found much that was instructive in his surroundings, and his new friendship with Mary and Fred Smith was most satisfying. But nothing could mitigate the ache in his heart engendered by his absence from Ann. He was aware that in the form of sleep, obtainable in this sphere, he made contact with her. He awoke with vague memories of having been with her but these were ephemeral and unsatisfying. For, like the veil that covers the life of mortals from the vision of Reality, there was another veil here to shield those in the Land of Illusion from the brightness of the higher life that would make their existence intolerable if it were reflected into their lives before they were ready for it.

So far he had made no reference to his desire to get into touch with Vera but he now broached the subject to Smith, who thought the matter over before replying. At length he spoke.

"The facts as I see them are these: We know that she committed suicide and the penalties for cutting short an incarnation are heavy. It does not matter whether it is your own soul or that of another, murder or suicide, it is defiance of God's will and therefore the law of Cause and Effect must have its way. There is another matter in that Vera short-circuited the spiritual sacrament of marriage and gave access to an incarnating spirit without the blessing of God. In that you have your share of blame. The imponderables are not so easy to calculate because we have no direct access to all the facts. We do not know, for instance, what previous incarnations Vera has undergone, if any. So much depends upon the root causes for her action."

"If she had been free," he went on, "the very fact of your wanting to help her would have brought you together. It looks as if she is in the hands of evil-minded people across the river. And that is an unpleasant state to be in."

"It all seems so unfair," burst out Michael. "Here am I, fairly comfortable and well looked after, while she is in heaven knows what horrible place. It ought to be me who should suffer."

Smith looked at him thoughtfully. "My dear friend, you must learn to look at these things from the right angle. Get out of your mind any idea of unfairness or injustice in the working out of God's plans. Injustice is an attribute of ignorance, due to lack of understanding of what is truth and what is not. It is one of the first steps in spiritual education to learn that injustice is an illusion. No one can alter the scales of the Great Spirit for they are adjusted to dead-centre. If we insist upon upsetting that balance then we must balance the scales again before we can progress. If your friend Vera is suffering

137

at this time, it is because her own spirit, in its highest plane of wisdom, has decided that through suffering she will gain freedom from something that is holding her back. It may be some past indebtedness or it may be some lesson she requires to learn in order to strengthen her character. But that does not mean that we may not try and rescue her, try and mitigate that suffering."

"All the same, I feel that it is largely my fault."

"Perhaps it was. Or perhaps you were merely the match that set light to the fire. Can you say that you were the fire? Can you call upon your intuition to indicate the motive that impelled you?"

"I—I don't know. I had no thought . . . it all happened so suddenly. I had no intention . . . ?"

"I thought as much. An occurrence such as this which has so dynamic an effect on an incarnation is rarely insignificant. It looks as though you and Vera were caught up in the toils of destiny."

Like a flash a queer thought went through Michael's mind of some old, old picture of a loom weaving the threads of destiny. He dismissed it as irrelevant and went on. "All the same I am conscious of an overwhelming desire to help her. I am certain that I can, if I can only get in touch with her. Surely it must be right to do all that is in my power?"

"Don't misunderstand me. It is not a question of not helping her. It is not even a question of helping her in this one plane of endeavour. What I want to ensure is that we help her on the highest plane possible. You can seek her out and alleviate the minor aspects of suffering, the pinpricks. You can give her friendship and ease and comforts and pleasure. That would be nice for her but it would not get to the root of the matter. I am, of course, assuming that she has injured herself deeply in the spiritual sense at some stage in her career, something even more negative than this suicide. So if we are to help her in the fullest sense you must make your effort on the highest possible plane of thought. And you cannot do that entirely without help. You will have to make your appeal to her spiritual mind rather than her soul mind. Do you get my point?"

138

"Yes, I think I see what you mean. To help her in my way would be rather like offering a bunch of grapes to someone suffering from cancer."

"That's the idea. Now if you will concentrate and send out a call winged from the highest aspect of your mind that you can contemplate, it may reach her. It is almost certain to. She may not be conscious of it and if her spirit does not desire to be so helped, it will have no effect. On the other hand, and a spirit seldom refuses such an offer, she may respond by impressing her soul mind to get in touch with you. I think that that is the quickest way of getting a real contact with her. Anything else would be superficial and probably have no lasting results."

"I say, you have acquired a lot of wisdom."

Smith shook his head. "The more one gets to know, the greater appears one's abysmal ignorance. There is no magic about what I have told you. When you have to deal with a few cases like this you soon become a psychologist. A human child regards the doctor as a sort of magician until it grows up and finds that he is just another individual with a knowledge of the human body and its ailments."

"Do you think that it is fairly certain that Vera is on this plane?"

"I think so. You will realize that there are very many towns and cities like this and a large tract of country that is part of this environment. But the tendency is for spirits to move in groups throughout their existence and the fact that you contacted Vera on Earth leads me to the idea that she will not be far from your own path."

"Is there racial discrimination over here? What happens to people of other races?"

"There is a racial distinction in the lower spheres but as soon as a spirit starts to move upwards in the scale of progress the racial differences disappear. They are put on with the soul body and discarded with that restriction. There are reception areas like this up-river which cater for different races. But the law is one of attraction only. If a Chinaman had a love for the British and their culture and social life, then he might gravitate here, just as he would probably travel to Britain when he was on Earth. But normally he would find the remnants of the social customs to which these folk still cling rather distasteful, and so he would prefer to join his own people. Then as he became refined through learning the truth about things and began to climb up the ladder of freedom, he would lose his racial identity and become just a spirit."

"Have you any idea how many planes there are? I have often wondered."

"I don't know, not for certain. They say there are as many as there are skins to an onion. But many of those must be intermediate conditions rather than distinct spheres of existence. Sort of halting places to get your breath, so to speak."

"It's a terrific conception, isn't it? Makes one's mind reel to think of it."

"Yes it is. But don't make the mistake of thinking of it in terms of locations. It is rather a matter of state of mind, of condition rather than place. A good simile is to think of it in terms of earthly society in Victorian days. The Royal circle, then the nobility, then the county families, the professional class, the middle class, the lower classes and finally the wasters, the criminals. All those categories inhabited one country at the same time, but there were unbridgeable gulfs between each of them. The difference here is that the qualifications for the different spheres are very unlike those for the classes; they are qualities of Spirit instead of accidents of birth or wealth."

"I can see that. You have a sort of divine socialism here. But rather different from our ideas about socialism on Earth."

Michael did his best to carry out his friend's injunction. He concentrated upon Vera as often as he could in the highest aspect of Spirit that he could visualize. From that niche he projected his thoughts to her and made his appeal that he should be allowed to help her. He found it a great struggle to keep out thoughts of doubt or failure, and to maintain his mind at that lofty altitude.

Of the purely physical attraction which had brought them together on Earth there was nothing left. But he still retained a comradely affection for her, born of their childhood's friendship. For the rest he felt linked to her by a deep sense of guilt, his contribution to the terrible conditions she must be enduring.

Nothing happened that could be attributed to his attempt to get in touch with her. On Smith's advice he sought outside distraction lest his concentration should tend to become too tense and thus nullify its power. He visited some of the many churches in the city. In some he found highly ritualistic services with much burning of incense, while there were others which embraced the simpler form of worship. It was strange to sit here and listen to the old theological arguments being trotted out as if there had been no such experience as death among the people who listened. In one chapel with the high sounding name of the sect which used it, he came across a preacher who was threatening his flock with all the fury of the fires of hell if they departed a hair's breadth from the path ordained by their narrow creed. To the faithful he offered the somewhat dubious reward of an existence in which golden harps and damp clouds appeared to play their traditional part. The flock, obviously aware of their own secure future, seemed to revel in diatribes against the lost sheep who were to be so utterly damned. Day after day these people would come here to listen to such inconceivable strictures, so bound by their old superstitions that they could only see their Creator through the eyes of fear. To Michael God was becoming more and more real and concrete as his mind expanded to understand the Omnipresence of the Great Spirit as well as His own inimitable Personality. The Love of God meant more to him now than anything he could imagine. His heart sank as he compared the petty conception of these victims of religious oppression with the glorious Reality. The minds of these people had never really been opened since childhood. They were afflicted with the sins of the fathers, based upon centuries of rule by fear, superstition and temporal power.

More than once he was able to help some unfortunate who seemed to be in a state of readiness to respond to his overtures. These he usually took to Mary's shop, for she was experienced in the best way of handling them. She had a surprising ability for sizing up the real awakening and for spotting the crafty individual who dissembled with the object of enlisting sympathy or gaining some material advantage. The City of Illusion has plenty of mendicants.

Occasionally he would allow his steps to take him towards the river, although Smith had warned him not to venture too far in that direction without an escort or at least a companion. He became interested in an old match-seller who stood on the near side of one of the bridges. The old chap had stood at such a pitch in London and now, after his transition, he had found himself unable to break away from the old habits and had drifted down to this spot. There he stood, day after day, with his tray of matches which nobody bought. Michael had found that the best way to get such people to realize their own position was to interest them in someone worse off than themselves. He spoke to the old man of Vera, and asked him to help him find her. But nothing would induce the pedlar to leave his pitch before it was time. He had a pathetic sense of duty.

"Aye, sir," the old chap said. "I'll have a look over the other side of the bridge when I go off my pitch tonight. I can go there safely enough. They all know old Luke the match-seller; they wouldn't do no harm to me. 'Cos why, I don't do them no harm."

Usually the old man stood apathetically at his post, taking no notice of anyone who approached. But on one occasion Michael reached his pitch just as the lights went on. Luke beckoned to him with some show of eagerness. "'Ere you are, sir. I think I seen her agoing into that pub over there. You stay along o' me and you'll see 'er come out in a minute."

Suppressing his excitement, Michael stood beside the old man, his eyes fixed on the dilapidated building opposite, where the equivalent of beer was sold to those who had formed such strong habits that they could not get on without a semblance of drinking. The place was brightly lit now the lights were on and it displayed some of the garish attractions of an earthly gin palace. Michael wondered whether it was used by the workers as a means of influencing its patrons to seek for something better. Then out of the swinging doors came a woman. The match-seller nudged his elbow and Michael's heart sank; this slattern could not be the trim little Vera he once knew. To his surprise she made straight for the match-seller and he was able to study the distraught, raddled features from close to. In her arms she cradled what appeared to be a bundle of rags as if it were a child.

"Have you seen the doctor?" she asked in a hoarse whisper, "my baby's ill. I must see the doctor."

"You're in luck, mother," said the old man with a wink at Michael, "'ere's the doctor." He jerked a grimy thumb in Michael's direction.

For the first time she looked directly at Michael and to his horror he saw that this indeed was Vera. She did not recognize him and he guessed that her mind was not functioning fully. He looked down at the bundle; it was a bundle and no more. A feeling of despair shook him out of his composure. How was he to cope with this wretched creature who was undoubtedly half demented?

"Vera, do you remember me?" He spoke gently.

She peered up into his face uncertainly. "Who are you, calling me Vera?" she demanded suspiciously.

"I am Michael. Don't you remember me?"

"Michael!" she whispered hoarsely. The name seemed to awaken some memory in her mind.

He had a sudden idea. "Is that our baby, Vera?" he asked, indicating the bundle.

Vera looked down at the bundle, then at Michael. A heavy frown creased her brows, puzzlement changed to alarm, then a look of fury spread over her features. She retreated, screaming foul abuse at him, utterances that he found it hard to associate with the gentle girl he had known. Then she turned and fled in the direction of the river. Michael made as if to follow her.

"Let 'er go, guvnor. She'll be acrost that bridge before you can ketch up with her. And there's chaps over there as'll manhandle you if they gets a chance. You wouldn't have no hope agin them."

Michael relaxed. The old man was right. From all accounts he could not hope to oppose the denizens of that murky rabbit warren of a place on the other side of the river, so dark that he could scarcely distinguish the outlines of the buildings from here. And if he did manage to catch up with Vera he did not know how to deal with her in her present condition. He would have to get advice on that matter. Deeply shaken by the encounter, he turned his steps towards home.

Chapter 5

REDEMPTION

Hardly had Michael left the vicinity of the bridge when a man overtook him. "I hope you will pardon me," he began, "but I was unwittingly a witness to your meeting with that woman. I am a worker in these parts and wondered whether I could help you."

Michael turned to see a man in clerical garb, tall and thin, with rather ascetic features. "That is very good of you," he said, thinking that this man might be able to help him get closer to Vera. "She was a friend of mine on Earth and I am trying to help her."

The parson nodded understandingly. "My name is Warner, Frank Warner. I have rooms near here, why not walk along with me?"

Michael gladly accepted the invitation and the two men strode off down the street. Warner's rooms were in a large tenement building, decidedly inferior to the house in the upper town where Michael dwelt. But his sitting room was clean and tidy and furnished with two comfortable chairs. Against the wall was a bookcase filled with religious works.

"Sit down, won't you?" invited the host. "And tell me in what way I can help you."

Michael hesitated for a moment, for he was not quite sure how to take Warner. Then in the queer way of the Spirit World the answer came to him. He saw the man opposite to him as one who is worthy in every sense of the word but who is so enmeshed in the doctrinal aspect of his religion that he has lost touch with its spiritual meaning. But he got the impression that it would be best to tell him the whole story of his relations with Vera.

"I knew this woman on Earth, she was only a girl when she passed over here. Her name was Vera Clark and I owe her a debt which I am trying to repay."

Warner nodded. "Good, good. I have seen this girl before and been struck by the misery in her face. I would have helped her but she wouldn't let me approach her. I understand that she lives across the river."

Michael went on to describe how Vera's and his destinies had become entangled on Earth and of the tragic results of their liaison. He did not spare himself.

"So you see," he concluded, "I feel responsible for her present condition. I feel that I cannot rest until I have helped her out of her present ghastly surroundings."

The parson nodded comprehendingly. "Yes, it is the old story; people do not realize what they are doing. This girl was evidently driven off her head with worry and is still unbalanced. We must try and get her on this side of the river and get a doctor to see her."

"But what I can't understand," said Michael, "is how she came to do such a foolish thing as commit suicide. After all, in these days it is not uncommon for an unmarried woman to have a child and she might have known that I would have helped her. And it does seem to me to be a rather harsh punishment to be incarcerated in such a horrible place because she was foolish enough to try and end everything."

Warner pursed his lips. "It was indeed foolish of her. But what matter so long as she repents, and you my son. The way is open for you, too."

Michael changed the subject. "Can we not go after her, across the river?"

The parson shrugged his shoulders with a helpless little gesture. "I have tried several times; there must be many over there to whom the Gospel would bring help. But they are a tough lot. It is a positive sink of iniquity, I believe. Whenever I managed to get across the bridge I was attacked by a gang of roughs who chased me back, telling me that parsons were not wanted over there. That made me try all the harder, but the last time they dropped me in the river. Luckily, I can swim."

"Jove, that's a fine effort anyway. How long have you been working over here?"

"I really don't know how long it is because I don't know how long I slept. To tell you the truth I find it all rather puzzling as I cannot find anyone who can explain satisfactorily what actually does happen when one—er—dies. I had a heart attack and when I regained consciousness I found myself in a churchyard somewhere out in the country near here. There were several old friends of mine, clerical men like myself, who said they had come to meet me. I asked them where I was; I guessed I must be dead because I knew they were dead. But they all seemed to have different ideas about things and immediately began a stiff argument. One had an idea that we must be dreaming because there was nothing in the Church teaching to cover this; he argued that if you were not alive you must be asleep as the Judgment Day has not yet come. I don't think he can be right though. One very nice chap wanted me to come up into the hills, where, he said, Heaven was situated. I thought hard over that but I couldn't believe you could get into Heaven as easily as all that; there must be a Judgment first. Another fellow who had been at Oxford with me said that he came from this city and described his work here. That attracted me because it sounded so much like my old work on Earth.

"Unable to decide the truth I went into the church and prayed. And light came to me. I went to the lectern and opened the Bible. St. Paul is quite clear about it in his epistle to the Hebrews. 'But now they desire a better city, that is a heavenly; wherefore God is not ashamed to be called their God: for He hath prepared them a city.' That was good enough guidance for me so I came here."

"Have you come to any conclusion as to where this city is located?" asked Michael.

"I really don't know. I think this must be a place of waiting until the Judgment Day. We used to teach that the sleep lasted until that time, but possibly we were wrong."

"You still believe that God will come to judge the quick and the dead?"

"Of course, it is the faith of the Church. There can be no question of that. And where did you wake up?"

"I didn't wake, I just walked out of the old world into this one." Michael sketched the story of his own transition.

The parson looked incredulous. "There must have been a hiatus of sleep," he averred, "no-one dies like that. Everybody here had the same experience as myself with minor variations."

"I am quite sure I didn't sleep between the two worlds. I just wandered into the Lowlands with my wife."

A puzzled frown crossed the parson's face. "The Lowlands? Never heard of them."

"Well, I can assure you that it is a very real place. It consists mainly of valleys and the high ground above is called the Uplands. I tried to climb up there once and got thrown back by nature spirits."

The parson sat up. He knew where he was now, he was used to dealing with cases like this. "My dear fellow, you must get all these ideas out of your head. I can see what happened now, it is as clear as daylight. You were killed in an accident and after a vivid dream you woke up in this city. All that about Uplands and Lowlands and gardeners is part of your dream."

Michael shook his head. "Not a bit. My wife was with me."

A look of sympathy came into Warner's face. "My dear chap, I am most terribly sorry. I am afraid your wife is still on Earth. You very naturally dreamed about her during your sleep after you died. If she had died too she would be here."

For a moment a terrible thought struck Michael. Supposing what the parson said was right! Could he really be in a state of self-deception? But his mind refused to hold the thought. He shook his head decisively. "No, that is impossible. I know that what I say is true."

"And I am equally sure that you are wrong," retorted the parson. "If there had been such places as the Uplands and Lowlands the Church would have known of them."

"In my Father's house are many mansions," quoted Michael suggestively.

"Ah yes, but, my dear fellow, this is not my Father's house.

148

You cannot say that God owns that fiendish place across the river. You are quoting about Heaven and we shall not know anything about that until and unless we are taken there."

"Where is Heaven, or Hell?" demanded Michael.

Warner looked hard at him. "When you were on Earth you didn't know of the existence of this place did you? Well neither do we yet know the whereabouts of Heaven or Hell. We shall be told when the time comes."

"And in the meantime?"

Warner's eyebrows went up. "We are in a state of suspension, awaiting the Day of Judgment, the Second Coming."

"How do you know?"

"By faith." Warner's chin stuck out obstinately as if to substantiate the permanency of his belief. "By faith in action. 'The substance of things hoped for, the evidence of things not seen.'"

"But don't you think," put in Michael, "that a static faith such as that implies that you have already found the whole of truth, and therefore restricts progress?"

Warner was quite firm in his reply. "Our faith rests upon the revelations of our Lord. If He had wished to give us further revelations He would have done so."

Michael was silent. He felt inadequate to pierce such armour as this.

"I wish," the other went on, more cheerful because he thought he had gained his point, "that you could see some of our work here. There are literally hundreds of souls who have taken this further opportunity of repentance since they arrived here and have become members of the Church. Why only last Sunday I had a large baptismal service."

"Sunday?" queried Michael, "do you have Sundays here?"

Again the puzzled frown. "Sundays? Why not? Why should not God's day be respected here as anywhere else?"

"But there is no sun, how do you tell when it is Saturday night or Sunday morning?"

The parson looked a trifle confused. "Why of course I know there is no sun. I don't know really where the light comes from. But they turn the lights on and off once a day and we go by that."

Michael made one last attempt to shatter Warner's convictions. "What about all these people across the river? Are they to be condemned to eternal punishment at the Day of Judgment?"

Warner's face fell. "That is the cross I have to bear. I lie awake thinking of all those souls in grave danger and trying to think how I may get at them. It is an enormous place, I believe. I am trying to plan some sort of massed invasion by our workers. I have tried alone, as I told you, and that was a dismal failure."

"I don't believe they are lost," affirmed Michael, "it just doesn't seem right."

"Who are we to say whether it is right? Our faith is quite clear on the subject. Of what use to tell the disciples to go out into the world and preach the Gospel if there was no danger of souls being lost?"

"But you believe that Christ died to save sinners?"

"Certainly. But through their repentance. It is the repentance which is the actuating factor and the sacrifice of our Lord which makes it possible. If we can only get these people to realize their plight and recant, then they will be safe." He got up and began to pace the room. "Oh, it is so little to do when one knows the implications. If only I could get at those people down there before it is too late. I know I could make them see sense."

"But do you mean to say that if I openly express my repentance of my affair with Vera I am relieved of all responsibility to her or anyone else?"

"You are never relieved of your responsibility for Christian charity. But through the act of your repentance you will be absolved from the consequences of your sin, our Lord has already redeemed you."

Michael got to his feet. "I am afraid we shall have to differ over that. I have learned a lot since I came over here and although I repent most heartily, I feel just as responsible as ever I was for her present plight. I wish that I could convince you of what I believe to be the truth, that we must bear responsibility and must set right what we have done wrong."

The parson shook his head emphatically. "No, you are

wrong there. Jesus Christ will shoulder that burden for you if you will let Him. Why else did He come to Earth, why else did He die?"

"I believe He came to show us the way to shoulder our burdens and to make God real to us by proving that life survives death."

"Then why didn't He say so?" expostulated the parson.

"How do you know what He said? The accounts of His life and ministry were written about sixty years after His death."

"Yes, by the hand of God. They were inspired accounts."

Michael laughed. "It is clear that we shall not agree."

Warner relaxed into a smile too as he said goodbye. "Anyway, whatever we believe we are at one in our endeavours to help your friend. I will certainly try and get in touch with her."

When Michael got back to the house, Smith showed great interest is his adventure. He seemed keenly distressed about Vera.

"Poor girl, things are worse than I thought. Seeing you must have struck a chord in her memory and the fact that she instinctively made for the bridge shows that she belongs over there. Those brutes across the river must have got a real grip on her. Now let me see. . . ." For a while he remained in deep thought. "Yes, I have it. I know one of the workers down here, a really advanced soul who has access to all the Records. He will be able to help us, I think, because he will be able to trace the original causes of Vera's condition. I rather think it is a case of *karma*."

"Tell me something about this *karma?*" asked Michael.

Smith smiled slowly across at him. "That would take quite a time. And really I don't know half of the story. It is a big subject. But briefly, it is the outworking of the law of Cause and Effect. 'As ye sow so shall ye reap.' I should imagine that Vera is suffering for more than the mistakes in one incarnation. I think she is working out something from a past experience."

Concerning Warner he was more emphatic. "I know him; he is a fine courageous chap and there are many like him. They have to cross over to this plane first because they are bound up in their rigid doctrine. Had Warner woken up in the

Lowlands and found that so much of his belief was based upon false premises it would have been a great shock to him and might have delayed his progress. Once he realizes the truth he will soon progress. He is not wasting his time, he is doing fine work where he is. It might sound strange to you but it is often better to tackle some of these ignorant souls by orthodox methods at first. The Salvation Army people are hard at work here and across the river, saving souls with their old persistency. It is the quickest way because it is what these people are accustomed to and expect. The real truth would be quite beyond their immediate comprehension. "Anyway," he added, "our plan worked. Your thoughts reached Vera and subconsciously influenced her to contact you."

Michael's hand caressed his chin. "I wonder," he observed thoughtfully.

"Not a doubt of it in my mind. I have seen it happen too often before. But the main point is that we have located her. The next problem is how to get her out of the power of those wretches across the river."

"Tell me more about that place."

Smith thought for a moment. "It is rather difficult to explain. I suppose you were taught all about Heaven and Hell when you were a youngster? Well you have stood upon the lowest steps of Heaven and I suppose we might call that place Hell, although the association of ideas is wrong. Neither God nor a devil created it, it was made by the people who sank into that condition. There is no doubt that an inkling of its existence got through to Earth and incarnate spirits greedy for power used the fact to frighten ignorant men. But it is definitely not a punishment centre. The only spirits to go there are those who are so weighted down by the environment they have created that they could not exist elsewhere. They are those who are trying to live entirely through the senses instead of through the Spirit."

"Has it always existed?"

Smith shook his head. "I don't think so. But it has been there as long as anyone here knows and I suppose it will remain as long as Earth continues to send us souls in a state of ignorance. Mortals think that when they have hanged a

152

murderer, they have finished with the business. But they have only 'handed the baby' to us. I can assure you that we view such an arrangement with anything but equanimity."

"And can't they break out of there?"

"Remember that we are dealing with a condition rather than a three-dimensional geographical aspect. You know something about the power of thought and what it can do, both for good and for evil. Well, negative thoughts generated by Earth people during thousands of years floated off into the ethers surrounding the Earth forming a belt of evil or negative conditions by reason of their density. In this belt is located the lower Astral plane and at its core is this condition we call Hell. And because the forces of Light are eternally warring against the forces of Darkness this belt of evil becomes compressed round the Earth from the continual attack of the Cosmic rays. This river that lies between us is far more potent that it appears, it is a band of steel confining the evil influences and gradually destroying them."

"But why does not God stop it, surely He has the power?"

"God does not work in that way. He has a plan for the Universe, a perfect plan. If His children, in their eagerness to experience, make a mess of that plan it would not speed their evolution to help them to avoid the issue. They would not learn their lesson without suffering. That is the meaning of suffering. And according to the depth of suffering so is the height of accomplishment made ultimately attainable. You may be surprised to hear that some of our greatest workers down here were once dwellers in the darkest corners of that Pit."

"I suppose it must be very difficult to get at these people."

Smith nodded. "It is indeed. There are many conditions of people in there. The best of them are those who are face to face with their Conscience, suffering terrible remorse. The others are those who have not yet awakened to the existence of Conscience and are merely revelling in the hideous perversions they practise. The use of Black Magic is quite common."

"You don't say so. I thought that was all moonshine."

"It is really. It can only affect those who let its manifestations register on their minds, where they accept them as real when actually they are illusory. But the rule of fear is the strongest weapon in man's armoury. You have learned something of the power of Spirit; well, if that power is used constructively it is White Magic, if it is abused and employed in a negative way it is Black Magic, that is all. There is nothing supernatural about it. White Magic is real and Black Magic is unreal except to those who let it affect them. It is all part of the lesson we have to learn."

"How do you place this City of Illusion we are in, it is not Hell, is it?"

"It is a sort of borderland. I suppose it came into being in much the same way as Hell did. There had to be somewhere for people to come who were not ready to enter the Lowlands and yet were not really bad, just ignorant. And it forms a useful resting place for those who are newly rescued from across the river. By contrast it seems a veritable paradise to them. It would never do to take such people direct into the Uplands. It would be like taking a prisoner from a dungeon and releasing him in a tropical desert. The sun would blind him and flay him alive."

Michael gave a half laugh. "Well, I must say I never thought I should find that Hell is a real place after all."

Smith made an expressive gesture. "It is only real to those who believe it to be so, to those who are so steeped in ignorance that they cannot respond to any higher stimuli. Nevertheless, I don't advise you to treat it too lightly. It can be a very dangerous place to those who are not prepared and protected. It is possible to allow the manifestations to so affect the mind that one comes to believe in their potency. Then the danger becomes real."

Suddenly Michael bowed his head in his hands. "Oh that poor child," he groaned. "I can't get the thought of her plight out of my mind. Whatever you say about *karma,* I was the cause of her getting into this awful condition."

"I know, Michael." Smith's voice was infinitely tender. "But you won't help her or yourself by giving way to emotion. Lift your mind into a positive assurance that you are going to rescue her; that will ensure success."

"Of course, you are right," agreed Michael, brightening. "I

can see you are more than you pretend to be. I don't know how I should have got on without you."

"Someone else would have helped you in that case. There is always the opportunity opening out to those who strive for it, whether it is for progress or retrogression. These things happen because they are subject to laws; they are not accidental."

"I can certainly see that God is working through you."

"As He does through all of us. Yet that is one of the hardest lessons people have to learn over here. The false modesty of Earth life is so strong that they can't believe that God is really working in and through them. It is very natural but it forms a stumbling block to the free flow of Spirit power through the individual."

"What a contrast there is between Earth and this life," exclaimed Michael as the other rose to go. "Here the ideal of service seems to be the only thing worth considering, while down there it is just the opposite, men are acquisitive to a degree, and anyone who lives a life of service is held up as a particular sort of saint."

Smith smiled as he nodded. "Yes, but we must remember that they have little conception of the glorious objective that is a little clearer on this side. They are struggling in the darkness while we are working in the sunlight. One must not judge them harshly. Well, I will leave you to rest now. Have another try to get in mental touch with Vera; this is no time to relax your efforts. I will see what I can find out about her condition."

When he had gone Michael lay on his bed and concentrated upon the task of directing his strongest thoughts towards Vera.

Two days later—that is after two periods of lights on— Smith came into his room bearing three robes and three staffs of wood.

"Here you are. I have seen one of the Initiates in charge of that area across the river and he seems to think that Vera is ready to come with us though her outer mind may object. We may have to use considerable force to overcome her resistance. We are to ask Mary to come too, she has mediumistic powers which may prove useful."

"Isn't that rather risky, taking a young girl there?"

Smith laughed. "No more than taking you. You must realize that a female spirit is just as tough as a male one. You do not need to be a *squire des dames* here."

Michael was forced to smile at that. "No, I suppose not. Curious how the influence of the earthly life gets one here."

"You need have no fear about Mary. She will merely be used as a channel for spiritual power, for the evil masters will undoubtedly try and keep their hold on Vera."

Smith was not opening his shop that day so they went down at once to see Mary, who readily agreed to accompany them on their errand of mercy. Michael was surprised that she showed no fear at the prospect. He wished he was feeling as calm himself. The rest of that day was spent in certain purifying ceremonies in case Black Magic should be employed by those who would resist their entry into the recesses of Hell.

As soon as the lights went out next morning the three donned the robes which almost obscured what little light emanated from their present garments, and with staff in hand, set out towards the river. Smith explained that the staffs were magnetized to deflect any form of unpleasant manifestation which might be conjured up to impede their progress. Along the river front was a thoroughfare faintly reminiscent of the Thames Embankment. The little party had to travel some way along this before coming to the bridge they were to cross. Michael noted that the area across the river was shrouded in a heavy haze and from its depths no sound came, nor did anyone emerge onto the bridges. It might have been a city of the dead. At length they came to the bridge they required and turned to cross it. There was a chill wind blowing from the water which swept in a turgid, uninviting swirl through the arches and almost instinctively the three wrapped their robes more closely about them. As they neared the opposite bank they could not resist the impression that from the frowning ill-kept buildings hundreds of eyes were watching their approach with malevolent regard.

The streets on this side of the river were quite dark and a faint glow from the flickering jets that passed for street illumination served only to intensify the gloom and offer deeper shadows beyond the feeble rays of light. As they penetrated into a maze of small streets they became aware of an occasional furtive figure flitting through the grey gloom.

"Best keep to the centre of the road," advised Smith, "then we have some chance of seeing what is happening. We shall get more used to this darkness presently."

They were just approaching a crossroads when Michael gave a cry of warning. A car came rushing towards them at great speed, braked suddenly and turned on two wheels into the right-hand turning. A sinister-looking bundle was thrown out onto the pathway followed by a quick rattle of machine gun fire from the saloon, then on it sped, as fast as it had arrived. Michael ran forward expecting to find a bleeding body on the ground. To his amazement there was nothing there.

Smith quickly joined him. "I should say that we have witnessed an astral repetition of some gangster outrage on Earth. There was no body, there couldn't be. But the villain, in his mad efforts to escape the consequences of his act, keeps on repeating the scene for which he has created an illusory car and gun with an astral body to shoot at. Of course it dematerialized as soon as it was beyond his control. I dare say the poor devil has been repeating that episode for years."

Michael gave a whistle of astonishment. "I suppose no one can help him?"

"I doubt it. Anyway the local workers will know all about him. He will go on doing it until he listens to them and accepts the fact that it is all illusion.

The little party hurried on and presently began to meet more people. For the most part these took no notice of them, being entirely absorbed in their own affairs. Since they had left the bridge, however, Michael had felt certain that some individuals were shadowing their progress and turned more than once to try and catch sight of some skulking figure. The feeling of being watched became more and more intense, and presently was emphasized by a man who had been watching their approach from a patch of shadow on the pavement. As they passed him, he stepped forward and gave vent to a burst of satirical laughter. The inhuman sound of it made Mary give a little shiver and press closer to Michael.

Suddenly she gave a scream. "Look!" she cried. Michael followed her gaze to see a large snake writhing sinuously towards them. Smith seemed unperturbed at the sight and simply pointed his staff at the reptile which reared up and swayed its head menacingly to and fro, its wicked little tongue darting in and out. Then it sank to the ground and slithered away into the shadows.

"Jove!" exclaimed Michael. "This is traditional Hell with a vengeance."

"Don't be alarmed," said Smith, "it couldn't have hurt you, it has no concrete existence. It was merely an astral shape conjured up by some evil mind to frighten us. It does indicate, however, that we are, shall I say—expected. A welcome awaits us."

"Well, if that thing can't hurt us what is there to be afraid of?" asked Michael.

"The principal danger is that some evil entity might try and obsess one of us, using a temporary state of fear to accomplish his object. That means try and get into our body and manifest through us. But we must not allow ourselves to be overcome by fear. And in any case we are well protected by the Hierarchy whose Initiates have given us permission to come here. The only chance of danger is in our *thinking* we had hurt ourselves, or were at the mercy of those who wish to injure us. Supposing that bandit's car had run into us, it would merely have passed through us. A queer experience, that is all. But supposing we were in such a state of fright that we thought it was a real car which had really run over us; then we might have accepted, subconsciously, the idea of being hurt. That might have made some impression on our etheric bodies and would certainly weaken our resistance to any further funny tricks they might have ready for us. It is really a form of suggestion."

By this time they were some distance from the river. Michael had no idea where they were but Smith seemed to be acting under some form of guidance. Presently he called a halt. "Now do carefully what I tell you. A lot depends upon the success of this manoeuvre. Stand back to back here, forming a triangle. That's right. Now send out your strongest thoughts to Vera's spirit. Tell her to answer you."

For a while the trio stood there, sending out the vital call of spirit to spirit. As he did so Michael could not help noticing that swirls of vapour wound close to his face. And, whether it was his imagination or not, these swirls seemed to take the shape of horrible grinning mask-like faces. He found it hard to concentrate and sensed that the object of those ghastly distractions was to prevent him from doing so. He was relieved when Smith told them to relax.

"Nothing happening," he remarked, "we must move on and try again. By the way, take no notice of those charming faces you may have seen. They are not real."

Once more the party advanced, travelling further and further into the depths of this city of evil. Sometimes they heard shrill screams from neighbouring buildings suggesting some horrible crime that was being re-enacted with age-old persistency. Once they saw a woman who passed along the street sobbing as if her heart would break. Michael wanted to go and help her but Smith sternly ordered him to desist. "You do not know but what she is a trap, a mere wraith set there by evil ones to entangle you. We have but one task at this time; let us resolve to stick to it."

A second time they formed a triangle and sent out the clarion call of rescue. Again the wreaths of mist wound their way into fantastic shapes and this time they were accompanied by flickering tongues of blue flame shooting about in the manner of phosphorescence. Michael could tell that Mary was deeply conscious of these manifestations for her slight form shivered against his shoulder.

They all heard it together: a long-drawn shrill scream of despair coming from the direction in which Mary was facing.

"Come on," said Smith, a determined note in his voice, and they set out in the direction from which the sound had come. When he judged they had gone far enough he called a halt and they formed a triangle once more. Thus, by a process not unlike the radio directional methods used to guide ships and aircraft on Earth, they came at length to a large dark building from which came not a ray of light.

"She is somewhere in there," announced Smith, gazing curiously at the building. This time they stood in a row and sent their thought call towards the building. But no answering cry of despair came to reward their efforts.

Smith gave a little expression of annoyance. "They must be holding the poor child down with their filthy minds," he muttered. "Well, we shall have to make an entry and see what is inside."

Leading the way, the valiant little tobacconist went up to the largest of the entrances to the building. The door was bolted but he soon disposed of that by means of keen concentration of thought. The bolt melted away and the door swung open. Hunching his shoulders, he said, "Here goes," and marched boldly in, his staff at the ready. Mary followed, with Michael bringing up the rear. Through the building they tramped, examining room after room. Once a veritable gale of derisive laughter swept down one of the corridors causing Mary and Michael to shiver with apprehension. "Don't pay any attention to that," cried Smith who was ahead, "whatever you do, don't think about it. Think only of Vera and success."

With an effort Michael switched his thoughts away from that eldritch screeching, though every fibre of his being ached to respond to this appalling manifestation. Suddenly, Smith, who had glanced back over his shoulder at Mary, faced about and stood regarding her. Then Michael realized that she was in a trance. Her eyes were closed and her face was set in severe lines as if the controlling entity were a man. She faced round to her left where there was a door. Her lips moved and Michael just got the word 'Vera' which they formulated. Again she spoke, louder. From inside the room there came the sound of a scuffle. Then there was a scream, rising to a shriek.

"Go away, I hate you all. I don't want you here. If you don't go horrible things will happen to you. Go! Go! GO!" The distraught voice rose into a shriek.

Michael, who had been eyeing Mary's lips, now began to notice that the swirling mists were taking advantage of the halt to gather again. The atmosphere became clammy and smelled abominably with a clinging foetid odour reminiscent of putrefaction. But Smith dispelled a good deal of that by use of his staff. The shrieking laughter began again behind Michael and this time it had a triumphant ring in it.

"Don't turn away, keep facing the door," murmured Smith in his ear. Not too soon, for Michael was on the point of giving way to an irresistible impulse to turn round and see who was laughing so uproariously. He concentrated his mind upon the door in front of him, conscious that attempts were being made to distract his attention. Insidious whispers just behind his ear made him long to turn his head just a fraction; the longing became more compelling than any urge he could recall. He had to summon all his power to resist.

Mary's lips began to move again. "Open the door," she commanded.

Smith pressed open the door and entered the room, followed by the entranced Mary with Michael in the rear as before. As he entered the doorway he saw a woman lying crouched on a bed of filthy rags upon the floor. It was Vera, her rag doll clutched to her breast. But this time there was nothing approaching recognition in those staring eyes. With horror Michael saw madness staring at him from their flaming depths. It seemed incredible that a human being he had known and liked, with whom he had been so intimate, could change into such a terrible personality. He heard a voice, it might have been his own common sense, telling him that nothing could be done. Vera was past help. Better leave her as she was. It really seemed the sensible thing to do and there was Mary who might be injured by too long a period in trance. . . .

With a shock he realized that it was the insistent voice outside the room which had been whispering into his ear. It was not his own self. Taking a pull on himself he shut out that impression and concentrated his attention upon the work in hand. Mary's control now began to take charge. In a voice that gathered in strength she ordered the two men to form a triangle with her, facing inwards and holding their staves behind their backs in a horizontal position so that they formed a wooden enclosure. This done she caused the wooden triangle to move bodily towards the obsessed girl who hurled a perfect tornado of shrieks at them, shielding her face with her forearm as if danger threatened. Finally the trio arrived in a position that enclosed the hapless Vera within the triangle. A commanding voice issued from Mary's lips. "Ignorant spirit, I command you to leave the body of this girl. Go!"

There was such power behind the last word, which was shot out with intense force, that Vera's body became convulsed. She groaned as if in agony. Mary's voice spoke again, and yet again. The third time Vera sprang to her feet and threw her hands high above her head, her features working with passion. Then with a shriek that jarred Michael's etheric senses, her body shook as if something were being drawn out of it, to fly upwards to the ceiling like a rebounding elastic. The girl's body swayed drunkenly, then collapsed in a heap upon the floor. Vera was free.

Mary gave a little shudder, gasped and opened her eyes. "Blimey!" she said, when she saw what lay at her feet.

"Are you all right?" asked Smith solicitously.

Mary raised her eyebrows. "Fine, how's the family?"

"Don't you know that you have been in trance, helping to rid poor Vera of an obsessing entity?" asked Smith.

Mary was astounded and looked it. She looked round her distastefully. "Nice place she's got here." She glanced down at her feet and for the first time seemed to sense the desperate need of the girl on the floor. Dropping down beside her she raised Vera's body so that her head rested against her shoulder and encircled her with one arm. She murmured words of love and pity as she pillowed the tangled mass of curls against her breast. With a shuddering sigh that wrenched Michael's heart, Vera opened her eyes, looked round with a fearful glance that spoke volumes, then came to rest them wonderingly on the kindly face so close to her own.

The return journey was far easier than the outward one. Although the dense nature of the atmosphere made it difficult for them to travel with the usual swift progress to which they were accustomed, they were able, now that their object was accomplished, to make themselves partially invisible to the denizens of the neighbourhood by raising their own vibrations.

162

Vera was left in Mary's charge and a spiritual healer was summoned to attend her.

As they returned home Michael observed to his companion that he would like to be alone for a while. Smith nodded understandingly.

"Yes, you have accomplished a great deal. You have much to be thankful for."

Michael's feelings were mixed. He was conscious of a feeling of elation at the successful termination of his mission. It seemed that at last Vera was out of danger and her recovery only a matter of time and attention. Yet the sense of freedom engendered by the rescue was burdened by the thought of that horror-haunted city across the river. Even now the lingering thought of that appalling stench assailed him. He pondered over the evil, layers and layers of it, that must have gone to the brewing of that vicious odour. It seemed incredible that man, own son to the glory that is God, could trespass so far, could sink so low and apparently be content to remain in such a condition. The thought sank deep into his being, where it was to have a vital effect upon his future planning.

It was some time before Michael and Vera were able to meet. Acting on the advice of experts, Mary insisted on keeping her quiet and without visitors during the time that she was having the attention of a skilled spiritual healer. There was much damage to her etheric body which had been 'wounded' by the antics of the violent spirit that had succeeded in gaining entry. At length, however, the time came when she was pronounced fit to meet people. Mary brought her to the open space which was dignified by the term 'Municipal Gardens,' and which boasted a few tired-looking flowers struggling for existence in the misty, fog-laden air.

Michael met her there. She came forward on Mary's arm. He saw that she had discarded the old rags and was wearing robes that became her; her hair was bright again and her eyes shone with new light. She looked more spiritual than he had ever seen her.

"My dear," he said, taking her hands in his, and leading her to a seat. "I am so happy to see you well again."

She conjured up a smile for him and sank onto the seat with

a little sigh. She was obviously still very depleted. Mary smiled down at her with a motherly air. "I am going to leave you with Michael for a little while." She turned to him. "Mind you take her home if you think she is getting too exhausted." With an understanding look at him she went off in the direction of her shop.

Michael sat down beside Vera and took possession of one of her hands. The action seemed to give her strength as if some power flowed from him to her. For a while neither spoke. There was so much to say, on so many planes of thought, that it was difficult to know where to begin. They were not in love, these two, yet they had shared in a deep experience which had created a bond between them with a corresponding mead of understanding.

"How are you now?" Michael began. "I cannot conceive what a terrible time you must have had."

For a while she regarded him silently, her eyes searching his for some means of breaking down the little wall of reserve which still remained between them. Then she spoke.

"I am beginning to forget, thanks be. The healer who has been treating me has told me a lot and I am beginning to learn the real truth about things. But first tell me about yourself. I hear that you are married and that your wife is over here too. Have you any children?"

Michael told her. He sketched the events of his life from the time he left home until the present. She listened with deep interest. He wondered whether he could speak to her of her son and his. Or whether mention of him would cause her emotional distress that might retard her recovery. He decided to tell her.

"I have some important news for you," he said gently. "News concerning our . . . child."

Vera's eyes regarded him blankly, some of the old misery rising in them.

"I have met him, he is a fine young fellow now," he went on.

"I don't understand," she gasped, the words coming in an incredulous whisper, "my baby was never born. I thought it was when I was . . . across the river, but I know now that I was demented and the baby was only a bundle of rags."

Michael tried to explain how an incarnating soul begins its life on Earth from the moment of conception and even if the mother dies before it is born into the physical world, it has already acquired its etheric body and can therefore be born into the etheric world, there to grow and develop under the loving care of women, many of whom have been denied the joys of motherhood in their own incarnation.

"So you see," he continued, "John went on growing at the same rate as he would have done on Earth and will continue to do so until he reaches the etheric age of thirty Earth years. I can tell you that he is a fine young spirit now."

Vera's eyes had been widening with the wonder of this news. It seemed that she was unable to absorb the truth of it all at once.

"Michael," she pleaded, her hands gripping his with the intensity of her emotion, "help me to believe this is true. You are not telling me this just to . . . cheer me up?"

Michael shook his head smilingly. "Why, my dear, I wouldn't do that. It is all very, very true, thank God. I have met John more than once and so has Ann. He is there, in the Uplands, getting a home ready for you to join him. He loves you so much, he is longing for you to come and teach him all that only a mother can teach."

A look of divine ecstasy flashed into Vera's eyes, as if a vision of unbelievable joys had opened up before her. "Oh, my dear, this news has made a new woman of me, it has taken me right up into heaven. Oh if I had only known this before. My baby—grown up." A pathetic look of yearning came over her face as she thought of the lovely years of his childhood which she had missed. Then she turned to Michael again.

"What does he know about me?"

"Not very much. You see he has no experience of Earth life and its difficulties and he wouldn't understand the meaning of deep emotions. Our story would seem rather futile and silly to him unless he were at the same time educated in the meaning of Earth life. He is filled with an intense longing to know about it all and it will be your pleasant task to teach him. You will find him a very willing pupil."

"Oh yes," she whispered, her eyes shining, "that would be heaven in itself. To teach my boy to be brave and fine and strong, not to hold the knowledge of evil from him but to teach him of the futility of evil. Oh I can teach him about that, I know, I know."

"Would you like to tell me about it?" asked Michael softly.

Her eyes flashed. "I would like to tell the world! I would like to shout my story from the housetops if it would help one single wretched soul from having to endure the hell that I went through. I have learned a terrible lesson. My story is a long one; the healer has been telling me about it. You know, I had lived on Earth before; this was my second incarnation. When I was incarnated the first time I was a Priestess in the days of Atlantis and I had endless opportunities for doing good and righting many wrongs. But I was proud and selfish and I delighted in torturing the poor wretches I ought to have helped. Well, after thousands of years of trying to work that out I was allowed to try again and I was given a test. If I passed that test satisfactorily I could take it that the account was squared.

"I don't suppose you have the slightest conception of the thoughts that occupied my mind that time in Belchester?" She smiled bitterly. "I was ambitious, I was determined I would not remain a nobody in Belchester. I meant to get on. I had designs on you from the time we were kids together. I could see you had it in you to succeed and I meant to share your success. I kidded myself that I was in love with you. I wasn't, of course, but it pleased me to fancy it that way. I knew you didn't care a rap about me for you were in love with your career. And that made me mad. I knew that what I was planning was wrong; I think my conscience was jabbing at me. And that made me all the more determined to have my way. I determined to possess you some way or other. I made up my mind to have a child by you and then force you to marry me."

Vera threw the words from her in the bitterness of self-abasement. For a few moments she was silent. Then she went on:

"I got my way, and I found to my joy that a child was coming. I knew my father would do all in his power to make you marry me or else turn me out. He was terribly proud and very hard. It didn't matter much which way things went for I knew my Michael. Things looked pretty good. Then one day I went for a walk along the river bank. I sat down to rest and must have gone to sleep for I had a queer dream. I woke up in a state of terror for I remembered some of my dream. I had seen myself in a mirror, as it were, and realized what I was trying to do. I knew I had failed to pass my test. In an agony of mind I determined that I would not try and ruin your life as well as my own. Oh, thank God, I did that. I know now that it formed a link between us that enabled you to come and help me. It was that little act which saved me from I daren't think what.

"I went home and my appearance must have frightened my mother for she soon had the truth out of me. Then my father came in and he was told. He flew into a passion and demanded to know who the father was. I swore I did not know. I told lies and pretended that I was a real bad lot and it might be one of several. My father went mad with rage and threatened to turn me out of the house if I did not tell. I got in a terrible state too and dashed out of the house. I went back to the place where I had my dream and . . . well you know what happened. I thought I was making an end of it all. Oh, my God!" She laughed bitterly. "An end! It wasn't an end, it was a beginning, a re-birth into Hell!"

She was silent for a while till she had regained control of herself. Michael possessed himself of one of her hands again and the action seemed to give her strength to go on.

"I woke up, down there, in that foul part of the city. I seemed to have had a dream that I gave birth to my child and then got separated from it. My arms ached for it and I wandered about disconsolate, looking for it. My heart almost burst with the strain of longing. I felt emotion and remorse more keenly than you can ever imagine. I knew that my horrible situation was due to what I had done to myself, taking my own life from motives of fear. Oh, Michael, don't ever let anyone commit suicide if you can prevent them. The consequences are terrible.

"Well, naturally, I didn't find my baby and so, hardly

167

knowing what I was doing, I made a doll out of rags and hugged that, thinking I might still the ache in my heart. But the rags kept on falling to pieces and I began to haunt the yards of the houses picking up what scraps I could. Sometimes I used to come over to this side to find better scraps, but I found the bright light here hard to bear.

"I don't know how long I was there, I had no idea of time. I met people and some of them spoke kindly to me and took me to their houses, but in reality they were filthy people. The debauchery, the horrors, the awful things they showed me. Then a man I had met at one of the houses began to hang around that building where I made myself a home. A horrible man but with unlimited patience and devilish persuasion. At length I was in such a state of despair that I didn't care what happened. The man used to follow me about; I couldn't shake him off. Gradually he got so close that we were never apart. Then somehow, I don't know how, he managed to get into my body and I was driven out. It seemed as if there were two of us in one body." She gave a shudder at the recollection and buried her face in her hands.

Michael put his arm protectingly about her. "Don't tell me anymore, my dear. Let us try and forget it." But she shook herself free and faced him with a sudden determination.

"I will finish, I must. It will help me to tell you. It became worse when that man obsessed me. You know that that place where you found me is only at the fringe of what they call hell. This beast made me penetrate further into the depths of that foul place. All the horrible things that the Earth has ever spewed forth are congregated in that obscene sink of iniquity. I was helpless, he had complete charge of me and I was carried along, compelled to witness all the depravity and perversion in which he indulged with a perfectly fiendish enjoyment."

"It sounds incredible, I know," she added bitterly, "but it can happen, I can assure you of that."

"But, Vera, my dear, surely all that did not happen to you because of your one indiscretion?"

She shook her head. "No it was not because of that. You see when I failed to pass my test and tried to end my life as well I released all the evil I had accumulated as a result of my past incarnation. I had the chance to get rid of that burden by showing that I had learned to control my lower self, but I hadn't. I failed. So I had to learn the lesson all over again."

"Oh, my dear child," cried Michael from the depths of his heart, "I am so terribly sorry I was so weak. How much I could have accomplished for you if I had been stronger."

Again Vera shook her head. "I don't think you could, Michael. I had to learn that lesson. If it hadn't been you it would have been someone else. I was determined to have my own way." She gave a deep sigh of relief. "I feel better for having told you all that. Perhaps it has helped to get some of its effects out of my system. Anyway," her eyes met his and lit up again, "I feel happier than I can ever remember. And what you tell me about my . . . John, lifts my heart right up out of that ghastly memory. I love him already although I have never seen him. But he has lain next to my heart. He is mine. Tell me more about him, Michael. What does he look like?"

He told her and as he did so her face began to soften and the hard lines were smoothed away. So Mary found them. She sat down beside Vera and put a hand impulsively over hers. A message passed between them such as only women who have suffered deeply can give to each other.

"My dear, you are looking better already. Michael must have found the magic elixir for you."

"Oh, more than that," exclaimed Vera happily, "he has told me about John."

Mary nodded enthusiastically. "Aren't you just longing to meet him?"

Suddenly Vera's eyes clouded and signs of a coming storm rippled her features. She dropped her head into her hands. Had she been able she would have sought relief in tears. Her emotions, so deeply stirred, had at last rebelled and momentarily overcome her weak condition.

Mary put an arm about her. "I am going to take her home," she said decisively. So, with Vera between them, the three paced slowly homewards. At the door Vera, now more in control of herself, turned to Michael.

"Thank you, Michael dear, for all you have done for me. Words cannot express all that I feel but some day I will try and learn how to thank you properly. Don't worry anymore about me. I am going right ahead, for there is a magnet in front of me that will never let me go."

Michael took her hand in his and on a sudden impulse, kissed her on the forehead. It was a kiss of benediction, an impulse coming from deep within himself. It seemed to set a seal upon the design that the weaving of their respective threads had made in the pattern of their lives. They had met, together they had experienced bitterness and joy, and now they were to part. Something had been accomplished.

When Michael got home he opened his door to an unaccustomed blaze of light. For a moment he had to shield his eyes to see who was standing there. It was Tendor. He had thrown off his dull cloak and stood, magnificent, glowing with a radiance that brought to Michael a nostalgic memory of his beloved Ann in that other life that seemed so far off in contrast to the depths he had just experienced. A cry of joy on his lips, he went to meet his dear friend with hands outstretched.

When the two had exchanged greetings Michael begged for news of his beloved. With his gentle smile Tendor said, "Have you not brought back with you any recollection of the many times you came to join her while your coarser vehicle slept here?"

"Oh, yes," exclaimed Michael impatiently, "I had vague memories. But that is not enough. How is she? Is she happy? and the children?"

"They are well, and they await your return eagerly. I have some good news for you. The Lords of Karma, they who hold the tangled threads of destiny and who watch the scales of Divine Justice, have decreed that you have earned your release from this place. You have earned the right to go back to the Lowlands where further opportunities await you."

Michael was so overcome by this glorious news that he could scarcely control his thoughts. "Oh, Tendor! Have I really reached that point?"

"The final adjustment to the scales of justice is not yet made but you are free from the chains that held you to this place."

"The Lowlands, and Ann." Michael softly breathed his thoughts aloud.

"Aye," put in the guide, "she will await you there, and the children will visit you there from time to time."

Michael found that the thought of reunion was almost too much to bear. From the time that he had entered this lower plane a veil had mercifully been drawn across the bright memory of the radiant heights where Ann dwelt with the children. But the arrival of Tendor in his pristine brightness had pulled aside the curtain and brought back reality. He felt an indescribable longing to get back to her.

Tendor, having arranged an appointed hour to call for him, took his departure. Michael then set out to say goodbye to the many friends he had made during his stay in the City of Illusion. Smith refused to say goodbye, saying that Mary and he were to attend his departure. Finally he sought Vera. She was looking brighter and happier than when he left her last and greeted him gladly. He told her of his impending departure.

She nodded her head. "Yes, Mary has told me. I am so glad." "Perhaps," she added wistfully, "you may meet my John. Tell him . . . tell him that I am striving with all my strength to win my way back to him, and give him all my love."

Michael promised that he would do all in his power to deliver the message. "I feel that I am leaving you in good hands," he added.

A happy smile came over Vera's face. "Mary is a darling. She is so good to me, I really don't deserve it."

For a while they talked of the future; neither of them felt inclined to recall her recent experience, even though it must be burnt upon her mind indelibly. They parted as they had met, with the unspoken sympathy of those whose paths have met in the mists of suffering.

It was just after the mythical daylight had broken over the City of Illusion that he and Tendor set out together, this time for the hills that lay behind the city. As they climbed the steep slopes Michael paused to look back at this queer metropolis where he had met with such varied experiences. In the half-light engendered by the overhanging mists, it looked like some artistic creation by a highly imaginative painter. Distance lent some enchantment to the half tones and veiled the air of disreputableness which characterized its closer appearance. A deep sense of thankfulness came welling up from within him that he had been enabled to rescue at least one poor victim from that darker hell which lay across the river. He breathed a prayer for those souls in self-inflicted bondage as he turned away to follow Tendor.

At length they neared the top and on rounding a corner came upon a little chapel that seemed out of place in these grim heights. It was a little gem of architecture and while there was little enough beauty in its setting, it seemed to light up its surroundings with a gentle radiance that gave promise of some wonderful quality within.

"What is this place?" asked Michael.

"It is a Chapel of Release," explained Tendor. "Here we shall meet the Initiate who aided you to rescue Vera. He is to help to speed you to a higher plane."

Michael entered the tiny building to find a lovely atmosphere that was deeply soothing. There was a dim quietness here as if some angel had his being about the altar. The contrast between the murky atmosphere he had just left and the clear though dimmed environment of this peaceful place made him feel as if he had shed some irksome garment directly he entered the door. To his delight he found Mary and Freddie Smith awaiting him. He greeted them both eagerly.

"I do wish you were coming with me," he could not help saying. He was finding that service in the common cause had its own rewards. He felt bound to these two by ties made enduring through achievement; the thought of parting from them was a sad one.

Mary smiled at him. She seemed to understand. "You wouldn't have me leave my friend Vera, would you?" she demanded. "I have you to thank for bringing us together. She and I are great friends and we are planning all sorts of things to do together."

Michael looked across at Smith. "And you, Freddie?"

Smith shook his head decisively. "My time will come. In

your happiness I see a reflection of what awaits me. With that I am content."

For a while they talked together, then Tendor beckoned to Michael. With a last farewell to his friends, Michael followed his guide up to the altar where a spirit in like sombre garments to themselves, awaited them. He greeted Michael with a ready smile, and explained that it was he who had spoken through Mary when they were combating the evil forces which held Vera down. Michael began to express his thanks but the Initiate merely smiled. "It was an opportunity to serve God and at the same time to help two spirits in distress. It is always a privilege to do that."

At his invitation Michael and Tendor passed beyond the altar rails and the Initiate moved to draw a curtain of thin transparent material across. Michael glanced back for the last time into the dimness of the nave. A smile from both his friends greeted the gesture, one that he carried as a precious memory into the future that awaited him.

When the curtain was drawn the Initiate bid them remove their outer garments. It was with a feeling of relief that Michael shed the clinging folds of the dark robe that had covered them since he arrived in this realm, and stood forth in the unaccustomed brightness of his normal attire. He gazed in astonishment at the brilliance that emanated from the Initiate when he too removed his outer robe. It was a splendour that transcended even that of Tendor.

The three then faced the altar and stood for a while in silent prayer. Accustomed to the almost materialistic reaction to divine influence which characterized life in his recent surroundings, Michael found a new aspect of God shining before him as he stood in the grateful freedom of his own personality. It was like coming out of long incarceration in darkness into the delicious freedom of the sunshine. Suddenly he became aware, with a conviction he had never experienced before, that God is truly in all things and the more a spirit expands in consciousness the greater will be the realization of this fact. Down the beams of light that filtered through the stained glass of the chapel east window, came a new assurance of spiritual power, a new understanding of God. A consciousness of a wonderful, all-embracing Power, tempered by the warmth of a Personal Love that sought out his individuality and made it at-one with joy and serenity. It was a moment of inimitable splendour far surpassing anything he had known before. He knew that he had taken a step forward never to retrace it again. He held a precious knowledge now that was pregnant with strength, for he knew that he was a part in very truth with the ultimate grandeur that is God. One by one the veils of illusion that stretched between him and his Creator were being torn away, to display Him in ever more glorious Reality. The ecstasy of that knowledge filled his whole being.

Gradually he brought his consciousness back into the focus of the immediate present. He became aware that the Initiate was even brighter than he had been before. The atmosphere was alive with life and movement, he felt himself growing lighter, rising of his own volition. The deep notes of an organ could be heard accompanying a song of praise, and among the voices Michael could distinguish those of Mary and Freddie, speeding him into the light with this last expression of their regard. The golden beam from the east window seemed to grow brighter, drawing him up into a heavenly splendour of light and colour and freedom. He was no longer conscious of the chapel nor of his companions, he lost all touch with conscious memory. . . .

Chapter 6

RESURRECTION

When Michael came to he found himself lying on the grass bathed in the cosmic rays of the Lowlands. It seemed so bright and airy and refreshing after the denser atmosphere he had become accustomed to, that he was content for a while to lie there in blissful enjoyment of the contrast. Then his mind began to readjust itself and a sudden thought struck him. He was here, in the Lowlands, near to Ann.

He sat up and looked around. Coming towards him was Tendor, who appeared to have been on some business of his own. Of the Initiate there was no sign.

"Come," said Tendor, and taking his hand, enabled the two of them to travel at a great pace over the countryside. After the arid nature of the lower plane, the brightness and verdancy of these surroundings offered a new revelation of the layer-like design of the Spirit World. Here in this realm, Michael could see much that was also present in the lower Astral plane, but with what a difference! Brilliance of colour, vitality of growth, quality of the atmosphere, even the very texture of concrete things, were in subtle contrast to their counterparts in that other, coarser world.

At length the home he loved came in sight. A moment later they alighted on the lawn and the children came running out to greet them with loud cries of welcome, while behind, her eyes shining with a joy she could not conceal, came Ann. The rapture of that reunion was something Michael had never experienced before. It seemed as if the circumstances of his stay in the City of Illusion had sharpened his ability to appreciate, and shown him how to live more fully through the finer perceptions of the Spirit rather than through the clamorous demands of the senses. Where before he had accepted Ann as his mate and companion, he saw her now as something more, a complement to himself enabling him to live more fully by reason of the reaction between them. This subtlety was much more apparent since his return from his redemptive experience. He was now able to plumb far more deeply and satisfyingly that spiritual at-one-ment which is the reality and core of what on Earth is termed 'love'. He knew now that he could not live and function to the fullest extent apart from her, and from the message he read in her eyes he knew that she too was aware of this glorious vital fact. The most radiant of earthly lovers never attained such heights as this.

Presently Ann announced that she would have to take the children back to their home in the Uplands, but promised to return at once. When they were gone Michael began to discuss his future with Tendor. The guide told him that he would have to remain where he was until he was revitalized after his stay in the depleting lower realm. It was to be in the nature of a holiday. Ann would be with him and from time to time the children would come and visit them.

"There is much to entertain you here," said Tendor, "there are many places for you to visit. Halls of music or the arts, workshops and experimental centres, laboratories or universities where you may study and discuss on almost any subject you wish. Any career is open to you; choose what you will."

For a while Michael pondered on this fascinating prospect. To have the means and the leisure to minister to all the desires of his heart, that was a thrilling outlook. "It is almost too good to be true," he observed. "Fancy being able to just sit back and think what one would like best to do or be. To be a good singer or a fine artist."

"Why, of course," smiled Tendor, "there are no restrictions here. Of course, inclinations and skill vary; it all depends upon the application you put into it. But the capacity is there, inherent in each one of us. And there are no tedious manual exercises to perform; it is just a question of developing mental ability. If you need facts, you have only to tap the Akashic Records where all the information you can possibly require is registered."

Thus for a period of the twins' career, the simple yet joyous pleasures of the World of Spirit claimed their whole attention. There was so much to do, so much to learn and acquire, that neither of them would have been conscious of the passage of time even if their lives had been subject to such a limitation. But in spite of these distractions Michael found his thoughts returning again and again to the plight of such as Vera in the underworld of the Astral plane. He was conscious of an intense longing to do something practical to help these unfortunates. Even the thought of turning that longing into action was an easement to the drain of sympathy that his contact with the lower Astral still drew from him.

"I think," he remarked on the occasion of one of Tendor's visits to them, "that I should like to undertake some form of service. I have been so blessed myself that I should like to help others to experience similar blessings. I think that would give me more happiness than anything else I can think of."

Tendor beamed. "You have chosen well, my son. You shall indeed serve the Great Spirit, and you speak the truth when you say that that is the way to true happiness. A way will be found for you, but not just yet."

Michael and Ann now found themselves impressed to study the laws which govern the Earth plane and the communications between it and the Spirit World. To their joy Tendor had been able to tell them that they could work together. In fact, as he observed, their joint power would be more than twice that of two individuals because of the strong, well-developed link between them. Sometimes Tendor amplified their studies by taking them on Cosmic trips into space whence they could observe the Earth and the peregrinations of the Solar system and its constituents. They also studied and observed the effects of the relevant Cosmic rays on Earth life.

Michael's ebullient nature had now recovered its full strength and with his usual impatience he demanded that the new work should commence without delay. But Tendor was not to be hurried. "There is a psychological moment for all things," he would say, with his enigmatical smile. "You must restrain that restive steed of yours. The Earth will not run away, and it will not change much in the time of waiting."

At length the time came for their departure to the scene of their new activities. After a last meeting with the children they made their final preparations. These consisted mainly in the preparation of the necessary robes which should enable them to function and be recognized on the plane where they were to work. It was understood that this would be on one of the sub-stratas of the Astral plane. The fashioning of these garments was accomplished by obtaining special fabric and constructing the robes which were then subjected to a slowing down process of their vibrations. Just as the whirling blades of an aircraft propellor are invisible at high speeds and on slowing down became visible as a thin shadow, so did these robes become dense in relation to physical senses as their vibrations or speed were reduced. As a result they became more opaque, and when donned, shut out much of the inherent light of the individual. Thus an inhabitant of the lower Astral plane is enabled to see and communicate with one thus attired who, without that garment, would be invisible.

Accompanied by Tendor, Michael and Ann made their descent into the lower Astral plane, using one of the prepared channels just as human beings use established tube tunnels and lifts to ascend or descend to varying levels. These channels are maintained by Spirit power which, working as a sort of beam of light, cleaves through the darkness of the lower planes and forms a bulwark against evil influences. The use of them saves much individual expenditure of power in preparation for such a venture, for workers can come and go more freely by this means than if they had to protect themselves on each occasion. Nevertheless descent into a lower sphere is never a pleasant affair; there is always a feeling of constriction and suffocation, together with the penetrating and often unpleasant odour of the plane concerned.

In due course the trio arrived at a large and important looking building not unlike a hospital. Here they were received and conducted to the superintendant. A spirit worker of great experience and wisdom, he questioned Michael and Ann as to their abilities and the work they desired to do. Finally he sent for one whom he referred to as Raphael.

Though not such a glowing spirit as the superintendent,

Raphael showed himself to be one of considerable attainments and much charm of manner. It was clear too that he was steadfast and determined, while the condition of his robes showed that he worked in some of the more severe conditions to be met with on this plane. Raphael now took charge of Michael and Ann and they bid a temporary farewell to Tendor. Their new guide led them through the long corridors and wards of the hospital, showing them the various degrees of patients catered for. He explained that these patients were mainly those who for various reasons came over in a state of unconsciousness from Earth life and are not ready to wake up for some time, or who require treatment on awakening. Nearly all of them appeared to be asleep as Michael and Ann passed by while about them flitted nurses and attendants.

"Some of these have been ill on Earth for many years," observed Raphael, "and would not understand what had happened if they woke up anywhere but in bed. Also some of them continue to demand the same attention and treatment they had in their last days on Earth. We try to give that where we can because it helps to give an air of normality to the environment when we try and explain to them that they are no longer in human bodies. Some of them take a lot of convincing."

"Goodness," exclaimed Michael, "they don't know when they are well off."

Raphael laughed. "That is very true, though many of them won't believe it. But we have a trump card which we play when necessary. We call upon some of their relatives who have been over here some time. When we produce someone who has already 'died' the patient usually gives in and accepts the situation. But some of these people won't wake at all and then it is no use trying to do anything. They come here convinced they have died and are sleeping the last sleep and awaiting the Day of Judgement. Nothing will convince them otherwise. We wake them up and try and get some sense into them but they think it is a dream and drop off to sleep again. A sort of laziness gets hold of them and they find it easier to believe something like that which makes no demand upon them; and there they are, slumbering nonentities."

"I should feel inclined to get hold of a trumpet and blow it," laughed Michael, "then perhaps they would all wake up."

"You'd better pass on your idea to sister Olivia," agreed Raphael, as a woman in the garb of a nurse came up. "Sister, will you tell these friends of mine something about your patients?"

Sister Olivia proved to be a cheerful individual with a merry twinkle in her eye. Michael observed when he was introduced that it must be very pleasant to be welcomed by such a cheerful person when they woke up. She smiled her pleasure at the remark.

"They are very funny, some of them," she said, "I call this the 'Incubator'; naughty of me I know, but the name fits. Some of them incubate so long that it is no wonder they are addled when they wake up." She took the party around her ward pointing out the cases which had some special interest. Then she led the way into her little sanctum and regaled them with stories of troublesome patients, which made them laugh heartily.

"Look out of the window," she said presently, "you see that long building over there? That contains what we call our 'mummies'. They are spirits who have been over here in a state of self-induced coma, some of them over a hundred years, and they refuse to wake up."

"Have they really?" said Ann, "and I have only been over . . . I don't know how long. It seems silly not to know."

Sister Olivia smiled at her understandingly. "It is difficult to get rid of the idea of Earth time, isn't it? We think in terms of progress here, not years. Otherwise we should get in an awful muddle. Think of my patients, sleeping away a hundred years or so. Time has stopped for them."

"Are these patients of yours all from one country on Earth?" asked Michael.

It was Raphael who replied. "We have no actual racial distinctions here but we cannot prevent our patients from bringing it with them. We separate them because we find it easier for them. They would find it strange and alarming to wake up among people of a different country. People here are mostly from British countries. Of course if they sleep for a very long time they have usually forgotten all about their Earth life when they awaken. Some of them have to be completely re-educated."

"Do most people have to pass through these hospitals when they die?" asked Ann.

"Oh dear me, no," the Sister replied, "we only take serious cases here, those which need long sleep or treatment. Ordinarily, spirits pass easily into this world, usually finding themselves in a garden specially designed for their reception. There they can rest and sleep if they desire and later on meet their loved ones. Often they are so surprised and pleased with it all that they forget they have passed through the dreaded portals of death."

"I suppose you were a doctor on Earth?" Michael asked Raphael.

Raphael laughed as at a joke. "Yes, but not the sort of doctor you are thinking of. I didn't carry a stethoscope. I was a Negro witch doctor." Seeing the incredulous look on both their faces he went on. "When we have been over some time we lose all identity with the earthly life. We are just spirits once more. You will be interested to know that one of my assistants here was once a king of England. The chief matron was once a washer-woman on Earth, while a once great military leader is now proud to be a doorkeeper here. To these spirits their earthly status was only a part they played. It is what they learned in the playing of those parts that matters. That is the wealth of the Spirit World."

Raphael now conducted his charges to the hostel where the staff of the hospital had their own quarters in which to rest or meet their friends. The buildings were not very impressive after the gracious design of those in the higher spheres, but all that was necessary to the comfort of a spirit in these conditions was provided. There were flowers in every room.

Michael and Ann spent some time at the hospital learning how to treat spirits awakening into their new environment. When they felt they had assimilated the rudiments of such knowledge they were taken before the regional Organizer, who in this case was a woman. She asked them many questions; it was, in fact, a sort of oral examination. Finally she smiled at them.

"I think you have earned the right to begin work on your own now with Raphael to guide and instruct you. Remember that upon the sympathetic understanding and treatment of each case may depend the advancement of the spirit you are trying to help. There must be absolute selflessness in all you do. Do not be in a hurry for results, do not short-circuit things in the hope of doing a greater service. Do not be too generous in your offers of love and sympathy; your patients are not accustomed to that and as to a drowning man who must not be given too big a meal immediately after his rescue, give your love in small but definite doses, like medicine. Otherwise you might do more harm than good. Now I am going to leave you to Raphael, he will know what to do."

Having taken their leave of the Organizer, Michael and Ann went out to where Raphael awaited them. He was delighted to hear of their success and told them that their first task awaited them. Without further explanation he led them to a small building which contained a number of cubicles, each fitted up in the manner of a dark room.

"We are going to assist at the transition of an old lady. Quite an ordinary case presenting no difficulties. Sure you don't mind participating in a death-bed scene?" he asked Ann as an afterthought.

Ann shook her head determinedly. "No, I am quite prepared for that."

When they were all inside one of the cubicles, he said: "Now, I want you to visualize the bedroom of Martha Blameworthy, for that is the name of the old lady. She has not been a bad woman, except that she was selfish and imposed upon all who were indebted to her. Being a wealthy woman they were many. She is afraid of death and of leaving the wealth and comfort and, above all, the power that she has wielded so long. She has no formed ideas about the life ahead of her for she is not religious and certainly is not spiritual. She is rather scared at the prospect."

As he shut the door there was almost complete darkness

except for a dim radiance from their spirit robes. There was a strange sensation as if they were moving and a slight feeling of suffocation. To distract their attention, Raphael kept on talking.

"This is one of our regular channels of communications with the Earth, of which you have already heard. If we tried to go down direct we should meet all sorts of unpleasant experiences as we passed through the lower Astral belt which immediately contacts the Earth's surface." Presently the sensation of movement, which in reality was due to the change in condition of their surroundings, became less and less and finally ceased. The light gradually grew in intensity though not to the extent of the illumination of the plane they had just left. Michael became aware of a bedroom scene that reminded him of a theatrical setting. It was strange to find oneself standing in the middle of a diaphanous wall looking into a room which had every appearance of being solid, yet which proved to be equally tenuous when approached.

The centre of the room was occupied by a bed on which lay the figure of a woman of about seventy years. Around the bed were a doctor, a nurse, and a man and woman who were presumably relatives of the dying woman. The occupant of the bed would sometimes murmur a few words and the light in her eyes showed that there was little wrong with her brain. Her busy fingers were fumbling at the counterpane.

As if sensing Michael's thoughts Raphael spoke. "She is not really ill, it is just old age. Her time has come. Look, see who has entered the door."

Michael glanced at the doorway and saw a Being standing there of so dignified and stately a mein that he guessed it could not be an ordinary spirit.

"That is an Angel of Mercy," explained Raphael. "He comes personally to perform the cutting of the life-cord which keeps a spirit chained to its earthly body. It is a duty which God only entrusts to advanced Beings such as he. He knows God's will and how and when to perform the function." Then he added, "See, the old lady has sensed his arrival."

As if she were indeed aware of the entrance of the Angel, the old lady raised her head slightly and gazed fixedly at the door. Then her face creased and tears began to pour down her cheeks.

"I don't want to die, doctor, I don't want to die. Don't let me die." The querulous voice ended in a wail of self-pity.

The doctor took her hand in his and murmured the things he would be expected to say at such a time. He knew that nothing could be done and that the end was approaching.

Reassured by the gesture she looked again at the door. Following her gaze Michael and Ann saw the features of the Angel change and become transfigured as a glow of love was projected like a beam of light towards the bed. The old lady's lips began to move as she tried to tell the others of what she saw, but the life-force was ebbing fast from the frail body. The Angel held out his hand to her. As if obeying the call the woman in a sudden access of strength raised herself into a sitting position, her eyes suddenly alight. In the distance they could hear music, from a spiritual source, probably relayed from the higher realms.

"Look behind the Angel," said Raphael.

There behind the radiant figure was a little crowd of spirits, all with welcoming smiles. They were friends or relatives of the woman making the transition who had come to aid her arrival and greet her in the new world. Something attracted Michael's attention to the bed once more. A thin wisp of vapour began to weave its way out of the top of the dying woman's head and hung there in a little cloud. Then the body dropped back suddenly and the hands dropped lifelessly upon the coverlet. Very soon after, a form, replica of the mortal body, was elevated to a position horizontally extended above the physical body and facing downwards. This wraith-like form gradually assumed a denser condition as the etheric forces were released from the physical body and builded themselves into the spirit body. When the process was completed the etheric body assumed an upright posture at the foot of the bed. Here the Angel advanced and placed his hands upon the eyes of the etheric form, then stepped aside. The life-cord still connected physical and etheric bodies but it was attenuated and was scarcely visible. Martha was free and in her new freedom was advancing to meet those who had come to fetch her. Exclamations of pleased surprise came from her lips. She began to respond to the greetings of these friends, the existence of some of whom she had almost forgotten. The little group began to move away.

"The Angel has not cut the life-cord yet," observed Michael.

"No," replied Raphael. "He will not do that yet, as it would be a shock to the spirit. He will guard the remains for a little time before he performs that last office."

The Angel now turned towards the retreating group and stretched out his arms towards them, obviously concentrating his thoughts upon them. Instantly the room vanished and after a momentary period of darkness, they all found themselves in the grounds of the hospital. There ahead of them were the old lady and her friends now approaching the entrance to the main building. She gave a yawn. Meeting friends had tired her for some time past and she felt that this strange experience must also prove tiring. So she was tired. Raphael stepped forward and spoke to the visitors. They seemed to respect his authority and made their excuses. A nurse came out of the building and to her Raphael gave charge of the new arrival. Then he rejoined the other two.

"Well," he smiled at them, "that was a very simple case. I showed it to you in order to give you some idea of what we aim at."

"Will she sleep for a long time?" asked Ann.

"I don't know; I haven't studied the case. Probably having recognized the faces of her visitors whom she thought to be dead, she will wake up after a nice refreshing sleep and realize where she is. Then it will be easy to get her to go off with her friends and learn how to live her new life."

"What about her selfishness?" asked Michael, "won't she have to make retribution for that?"

"Assuredly. But God does not demand payment on the nail. She will first be made aware of the fact that she does owe a debt. And conceivably that may take a long time to sink in. Then she will have to entertain and express a desire to make retribution. Then, and not till then, she will be shown how she may make that retribution. She may shy at that and refuse.

185

Then it will be a case of waiting until her spirit grows strong enough to enforce its will. Oh yes, it may be a long business. We do not try and hurry things here. That is a great mistake."

"Supposing she had been very bad indeed," suggested Ann.

"In that case we should not have been able to get near her to help. She would have sunk, by the weight of her negative thought forms which surrounded her, down to the lowest Astral plane. We could not have done much for her then, though there are workers down there who meet such cases. On the other hand, we have many grades of hospitals and reception gardens and we try to arrange for a new arrival to enter by the most suitable environment for his state of development. If there is no need for hospital treatment the visitors would probably be allowed to take their newly arrived friends straight to the plane where they are to live and possibly to the house already prepared for them. We don't have to worry about such arrivals; the regional Organizer knows when a transition is due and the relatives are warned. One of these goes to the Organizer's headquarters and makes the necessary arrangements. Quite businesslike, isn't it?"

"Why yes," agreed Michael, "but what about cases where there is a lot of grief. I have heard they are difficult to handle."

"They are the most difficult of all," replied Raphael. "Grief forms a deadening wall around both the passing spirits and those we would help who are bereaved. It actually drags the spirit back and makes it almost impossible for us to tear them away from the scene of the transition. If only we could get that fact known on Earth, what a difference it would make! If only humans would realize that a transition ought to be a happy speeding on a delightful journey instead of an occasion for a parade of grief. So many would think it disrespectful to the dead not to weep and mourn. But that will change in time. In the meantime we have to plug away and try and pierce the armour of grief which ascends from the mourners and surrounds the passing spirit. It is a terribly low vibration. Often it is not till long after the funeral that we can approach the afflicted soul."

"What about Martha?" asked Ann, "she was crying at the idea of passing."

Raphael smiled. "There was no one to regret her death except herself and she soon got over that when she saw her old friends. Her surviving relatives were mainly concerned with the amount of money they were going to get. It is the real emotional grief that condenses into a cloud around the spirit leaving the body."

There were many more expeditions to follow on which the three spent much effort, and Michael and Ann learned a great deal about the depth and shallowness of human nature. At length Raphael expressed himself as satisfied with their work and ability to work alone.

"I shall always be ready to send you advice if you are in any difficulties. I shall communicate with you by telepathy."

"But neither Ann nor I are any good at that," expostulated Michael, "not at a distance."

Raphael chuckled. "It is just the same as thought language. I think you will be able to understand what I mean." A moment later he disappeared. Neither of them saw him go, he just wasn't there.

"What on earth . . . ," began Michael.

"Wait a minute," cut in Ann, "something is happening. Listen."

Michael listened. He heard nothing. They were standing outside the hostel and he felt an urge to walk towards a clump of trees away to a flank. Obeying the impulse he started off and to his surprise he saw that Ann was also moving in that direction. She looked at him enquiringly as she went.

"Can you hear it?" she asked.

"I can't hear anything, but I feel that I want to walk towards those trees." About halfway there, he suddenly began to think of the sunken garden and of some particular orange-coloured flowers that grew there. Still obeying the urge he turned and retraced his steps. He found that Ann was doing likewise. As they arrived at the sunken garden Raphael came smiling up the steps.

"I think that was all right; you got my messages?"

"Yes I did," said Ann, "I got your thoughts quite clearly."

"I didn't get anything," Michael said ruefully, "but I know someone was making me do a route march around the garden."

"You got the impression all right, you will soon get the thought direct like Ann. In the meantime Ann can interpret to you if necessary. Just call me mentally when you want help. If it is really necessary I will come in person. Now I have just heard of a case which will be a real test for you both. Come along with me."

He led the way to the darkrooms. "I have information that a man is contemplating suicide," he went on. "You know what that means," he added with emphasis, addressing Michael. "Try and prevent him if you can."

This time Raphael did not enter the room with them but prepared to shut the other two in. "I want you to make your minds receptive to the thoughts that I shall send you. I will visualize your destination and you must link your thoughts with mine. Just concentrate on me and you will arrive there."

As the door shut, Michael and Ann cleared their minds of all obtruding thoughts except that of Raphael's personality. Then they began to see, in the mind's eye, a room furnished as a study and library, for the walls were covered with books. In the centre was a table and at that table a man was sitting. . . .

The walls of the darkroom melted into the dull light of the Earth world with which they were now becoming familiar. Around them were the features of the room which they had seen clairvoyantly a moment before. At the table was seated a man as in the vision and at once Michael felt his attention arrested by the look on his face. He was a dark-haired man of about fifty odd with rather broad features and a prominent jaw. Fear, distraction and grim determination were written among the ravaging lines of bitter experience. It was obvious that the situation of this man was one needing desperate remedies. In front of him lay a revolver, while at the back of the table, resting against the inkstand, lay an envelope addressed to the coroner. On the table were a number of account books and slips of paper covered with figures. The story was clear enough. The man smoked cigarette after cigarette and beside his right hand stood a half-empty glass of whisky.

Ann's voice at his elbow broke in on his examination.

"Michael, we must do something quickly. I believe he is on the verge of committing suicide now."

"Yes, but what?" Michael demanded. "We have no means of making our presence known."

"Let's send a message to Raphael, he will know what to do."

Michael was rather loath to call on their friend and instructor so early in their career on their own, but the obviously urgent need for drastic measures was too apparent for delay. Together they concentrated on Raphael, and made an effort to describe the situation through the flow of thought. Back came the answer, aurally to Ann, by impression to Michael. "All you can do is to concentrate on him and impinge your thoughts upon his mind urging him not to take his life."

Acting on this advice Michael and Ann bent the whole of their mind force upon the unfortunate man. Once or twice he looked up and glanced enquiringly around the room as if someone had called his name. But the reaction was transitory and once again the haggard look came into his features and he would shut out all external influences.

Presently he took up the revolver and examined it, caressing it as a little smile creased the rigid corners of his mouth. Obviously he regarded the weapon as a way out of all his troubles. A sudden look of action came into his features.

A little gasp escaped from Ann. "Oh, God help us! What can we do?" There was a despairing note in her cry. As the man raised the revolver she sprang forward to snatch it from him, forgetting the change in dimension that separated them. Her arms passed right through the grim figure and she retreated, crestfallen, to Michael's side.

But her action seemed to have temporarily upset the man's intention. Once again he began to play with the weapon, trying out the best position in which to point it. Then he laid it down and took a last drink from the tumbler, after which he grasped the revolver resolutely, seeking to use the momentary courage the spirit gave him. Ann tried to interpose herself between the man and his weapon, while Michael redoubled his efforts to impress the man's mind. Her efforts were fruitless, his

189

intention remained unaffected and Ann felt herself thrown back by a sudden gathering of his will. He raised the weapon, and with a scream on her lips Ann turned and buried her face on Michael's shoulder. When she heard the shot she shuddered convulsively and did not turn until some moments later when the body had ceased its twitchings and was still.

With a deepening sense of failure they watched the etheric form of the suicide rise from the crumpled figure and stand erect, gazing around in amazement. He looked down at the mortal remains at his feet then an expression of horror spread over his face. He was realizing the terrible truth that he had not annihilated himself after all, but was still very much alive. With one fearful look around, the suicide tried to get back into the body but eventually he decided that this was impossible. At length he looked up and saw Michael and Ann. For a moment he was too astonished to show any reaction. Then the look of surprise was followed by one of fear and before Michael could get out a word, he gave a scream of despair, and dashed out of the room.

Michael would have followed him, but he got the impression that Raphael was urgently recalling them. Ann corroborated this, so with heavy hearts they made their way back to the hostel.

Raphael came to meet them, wearing, strangely enough, a smile of satisfaction. "Well done, my friends, you have passed that test well," he announced.

"But why?" demanded Ann, still somewhat shaken as a result of the experience, "we failed to save that poor man. It is our fault he did it."

Raphael shook his head emphatically. "Not a bit. I knew when I sent you that the case was hopeless and for that I ask your pardon, but I thought the exertion of your whole-hearted efforts would be good training for you. The man was a solicitor who had robbed his clients and created terrible misery for many innocent people. He was a coward and afraid to face justice, so it was easy to see that he would take the coward's way out. Don't worry about that, it will prove the shortest way for him in the end. So you see, I gave you this experience purely from the point of view of training. As you may guess,

190

we do not trust our would-be suicides to incompetent hands. Had there been any chance of saving him from his folly the powerful influence you exerted would undoubtedly have done so. In any case your efforts are not lost, for when he begins to see reason your influence will react on him. That last vision he had of you two has been burned into his memory and will never leave him. It will act like a goad to him in his misery and remorse."

"Will he have to go to that awful place—to hell?" asked Michael.

"He is on his way there now. He will have his last chance, he will be met by workers who will try and persuade him to realize what he has done. If he accepts what they tell him and honestly tries to face his position and sets to work to undo what he did, why then he would escape the worst. But I don't think he will. He is too obstinate and fearful. All that he is thinking of at the moment is to put as great a distance as possible between himself and those he has wronged."

"It does seem so terrible that suicide should be such a crime," said Ann, with a still lively sympathy for the unfortunate.

"Well, you see, it is a crime. He has committed murder, he has murdered himself. God had ordained that he should spend a prescribed number of years incarnated on Earth. He has defied that law, he has shaken his fist at God. It matters not that he did it without being aware of the consequences. The immutability of God's laws is not affected by the state of man's enlightenment. It is the motive that fixes the extent of the blame and in this case the motive was purely selfish. If it had been pure, if the suicide had been in the nature of a sacrifice, he would not have been hurled into the darkness as he was. The taking of life must have its repercussion, the cause must have its effects, and therefore he would not have escaped, however pure his motive; his advance would have been slightly delayed; he might have had to stay a while on a lower plane, but that would have been part of the sacrifice. He would not have suffered unduly. And by making that sacrifice he would have learned much through the suffering which he did have to endure, thus drawing to himself compensation beyond his wildest dreams. God's justice is perfect, there is nothing to be gained from looking for flaws in it."

"This man," he went on "drew upon himself the full force of the law which you saw in action. You saw him literally hurled out of your presence. And as long as he refuses to recognize his own blame in the matter, the law will continue to hurl him further and further into the darkness, even into the depths of what you call hell."

"And then . . . ?" Ann scarcely dared to ask.

"Some day his spirit will succeed in getting through an impression of the true state of affairs. Then the etheric mind will cry 'enough'. The Spirit of God that burns within man cannot be destroyed, for it is divine. Of its own inherent power it will some day burn its way through the etheric casing that encloses it. Then there will be the reckoning and the redemption. For every soul must be redeemed; that too, is the law. And after all what is time in eternity provided the object is gained?"

But neither Michael nor Ann were able to share in this complacent attitude. To them the fact of a soul being thrown into torment whether of man's creating or not, was a matter for sombre reflection. They had yet to rise to that point where they could watch, unmoved, the manifestations of the law of Cause and Effect. Both of them were thankful that no more suicides came their way for some time. In the meantime they continued, with growing enthusiasm, the work of receiving passing spirits whose incarnation was at an end. Almost every case had its interesting feature, for the reactions of spirits emerging into the strange wonders of the World of Spirit, are infinitely variant. And through all their work ran, like a golden thread, an inward joy and satisfaction which no other form of occupation could engender. At times they would ask, and readily obtain, permission to go back to the Lowlands where they would seek rest and recuperation and the never-failing absorption in the development of their children. Stephanie and Peter were fine young spirits now, becoming more and more self-reliant. Soon they too would be deemed fit to take their part in the great work of redeeming mankind from the octopus grip of Self.

192

It was after one of these visits that Michael and Ann received a call from Raphael to attend an urgent case. They were in Ann's quarters when the call came and Michael, whose aural faculty was now developing, heard the incisive tones of Raphael's voice say: "Do not await the usual channel for reaching the Earth, but go direct on the thought ray I am projecting for you. One Jim Walker has met with a street accident and your assistance will be required to help him pass over."

Neither Michael nor Ann had previously tried to obtain access direct to the Earth, which meant passing unguarded through the dense regions of the lower Astral plane with all its unpleasant associations. Always before they had made the journey through one of the prepared tunnels which made the trip so much easier, but which took some time to achieve. It was possible, they knew, to make the journey almost instantaneously but in such a case they would not be able to remain long in the Earth environment as they lacked the necessary preparation. It is rather like working at the bottom of the sea. A pearl diver can dart below the surface and remain at considerable depths as long as he can hold the air in his lungs, but for longer periods a diver with suit and air pump is essential.

The reason for the urgent summons was not apparent, but the twins were used to obeying Raphael without question, so great was their trust in him. Hand-in-hand they stood, concentrating their thoughts on the mind of their instructor. Almost immediately they began to feel the lift-like sensation, and the familiar aspect of Ann's room faded. When next they could discern objects they were aware of considerable movement around them. The lift seemed to be going downwards and queer visions began to pass upward before their eyes. It was like descending into the depths of the ocean in a submarine with a marine window enabling one to watch the monsters of the deep where the rays of the sun never penetrate. Sometimes they would see misshapen figures in human form that seemed to be empty, lifeless shells, at others the fantastic creatures undoubtedly were alive. As far as the dim light revealed, the verdure of this sphere was of the exotic nature to be seen in the tropical depths of the ocean. The atmosphere was opaque and of a dull inky blue giving visibility for only a short distance. All about them seemed to be peering eyes which regarded their passage with malevolence or with no more than a fish-like indifference. Everywhere was a foul smell that penetrated the miasma like the odours of the marsh swamps.

At length the horrible journey was accomplished and the haze thinned into the light of Earth. The sensation of moving ceased and Michael and Ann found themselves standing on the pavement of a busy street. In spite of his many experiences of visiting the Earth, Michael could never forego a thrill at contacting once more the material surroundings which he had once regarded as representing the limits of individual experience. The comparatively slow movements of the pedestrians, after the swift easy motion of the Spirit World, seemed like a motion picture slowed down, while the sight of cumbersome vehicles threading the streets in a slow pulsating progression, made him realize more and more the great amount of effort required in physical existence to produce even a small result. Nevertheless the thrill was there, emphasized perhaps by something that was absent from the life of Spirit, the conception of a time limitation, the idea that everything has a beginning and an ending. The thought of a possible ending in sight to any and every accomplishment gives to the earthly people an illusion of security. To the human mind the thought of life based upon an eternity that is unending and an affinity that is boundless would cause dismay. To Michael's widening consciousness this three-dimensional world now brought to him a sense of wonder that he could ever have conceived of its limitations as real.

Gradually the street scene resolved itself into focus and Michael became aware of a little crowd close by, the inevitable gathering of rubbernecks after a street accident. Passing through them as if they had no existence, he paused at the recumbent figure of a slightly built man, crippled as was evident from the shortness of one leg and the crutch at his side. The man was unconscious and even as he watched, Michael saw the etheric evaporation commence, presaging the release of the spirit. Presently the etheric body stood clear, the spirit gazing round in astonishment at the crowd and their obvious ignorance of his presence. Before he could look down at the pathetic remains Michael drew him clear of the crowd and led him gently away.

Meanwhile Ann had made it her business to locate the earthly end of the nearest spirit tunnel by which they might return. She scanned the neighbourhood, gazing through the buildings as if they were made of netting until she saw a familiar glow. Speeding to the spot she found a small upper room dedicated to spiritual work. Clearly there dwelt here one who was alive to the existence of the two worlds for from this room led one of the tunnels that pierced the Astral plane. In a moment her part was accomplished and she was back to meet Michael and the newly passed soul emerging from the crowd on the pavement. Taking the scarcely conscious spirit by the arm they conveyed him to his destined plane.

In a field of luxuriant green patterned by wild flowers, the spirit opened his eyes, gazing round in astonishment. City bred, he saw the beauties of nature revealed in a way that was miraculous to his untutored mind. Suddenly a flying figure came in sight and with something between a gulp and a cry of welcome, a girl of about fourteen threw her arms about him with all the joy of a mother for her long-lost child. Watching the affecting reunion Michael gathered that they were both waifs of the physical world judging by the state of their garments.

Presently the child relaxed the ardour of her greeting and stood back to view the new arrival possessively.

"Oh, Jim," she cried happily, "I did miss yer when I came 'ere, and oh, I did wish you was coming 'ere too. Then a lidy come along and I told all about you and me, and she said she'd see what she could do to get us together agin. She done it too. Well, 'ow are yer, Jim? Yer lookin' thin. It's a lovely place and all, 'ere. Why there's fruit on them trees over there and no one stops yer pickin' it. Ain't seen a copper since I come 'ere." Suddenly she noticed that they were not alone. For a while she was struck dumb, eyeing Michael and Ann with sullen distrust.

It was Ann who explained the position and tactfully made it clear to Jim that the old life was done with.

Jim listened attentively though he gave a quick look round from time to time as if he was accustomed to a world in which danger stalks close at hand and where preparedness is a better ally than trust. But the pastoral air of peace and quietude evidently reassured him for he turned his attention to Michael.

"Yus, seems like I've conked out, don't it. Ain't a bit like what I hexpected though. Still I must be a goner, for this 'ere kid died larst year and I went to 'er funeral."

"Ah," concurred the girl, "an' I see the luverly flowers you put on me coffin."

Jim looked at her a bit blankly at that, then he dismissed the thought in his mind with a little frown as if with the notion that his thoughts were a bit scattered as yet. He made a slight movement and Michael noticed that he still limped though his legs were now both perfectly proportioned. He had his crutch tucked under his arm in its old familiar position.

"By the way, Jim," Michael mentioned with a casual air, "you can throw that crutch away. You aren't lame over here."

A look of incredulity passed over the man's face, to be followed by a pitying smile.

"Cheese it, guv'nor, you're a bit off the mark there. I bin lame since I wos a nipper. Fell off'n a wall trying to get away from a copper. I'll always be lame like that."

Michael shook his head. "No, Jim, you have left that lame body behind and got a new one here. See, the two legs are the same size."

Jim glanced down and a comical look of amazement spread over his face. There was a gasp from the girl.

"Lor love a duck," he exclaimed, "so they are. 'Ere, Lizz, take yer arm off'n me." He threw away the crutch and essayed a few steps. As he shuffled along, trying to adjust his mind to this unexpected freedom, the girl followed with the anxious concentration of a mother witnessing the first steps of her child. With many exclamations and chuckles Jim began to step out and then to hold himself upright, a forgotten posture to him. There was a great light in his eyes as he cried: "Glory be! This beats everything this does. How's this, mate?" He lifted up his feet and actually began to hop along in an endeavour to run.

"Splendid, Jim," called Ann, her eyes shining, "keep it up, you'll soon be running in a race." Lizz turned wondering eyes on her as she said it.

Moving with hardly a trace of a limp, Jim now came back to the others. "Well if that don't beat the band," he announced. "To die and be able to walk and run and to get me Lizz back, all at the same time. Young Lizz here, she looked after me in 'er spare time like, for nearly three years, ain't you Lizz? Time's me back used to 'urt somethink 'orrible and I 'ad to lay up in bed. And Lizz, she used to come and do for me. Reglar good un at it she was." He looked affectionately down at her. And Lizz, the humble child of the gutter, drank in his praise with the wide-eyed devotion of a dog. Despite her ragged clothes and wretched shoes, despite her tangled hair and grimy paws, her etherealized body glowed with a light that was lovely to behold; it seemed to radiate pure love.

Presently Ann suggested that they should all go to the hospital. But at the word a look of terror came into the child's eyes.

"You're never going' to tike 'im to 'orspital? 'E'll die there as sure as eggs. Straight 'e will. I got a place 'ere all ready for 'im in case 'e should die like me. Look, it ain't far."

So saying she led the way across the field and down a narrow lane to a small thicket in the shelter of which she had constructed a hut from materials collected from heaven knows where. It was spotlessly clean and evidently she had scoured the neighbourhood to find oddments that would serve as household necessities. It was the sort of habitation a child would make in the garden for a game of make-believe.

"That is awfully nice," Ann commented, "but I think Jim needs special care . . ." then she stopped suddenly.

Michael got the injunction at the same time. Raphael was sending them both strong thoughts to leave the child and Jim to their own devices. So bidding the two waifs a cheerful farewell, Michael and Ann made their way back to the hostel where they found Raphael awaiting them.

When he had heard their story he said: "The love that child has built into that unpretentious shack will be worth more than all the attention we can give Jim in hospital. Let them be. We will be ready to help them when they are ready to receive it."

Then he asked Ann what she thought of the journey through the lower Astral plane. She made a grimace. "I never imagined such horrible creatures could exist outside a nightmare."

Raphael laughed. "You are right, but we soon get used to them. Many of them are astral shells, devoid of life. When a spirit leaves its mortal body for the last time, there is a shell or envelope much the same shape as the physical body, which is freed and floats away. Where the physical life has been on a high level the shell soon disintegrates but when the life has been material the shell is thicker and takes longer to dissolve. So it drops to its own level in the lower Astral plane and there floats about aimlessly. But sometimes mischievous or evil-minded spirits get hold of these shells and occupy them, even using them to materialize for Earth folk and deceive them into thinking it is the spirit of their one-time friend who has returned. That is the origin of most of the stories of ghosts and earthbound spirits you heard."

"Ah!" exclaimed Michael, "I thought it might be something like that."

"A most unpleasant habit," observed Ann. "One can see how all sorts of complications might arise."

"They do indeed," observed Raphael. "It makes the task of communicating with the Earth much more difficult. But it can't be helped, and if one is aware of the existence of these interlopers it doesn't really matter. If the communication is on a high and constructive level these wraiths cannot interfere; they cannot reach the necessary level to manifest."

Soon after this Raphael took them to a lecture where further information on the subject of the relation between the Earth and the Spirit World was given by a spirit teacher of high degree. The object of the speaker was to show the perfection of the Divine Plan. He took his audience right back into the dawn of earthly history, to the point where incarnate man first began to use his then great powers for the furtherance of his own personal interests, thus interfering with the progress of his fellow men. Gradually the leaders of the revolt gathered followers about them in whom they instilled authority through misrepresentation of the truth and by means of fear. Such action, if unimpeded, would have caused a serious deviation from God's Plan, eventually leading to chaos. So to save man from himself God had to enclose the Earth in a protective envelope, thus preventing the contagion from spreading through the Universe. This envelope had to be an obstacle to Spirit power, whether good or evil. So the situation on Earth was bound to deteriorate through starvation of spiritual food, until such time as sufficient spirits of high degree could incarnate onto the Earth and by their united influence cause the Spirit of man to desire freedom from the thraldom of Self.

He went on to show how in the meantime spirits must go on incarnating; the wheels of the Cosmos must go on turning because the Earth is not alone. It is part of the Cosmos. Thus the endless cycle of birth and death went on, many of the spirits kindling one more glimmer in the illumination which in time will free the Earth once more. There is always the divine urge in the human heart and in time it will burst through the opaque envelope and admit the Spirit radiance which God sends forth eternally.

The lecturer explained that the time for the rending of the veil between the two worlds was rapidly approaching and much had already been accomplished. In the hearts of men the urge for the spiritual was already manifesting to a marked degree though few realized the nature of that urge. The final struggle between the forces of Light and Darkness was in full sway and the manifestation of evil within the envelope was in rising crescendo owing to the fury of the etheric strife. But the forces of Light were winning, crushing in the dark miasma of ignorance.

A sudden light burst in on Michael's mind as he listened. He began to see the meaning of much that had puzzled him. All this labour on the lower Astral plane, all this suffering that incarnate and discarnate souls were undergoing, was not merely the rescue of individuals from a sort of 'witches' cauldron'. It was a mighty work of redemption of the whole world. The very thought made it all seem worthwhile. Though indeed the grave condition of the Earth was due to the 'sins of the fathers', this wholesale effort of rescue caught the imagination.

Discussing the matter afterwards with Raphael, Michael

could not help exclaiming: "But this puts new life into me. I feel that nothing is too much to overcome if we have this great object in view."

Raphael nodded his head gravely. "That is what we understand to be God's Plan for the Earth and all the lower spiritual planes associated with it. You cannot consider them separately."

"But this is wonderful!" exclaimed Michael, still stirred by the revelation.

Raphael smiled at his enthusiasm. "We all find that as we progress new revelations such as this are continually given to us. You have only experienced the first glimpse of what waits to be revealed to you. As your consciousness, or power of understanding, is opened out by the flow of Spirit through you, new visions of God's wonders will be given to you, wonders that you couldn't possibly begin to comprehend in your present stage of development."

"What a conception!" agreed Michael. "Like a series of transformation scenes, each transcending the last. And yet this one glimpse I have had convinces me that it is true. What a pitifully inadequate idea of God we had on Earth. But tell me, what is the immediate plan for getting this truth through to the Earth people?"

"To go back a little," said Raphael, "we first had to pierce the envelope round the Earth with tunnels so that we could carry our message through to the people. For the past hundred years of Earth time we have been making these tunnels by projecting powerful Cosmic rays which cut through the mists. These tunnels we lined with etheric substance which prevented them from filling up again. Thus we are able to travel up and down with a minimum of effort or waste of power. Our next task was to find incarnate spirits with the necessary psychic power to act as receivers or mediums for the messages we had to give. Often the person who had the most promising gifts was unwilling to co-operate owing to fear of public opinion, while others, who were much less able, thrust themselves forward. We had to choose where we could. When we had trained them over long periods they would sometimes suddenly tire of the notion and give it all up and our work was wasted. Some mediums were actuated by anything but spiritual motives, while others were so carried away that they insisted on obtruding their own mentality and thus distorting the messages. But always there was progress of a sort. At first these tiny points of contact were like single lights in a great gloom, but gradually the number and power increased and the gloom has become a grey dawn with thousands of twinkling lights glowing like the Milky Way."

Michael's eyes were shining with eagerness. "That sounds fine," he exclaimed. "I should like to help in that work."

"Don't be too sure about that," laughed Raphael. "It is not so easy as it may sound. It is like working in a diver's suit deep under water. Much of our consciousness we have to leave behind us as it were. We cannot function fully and freely at the end of our lifeline. And when we do we have to humble our pride and summon all our faith to enable us to appear before the bar of intolerance. We have to face meetings where we are termed spooks, entities, wraiths, and even envoys of Satan. We have to face abuse, certainly unbelief and often indifference. We have to prove our identity to critical minds and egotistical research workers. Or we have to listen to people who want lost handbags found or errant husbands retrieved or wandering wives shadowed. We have to be patient with these people and gently inspire their minds to desire something higher."

"Sounds a bit grim, doesn't it," agreed Michael. "But I suppose there are compensations?"

"Of course. The willing and loving comradeship of many incarnate spirits, some of them undergoing unavoidable suffering, is ample compensation. We can endure all that I have described if we remember always that these people are labouring under terrible handicaps: 'the sins of the fathers'. We have successes to bring us joy, and there is the healing that gifted spirits are able to give through suitable mediums."

"Why is it so difficult to prove your identity?" asked Michael.

"It is never very easy," replied Raphael, "and even when you have produced evidence it is very likely the sitter will say it is thought-reading or pre-knowledge. If he doesn't say so he may think it. Imagine I am an incarnate sitter and you are speaking through the mentality of a human medium. I ask you to prove you are who you say you are. How will you set about it?"

"Why I . . . that is, I . . ." Michael broke off, nonplussed. He suddenly realized how far he had drifted from the objective details of his Earth life. It all seemed so far away. Of the subjective influences in his incarnate life he was well aware. He could recall the mistakes he had made, the lessons he had learned. But it was like the recollections of early childhood: only the highlights stood out. The humdrum details of existence upon which a finite mind would rely for cognate evidence had faded into an indefinite background. It was difficult to recall anything that could be used as cast-iron proof of identity.

Raphael smiled at the tacit admission. "It isn't easy, is it? Almost impossible for most people without the assistance of experienced controls who know how to jog your memory. Of course a lot of it comes back when you contact Earth conditions once more."

"Still, I should like to try it," said Michael.

"Very well, you shall. It is by refusing to be beaten that you will succeed. And remember, as I told you, the rewards are great. If by striving you use all your endeavours to render service, you will open up your consciousness in a surprising way and thus find a newer and deeper meaning in everything you do and experience." And with that he took his departure.

There followed numerous and varied experiences for Michael and Ann, experiences which demanded all their wit and ability to handle. They met all sorts of conditions and tasted of both joys and horrors, successes and defeats. They presided at beautiful scenes of reunion between loved ones, between the lover and his mate, between mother and child. They witnessed the release of spirits from human bondage seemingly beyond endurance, to the glorious freedom and surcease that awaited them. They watched, with leaden hearts, the transition of souls laden with the harvest of human ignorance drifting down into the welter of that limbo in which they would have to struggle so long and so hard for release.

Together they wandered through the dark recesses of the lower Astral pleading with earthbound souls to listen to their message of hope and light and freedom. So often they failed. Yet sometimes they succeeded, and the joy of one success would make up for endless toil and despair. The sight of an earthbound soul emerging into the light and warmth of the real Spirit World was something to treasure. Such experiences as these were epics that far transcended any earthly tale of adventure.

In one experience they met with a spirit held inert beside his mouldering corpse. He had held such strong views on the importance of the physical vehicle and the impossibility of the existence of a soul, that he found it impossible to get away from the only thing he had held to be real. They tried to approach him but he shied away from them and shut his mind to their persuasions, believing them to be demons. His dull eyes held little intelligence and his etheric body was turgid with negative thoughts of a purely physical nature. There was clearly nothing to be done so he was left to his dreary vigil.

Ann, especially, found it necessary to keep her feelings under control, for any excess of emotion or sympathy affected the spirit undergoing transition. On one occasion they were helping a shipwrecked sailor who was suffering the last pangs of torture by thirst. His wretched condition so affected her that she could see the effect of her emotion working on his auric condition and increasing his sufferings. She managed to control herself and was able to help the man by suggestion, but she was relieved when she saw the Angel of Mercy approach to effect the final transition. Freed from his burdensome body the sailor bounded up and greeted the friends who had come to fetch him with boisterous gaiety.

Some incidents were not without pathos. A lady of title, well-known in the social and political firmament, whom we will call Lady Blank, was passing over as a result of illness. Aware that she had not been prepared for transition, being self-centred and purse-proud, Michael and Ann led her to the neighbourhood reserved for such individuals. By the law of Cause and Effect such people can only exist in mean habitations for they have not provided in their Earth life the essential spiritual materials for building anything better. When she beheld the miserable cottage allotted to her, Lady Blank was highly indignant and refused to enter. Suppressing the contempt which he felt for this selfish woman who, he was aware, had never spared a thought for those less fortunate than herself, Michael answered courteously.

"I am sorry, Lady Blank, but we have done the best we could with the materials you provided. We can only create houses with the spiritual material we are given."

"What do you mean?" she demanded, "why should I provide you with materials? I am ready to pay for my accommodation."

"What with?"

"With whatever you use for money here. I am a very wealthy woman and my husband is . . ."

Michael broke in with a deprecatory gesture. "We know who you are, Lady Blank. But you must realize that titles do not count over here and the money that you once enjoyed does not exist anymore. The currency that we use is love and service."

"Then perhaps you will see about getting me some service. I shall need a personal maid and . . ."

Once more Michael intervened. "I did not mean that kind of service. There are no menial servants in this place. Those who render domestic service of any kind do so out of the love in their hearts and it is received in the same spirit. It is one of our first lessons here that service is a means of progress; no one can demand it for their own use. Besides, you will soon find that there is no need for the kind of service you are thinking of."

"But," expostulated the smartly dressed woman, "who is to look after my clothes, who is to get my bath and so on?"

Here Ann came forward. "You must let me help you, Lady Blank. You will find clothes an easy matter over here." She gave the woman an intimate smile. "But we women still contrive to introduce some element of fashion into our spirit robes though we have little control over the quality of our materials; that is determined by our state of advancement. You will soon want to exchange these garments for something more durable.

Earth clothes don't last very well in this atmosphere. See, the material of this coat is already affected." As she spoke she brushed at the shoulder of Lady Blank's expensive looking coat. Wisps of material rose into the air as she did so.

An exclamation of horror and disgust rose to Lady Blank's lips. "My dear, how awful. This is a new coat, it only came from Bond Street a few days ago. I shall make them replace it . . . oh . . . I forgot."

Ann smiled sympathetically as she took the other woman's arm. "Come along into the cottage and we will see what we can do, you know. . . ." Her voice died away inside the wretched little building and Michael turned to see a group of people approaching. These were the relatives of the newly arrived spirit, coming to welcome her.

So the work went on, a vast labour imbued by an ideal of service that Earth people can only dimly comprehend. A vast concourse of workers all bent upon their task of breaking down the veil between the two worlds and with it the intricate mass of prejudices, superstitions, doubts and fears which divide man from his God. Were the vision of incarnate souls to operate with equal freedom in either dimension they would be so impressed by the astronomical efforts made throughout the spheres surrounding the Earth, that worship of the Self would die of atrophy and man would tap the mighty powers open to him for the relentless pursuit and destruction of all that opposes his progress towards the light. Every spirit laboratory, every seat of learning and wisdom, every landscape, held its quota of figures bent on research, figures studying far ahead of their fellows on Earth, figures hurrying in their thousands on this great errand of mercy, this great labour of tearing down the edifices of the past, so that the great Cosmic Command which rings through the Universe, 'Let there be light', might once more cleanse and revitalize the Earth, many inhabitants of which gaze obliquely at one another and affirm: 'There is no God! The dead are dead!'

At times the task allotted to Michael and Ann was varied. A guide would be allotted to them to take them to the various Senates or Parliaments on Earth where they would engage with others in the uncongenial task of spiritual lobbying. This entails influencing subconsciously the minds of certain responsive members, to press for certain constructive measures making for freedom and progress. Usually the guide was a one-time leader of the house in question and often he would brief his assembled spirit workers with all the fire of his old oratory. Sometimes the guide would directly inspire a politician who got up to speak on some controversial subject. The politician would get up, notes in hand, speech thoroughly rehearsed, and deliver himself of an oration which had little in common with his notes. But this could only happen in rare cases where the spirit of the member gave explicit sanction. More rarely still pre-arranged connivance would result in a speaker being smitten with a sudden confusion so that he omitted to dwell upon a certain point. Care in delegation of such permission is engendered by the fact that nations and corporate bodies have to follow the line of self-determination just as individuals have to learn and progress by the light of their own mistakes. It would not do to substitute spirit rule for self rule. But whatever of the light of spiritual understanding showed in the aura of a member of government, that capacity was made use of to impress the individual with a point of view that was selfless and far-sightedly constructive.

One amusing incident occurred when Michael was listening to a debate in the House of Commons. It is not easy for spirits to get the meaning of human speech and to facilitate his reception of an important dissertation Michael drew nearer to a member who was, probably without knowing it, a natural medium. The power of this man acted as a magnifier and gave clarity to the speech. He must have seen Michael clairvoyantly, as he took the vacant seat beside him, for he leaned across and said: "Did you get that point about fiscal control? I heartily disagree, don't you?"

Without withdrawing his attention from the orator, Michael answered in thought language, "I think he is quite right." The member of course did not hear the answer and repeated his question. He seemed annoyed at Michael's apparent churlishness and to avoid giving him further offence Michael removed himself. But he could not help noticing from his new vantage point, that the member kept on glancing uneasily at the empty seat beside him.

Many times since his transition, Michael had paid visits to his parents, still living at the old home at Belchester. His father was an old man now and relied more and more on Clark to manage the mill. His mother was a little more careworn but still maintained her placid outlook on life. It was clear that she did not regard him as having any objective existence, for she relied entirely upon the precious memory of him that she carried in her heart. He made several attempts to draw their attention to his presence, but it was no use. Their minds were entrenched behind such a formidable rampart of conservatism and bigoted belief that it was hopeless to try and pierce it. He knew they would have nothing to do with mediums.

True to his promise, Raphael came to the hostel during one of the rest periods to announce to Michael that he had arranged for him to attend a séance. The two set out together. Descending through one of the ray tunnels, they found themselves in a room which seemed to be constructed of plastic glass. It was more of an enclosure than a room, for it was bell-shaped and of pink translucency. As his sight became more accustomed to the surroundings, Michael discerned that the glass enclosure included a room in a material house. He heard voices speaking English and in the dim light saw a group of people seated round one at their head who was obviously a medium, from the bright globe of spirit light that shone above his head. Michael's gaze, travelling round the circle, came to rest on a familiar face. It was Davis, his old partner, perceptibly aged, but blunt and impassive as ever. Raphael, at his elbow, told him that the woman on Davis' right was his wife. Michael regarded her with interest, for Davis had been a bachelor when he knew him. Mrs. Davis was, he surmised, the real reason for Davis' presence here. It was she who appeared to be at home in these surroundings while her husband displayed every sign of antagonism to his environment.

At this moment someone drew the curtains, and the séance commenced in a dim light. As the medium went into trance Michael observed a figure with features suggesting Egyptian descent approach the medium with two other spirits, who proceeded to collect some plastic sort of substance which issued from the medium's side. This they manipulated into a queer instrument which Raphael told him was a voice box, or mechanical larynx, through which manifesting spirits could speak in what amounted to a human voice. As soon as this was accomplished the Egyptian stood close to the voice box which had been suspended in mid air, considerably above the head of the medium. He began to speak, greeting the sitters and explaining the object of the circle. He then offered up a prayer to the Great Spirit, dedicating the work of those present to His service, and asking His blessing on the proceedings.

While this was going on Raphael conducted Michael round the circle. First of all he showed him the plastic substance from which the bell-like structure was made. It appeared to be elastic, but very strong and quite transparent. It was of course not visible to human eyes nor an impediment to human touch. Michael was warned to make no attempt to pass through it. But he could see through the pink transparency a great host of spirits drawn here by the unaccustomed lights of spiritual beings who were making the purely mechanical arrangements for the séance. Like eager children pressing their faces against Christmas time shop windows, they gazed in wonderment at the proceedings afoot within the structure. Raphael explained that these were spirits from the lower Astral who came out of curiosity and many remained to take more than a passing interest. The desire to return to Earth conditions was always strong in the lower Astral dwellers, and the workers in these conditions used that fact to influence those who appeared ready for it.

Inside the bell structure were more spirits. These, it was explained, were spirits who had come down from higher realms to use the medium and give messages of love and encouragement to those in the circle.

The Egyptian had now finished speaking and his place was taken by a young girl spirit, who was amusing the sitters with quaint jokes and making fun of some of those with whom she was on intimate terms. It was observable how the laughter lightened the conditions, for as the tension relaxed, the haze seemed to clear from the circle in all directions except that of Davis' chair. He sat there, grim and unbending as ever. Following the child, two spirits spoke to friends in the circle. Adept at this work, they used the artificial larynx with skill and ease. While they were speaking Raphael introduced Michael to the Egyptian. He greeted Michael warmly and explained that, as Davis' wife had persuaded her husband to attend this circle, they thought it would form a good opportunity to give Michael experience of this type of work, and possibly exert some influence upon Davis himself, although he was deemed to be an unsympathetic sitter.

"What a hope for me," said Michael, smiling ruefully. "I don't see how I am going to have any effect on old Davis. He was always a pretty blunt man, who knew a spade as a spade and nothing else. However, I am always prepared to try."

"We do not propose that you should use the larynx tonight. It is not easy to use without practice. When the time comes I will show you how to occupy the medium's body and use his own larynx."

While he was waiting his turn, Michael noted there were several spirits going round the circle carrying different coloured lights in their hands. Raphael explained that these were workers who were giving something to each of the sitters, healing to one, spiritual development to another, consolation to a third. One spirit produced a bunch of flowers having a pungent scent which she placed in the lap of Mrs. Davis, who immediately began to move her head and sniff the atmosphere as if trying to locate the scent. She whispered something to her husband who was obviously scornful, because his own senses did not respond to the etheric odour. Michael smiled grimly to himself; it was evident that he was not going to have an easy time proving his identity to Davis. He began to cast around in his mind for something to say when the Egyptian beckoned to him. The child control was speaking through the etheric larynx again, and the Egyptian informed him that he would be the next to speak.

In some trepidation Michael approached the man whose mortal body he was to control. From the side of the body he could see the thin life-cord stretching away up out of sight to where the medium's spirit, temporarily bereft of its human vehicle, was functioning on another plane. Following the Egyptian's instructions he concentrated upon the head of the medium, then he waded right into the physical body as one wades into deep water. For a moment, he had the sensation of a wave passing over his head. He became conscious of the odour of human emanations, which to his refined spirit sense was rather overpowering. At length he had 'thought' himself into the new garment and began to make use of the physical limbs. They felt heavy like limbs that have 'gone to sleep' through sitting too long in one position. But gradually his strength and confidence increased and he was able to operate the body without effort. He bent down to gaze through his own clairvoyant sight at the material of which the medium's coat was made. He patted the solid flesh of the wrist.

A warning message from the Egyptian caused him to notice the slumped attitude of his body. He straightened it and raised the head so that he could face the sitters. Now that he was in a physical body he was unable to see them so clearly. The outline of the circle was confused and their faces were blurred. He managed to focus one sitter at a time but it demanded an effort and he abandoned it. The child control had finished speaking and as she left the etheric voice-box she laughingly whispered in his ear.

"Your turn, Uncle Michael. Keep your spirits up."

He realized that the moment had come and that he must do something. His lips moved but for the life of him he could not think what to say. He was conscious that kindly thoughts were being extended to him from a number of the sitters, but there was one stream of antagonistic thought from Davis' intellect that stabbed his mind and paralyzed any inspiration he possessed. Suddenly he felt the concentration of the powerful mind of the Egyptian and a wave of power and confidence swept over him.

"Good evening," he said, with the aid of this external stimulus. It sounded fatuous, but there was a chorus of responses from the sitters that gave him added confidence. He began to speak of himself and his work in spirit life, of the things that were so real to him. The circle listened politely but he sensed that he had not captured their interest. No doubt, as Raphael had warned him, they would rather hear about themselves and their immediate problems. As he paused uncertainly, one of the sitters asked his name.

"Michael," he replied promptly. Then he realized that he ought to add his surname and opened the medium's mouth to give it. To his horror he could not remember it. Everyone called him Michael and as spirits rarely used his surname it had just floated out of his etheric memory. His face must have given away his predicament for the sitter asked again, encouragingly, "Can you tell us what your work was on Earth?"

That was better. He knew very well what his work had been. It was . . . what did they call it? He could see the whole thing, the materials, the machines, the finished articles. He could have given any spirit a complete exposition on the subject together with the employment of its counterpart in the Spirit World. But that was thought language, so complete and comprehensive, so effortless. What in the name of fortune was the name they used on Earth? He temporized.

"I was engaged in the manufacture of certain articles you use in your Earth life. Articles for construction, yes, that was it, construction. Just as our scientists, whom I see going round your circle, and collecting the ectoplasm from the medium and the sitters, fashion it into the semblance of a human larynx, so we made moulds and fashioned articles for earthly use." He paused, for his attention had been distracted by the sight of a finger clairvoyantly displayed before him, tracing something. It was a word. "P-l-a-s-t-i-c".

"That was it, plastics, my business was in plastics," he exclaimed trying to keep the note of relief out of his voice. He could see Davis leaning forward in his chair, staring at him intently.

Michael became conscious of another clairvoyant vision. It was a long narrow book, and he recognized it for a chequebook. It was open and a signature was scrawled at the foot of a cheque. "Michael Blair."

"Blair was my name, Michael Blair," he announced, almost in triumph. He saw Davis give a slight start and draw his brows together in a puzzled frown.

Michael decided to challenge him. "I think there is a friend of mine here, by the name of Davis."

Davis froze. "I used to know a man named Michael Blair," he replied in an uncompromising voice. "But his voice and manner were not a bit like yours."

Michael thought for a moment. He felt he wasn't being very adequate. "You must realize that I am using the body of this medium and am speaking through his larynx. It is the vibrations of his voice that you hear. Also this is my first attempt to manifest in this way and you must forgive me if I am not very good at it."

"Can you give me any evidence that it is really you?" asked Davis.

"I am Michael Blair, I passed over here as a result of a motor car accident together with my wife. My two children were burned to death in my house shortly before my passing."

"Yes, yes," returned Davis testily, "but these things are known generally. The medium could easily find out about such events. Tell me something that is known only to you and me and I will believe that it really is you." He sat back in his chair with the air of a man who has propounded an unsolvable problem.

Michael was nonplussed. Frantically searching the almost abandoned limbo in which were recorded all those faded symbols of a half-forgotten journey, he tried to fit together some incidents of his earthly life that would prove convincing. Why on Earth couldn't Davis take his word for it? It was degrading to have his identity doubted. There was so much he wanted to say, all the wonderful realities of his present existence clamouring for expression. He thought he might say something about Vera. Then he realized that Davis knew nothing about the girl. Time was passing, the power seemed to be lessening, and the challenge Davis had flung at him remained unanswered. It was almost with a feeling of relief that he heard the child control speaking again through the voice box and felt himself being withdrawn from the medium's body.

At length he was clear and stood facing the Egyptian. "I'm terribly sorry," he began, "I'm afraid I was a complete failure."

The Egyptian smiled understandingly. "Do not be dismayed. It is always difficult the first time, and some of these hard-headed sitters are difficult to deal with. Your friend Davis did not want to come, but was dragged here by his wife. It is better to take a newcomer to a clairvoyance séance where a practised medium, using her own consciousness in conjunction with us to get through evidential messages, has a much better chance of success. But your effort will not be wasted. Although your friend is not yet ready for spiritual truth, he was shaken by what he heard and that puzzlement may someday blossom out into a desire for further proof."

Feeling somewhat depleted by his experience Michael did not wait for the end of the séance, but departed with Raphael for the hostel where he was soon engaged in telling Ann of his adventure.

As Michael and Ann furthered their experience and knowledge, so did their development progress. They remained themselves, just as they had always been, but in accordance with the wisdom they acquired, their characters expanded. Their ability to appraise and to grasp deep significances and the inner meaning of spiritual truth broadened and deepened. They began to realize that what they had understood as Truth, ultimate and unalterable, was but the bud opening and blossoming with ever-increasing beauty and splendour. Each new conception brought them added tolerance, increased understanding, and that measure of pre-vision which is an attribute of the spiritually developed. The focus of their sight widened until it began to take in and outline the broad processes of an evolving world. At each turn of the kaleidoscope the myriad pieces that made up the Universe they knew rearranged themselves in a new and even more wondrous pattern. The manifestation of God through this growing and out-working development of

His 'many mansions' showed it to be something that was pulsating with life and colour and vitality, growing and expanding through the impulses of Spirit power eternally projected from the Source, working outwards in cycles that widened like the ripples on a pond.

Apart from the happy times of their vacations, all Michael's and Ann's energies were now devoted to the pursuit of the work to which they were dedicated. They studied the nature of spiritual matter and the source and transmission of the powerful Cosmic rays that beat upon the physical worlds of the Universe. They were given the secrets of inter-planetary attraction and repulsion and they learned something of the lives of those spirits who incarnated on other planets. Much they found to marvel at in the history of the sacrifice and redemption of those spirits who were giving all, that the dire situation of the Earth might be retrieved. They stood amazed at the endurance and courage displayed by those spirits who incarnated into a life chosen by themselves for its great suffering or seeming failure in order that they might, by their own spiritual strength, demonstrate how to meet and endure or overcome such disabilities.

One such case they encountered in this manner. They were present while a spirit was freeing himself from a body which was deaf, dumb and blind. They were surprised to see the grief and affection displayed by the friends of the passing spirit, grief which did much to hamper the disentanglement of the etheric body from the physical. As soon as the spirit was free they approached and offered their help and instructed him how to use the etheric senses which were now ready to be used by one who had forgotten how to employ such means of communication. To their surprise the spirit threw off the dull etheric body which he wore and revealed himself as a being of very high degree as evidenced by the brightness of his spirit vehicle. Its translucent radiance almost dazzed the beholders and they realized that here was one who could not be confined to these lower realms for long in his present brilliance. He thanked them for their loving care and assistance and explained that he had incarnated for the special purpose just described, simply as a thank-offering to God for the joy of

214

living. He explained that, through the interest and pity that his condition had aroused, he had been able to regenerate much of the despair that he found in his surroundings, to heal many afflicted bodies by the power emanating from him, and to uplift all with whom he came in contact by the Spirit that shone through him, voiceless but pregnant with authority. He said this without a trace of self-consciousness, for spirits of high degree are not subject to the limitations of conceit, knowing long before they reach such status that all power emanates from one great Source and that individuals are but bearers of its blessings. Then with a smile that radiated the pure love of Spirit, he made a graceful gesture of blessing and, gathering his glowing robes about him, precipitated himself into the sphere where he had his real being.

So Michael and Ann learned not to judge by appearances but to subordinate their judgment to an ever-growing power of intuition. One by one their existing prejudices began to fall away from them like overripe fruit. It was the loosening of the etheric body they wore and the prelude to the ultimate severance of themselves from the Self that alone held them back from that reunion with the Father which was the substance of the urge that impelled them through life. They were gathering, too, a new awareness of God. From being a powerful Deity, infinitely far off, infinitely unattainable, He was now coming into the prominence of their lives with a new meaning. They saw His manifestation in everything they met, in everything they sensed in the etheric world about them. His was the mysterious light of the Cosmos that was also an activating power, His were the still more mysterious rays that were a direct emanation of His Person, the rays that drove the Universe, that created and destroyed worlds, that determined the colour of a leaf or held in check the great rampaging powers of evil. Yet in all these things they were aware of a benevolent Personality, of a great Love beyond understanding or reciprocation, of One who was responsive to thought, rather than the Spirit of a Perfect Law. The two seemed to be combined in one great Omniscience. They knew that the greater their progression, the greater their wisdom, the deeper their understanding of Him, the more love He drew from their hearts, the more they felt at-one with this Radiant Being who was their Father.

Tendor had visited them on several occasions while they were resting in the Lowlands and told them that their continued service was earning for them the right to enter the Uplands of Heaven where their children dwelt. It would, however, be necessary to remain there for some time once they made the decision to enter this new life. And because of the absorbing interest in their work in the Astral, fanned by a growing understanding of the Great Tragedy of the Earth, they had put off the glowing promise of this forward step.

But now the great moment was approaching. New work lay ahead and they discovered that the work they were doing could as easily be performed by those who came after them, while they themselves could best render service by first increasing their own capacity to serve, that is by enhancing their own advancement. They knew that the progress of spirits through eternity is like the steadily advancing waters of a great river. Though single drops may tarry in quiet backwaters, though whirlpools may whirl with unending persistence, in the end each drop must move onwards to its final mergence with the ocean.

So now they left the Astral and confined their efforts to study on the plane of the Uplands. Ann was studying incarnation and reincarnation, a deeply absorbing subject. She asked Tendor to tell her if the children were likely to be incarnate again. But the guide smilingly refused to be drawn.

"It is a matter on which they must exercise their own free will," he said. "I cannot say what they will choose. When they are ready for it, they will be shown what they lack in experience and the way in which that experience may be gained. It will then be for them to decide which of the alternative suggestions they are ready to adopt. It may be that they will be able to learn all they need without another incarnation."

Nor would he enlighten her as to the children's respective affinities. "I do not know," he said in his grave dignified way, "the whereabouts of those spirits who shall, in God's own time, reunite with them to make the longed-for One. But I do know that for every one of either sex there is the mate. Thus did they emanate from God, thus will they return to the Heart of God. Somewhere in the Cosmos are the mates of your two children and love will draw them together as soon as the threads of destiny allow. That is the function of unity or love, which is the same thing."

When all was ready Michael and Ann accompanied their guide up the ridge which Michael had essayed to climb so long ago. As they neared the top Tendor told them to pause and look back over the Lowlands. It is difficult to impinge this fact upon a finite point of view, but the opening of their consciousness had now become such that they were able to embrace comprehensively, the whole of this plane of endeavour. They were in possession of all it could teach them, they held its secrets and knew its limitations. In one sweeping glance they could encompass in their understanding its place and its meaning in the scale of progress. They had learned to see life through its eyes, now they were about to rise external to its limitations. Now they would see not only the effects that manifested in its confines, but the causes which animated those effects. They would see behind the scenes, not only the obverse but the reverse, not merely the objective but the sub- jective. As they gazed out over the scenes of their late endeavours it seemed as if all the pent-up desires of their hearts flowed out of them and in their place rose the quiet waters of Spirit, giving them an infinitely finer degree of per- ception and a new understanding of what they saw. The values of life, the yardstick of their expression, changed and refined, shed a new light upon their environment.

As they trod the summit of the ridge a new world burst into view. Resplendent to a degree impossible to describe to phys- ical minds, they felt the new freedom, enabling them to look forward, upward, wider, opening their hearts to the beauties and joys of this grander, more satisfying life that met their wondering gaze. Happy as their lives had been in the past, that existence seemed by comparison cold and comfortless as they went forward like frozen creatures drawn to the comfort and warmth of a fire.

Though Ann had visited this plane before with the children, she had not seen it with the widened vision of this Initiation.

To Michael the grandeur and wonder of it was such that he felt something slip off him like an old garment. Before him was a new dawning, redeemed from the mistakes of the past, a new sunrise to all his hopes and aspirations, opening up new opportunities for the expression of all the desires that rose within him. The door of the past closed behind him, even as the door of the cottage had closed upon his Earth life, setting a seal upon what he had accomplished. The magnets of the Earth no longer pulled at him.

Into the consummation of the new joys Michael and Ann stepped, faced with a realization that but a little while ago would have been impossible for them.

Chapter Seven

ASCENSION

It would require many volumes to record the experiences of Michael and Ann in their new environment, which they faced in the light of a new perception, refined in the crucible of a past that now fell away from them like the spent thing that it is. And the story would fade in the telling if an attempt were made to translate the brilliant range of colouring which illumines every phase of that life into the crude pigments to which earthly minds respond.

On their arrival in this sphere Michael and Ann had found the prototype of their house waiting for them and here for a time came Stephanie and Peter to dwell in joyous harmony with them. It was a time of great beauty and fulfilment, this family reunion, founded on the rocks of a deep and abiding love and understanding. But the time came when these two young souls became athirst for new adventure and new means of acquiring wisdom and experience.

So, as their parents had done, they too set forth into the realms where there is infinite opportunity to choose and to decide, to profit and to lose by experience, into that wonderful Cosmos which is an infinite repository of every experience that an evolving soul can need for the shattering of its illusions and the perfection of its knowledge of its own inherent goodness. We have no wings to follow them so we must content ourselves with sending them God-speed to help them on their way till they meet those who are a part of themselves, to mate in their turn and complete their journey home.

From time to time Michael and Ann descended into the lower realms for special service or to meet those whom they loved who were making the great transition. Robert and Mary

Blair were both met and conducted to the plane most suited to their needs and it was Michael's joy to teach them much that he had learned himself. In due course John and Vera were able to meet and abide together and it was interesting to watch the law of Compensation at work. That which John had missed as a result of his frustrated incarnation he gained in double measure through his mother. Fred Smith and his beloved Kate, refined by the fires of his devotion, also made their appearance in a new environment, while Mary paid the twins a visit before departing into the Cosmos in search of her mate. From her they learned of much progress in the rescuing of those who were stuck in the morasses of the City of Illusion or embedded in the deeper snares of the land across the river. From all sides came news of the endless resurrection, the eternal upsurge of spirits on their way back to God through infinitely varying channels. To Michael and Ann and their contemporaries, this resurgence was a constant source of wonder and delight, for they were able to view it from the vantage point of a widened comprehension, seeing the record of what was behind it all, able to marvel at the depth of experience through which some of the persistent travellers had come.

The twins were enabled to study here the essences of matter. Here was shown to them the common denominator of all that externalized into outer manifestation in so many different guises. The material things of the Universe were here reduced to a common source, almost to their true origin, the initial Source of all. Juggling with the protons and electrons of the atom, they were able to accomplish the transmutation so much sought by the ancient Alchemists. For in this realm processes are ultimate; it is nearly at the centre of the circle. They learned, too, that matter is not active of itself. It was shown to them that the chemical ingredients of sea water, artificially put together, are not sufficient to sustain marine life. Here was proof that the manifestation of the Life-Force of the Creator is needed if life is to be preserved. Together they traced this principle through all the workings of the Universe.

Freed now from the magnetic pull of the globe on which they had tasted of the deepest form of experience, Michael and Ann were now better able to extend their visits to outer parts of the Cosmos. Much they learned that has not yet been given into the keeping of man and so can find no place here. It was part of that learning, however, that they found themselves able to identify themselves with it. All that they saw and learned became part of them for the rest of their existence. They were learning to recognize Spirit as a power that motivates the Universe and all that is in it, running through every atom of it like a divine spark. They were becoming at-one with their environment, which is the last step before becoming at-one with God.

Although the twins were now clear of Earth influence they still retained a lively interest in all that befell the dark planet. Tendor, who was now habitually with them, now announced an event of great importance. He took them to a rendezvous deep within the Cosmos to where a mountain rises in its pristine glory. It is the Holy Mountain of Spirit, mention of which is so often made in esoteric writings. At its base lies a vast amphitheatre surrounded by a low range of hills. The mountain appears to be of purest snow, glowing rosily with the light that emanates from it, while the surroundings are of a verdant green never before seen. When they arrived the amphitheatre was empty, but the low hills were crowded with an ever-growing mass of spirits in splendid garb. An air of expectancy swept over the assembly.

Presently there came, from the infinite distance, the strains of martial music, and as the sound grew in volume, from both sides of the base of the mountain came great armies of marching men. They marched in divisions, each in a uniform of different colour. All were brilliantly garbed and each soldier carried a shield upon which was emblazoned a fiery cross while he carried a sword which glittered like molten gold with every movement. At the head of each division rode a mounted leader, even more brilliantly accoutred than his men.

"These are the armies of Light," explained Tendor. "They are composed of men who have fought on Earth in the past for great ideals, and now they fight on in a similar capacity. Do you see those leaders? They are spirits who were inspired leaders of the past who now organize this powerful spiritual army in the service of God."

221

"Much of the work of God," he went on to explain, as the serried ranks ranged themselves in perfect symmetry, "is carried on by the Masters and the Initiates, aided by the Angels, a race of beings which evolves separately from spirits like ourselves. But certain work on a specified planet can be better accomplished by those who have some link with that planet. I must tell you that war has broken out on Earth. There has been war on the lower Astral planes for a very long time, as you know, war between the forces of Light and those of darkness, and now a great effort is being made to clear up the effects of centuries of revolt. The struggle has come to a head, and the resultant stirring up of evil forces has precipitated war upon the Earth. There is war all over the globe. And word has come from the Masters of Karma that the Earth is now ready for the thinning of the veil so that the Light of Spirit may shine through and illumine the starved souls of men. This must be done on a wavelength that men can receive and respond to and is best done by the soldiers of Peace, who have manifested in human bodies and can still operate on the wavelength of a human mind. Watch what happens."

As he spoke the last of the divisions came to a halt, facing the mountain. They stood at rest, a vast concourse of disciplined soldiers, filling the huge arena, silent yet vibrant with life, a tremendous power held in leash. It was an inspiring scene, far transcending any pageantry that human endeavour could present. Suddenly, there was a blaze of light from the summit of the mountain. A single herald appeared and rode forward to sound a clarion call upon a silver trumpet. It seemed to those who watched that the echoes of that call rang through the Universe, as if it were a mighty cavern. Then appeared another Figure riding a white horse with the air of a splendid Conqueror. So transcendent was the vibration upon which He manifested at this time, that even these advanced spirits found it difficult to hold Him in their vision for long. There was no need for anyone to be told that here was the Master Himself, in the Majesty of His real Being. As He appeared, the whole assembly, soldiers and spectators alike, gave a mighty shout that raised the echoes again, while the soldiers raised aloft their shining swords in a single flashing movement which made the whole amphitheatre seem a sheet of living flame. Behind the Master rode a shining throng, all of them spirits of high degree. Among them was a White Knight, he who is known as St. George. Clad in armour of dazzling whiteness, he held a sword whose blade caught the shafts of light and hurled them to the confines of the Universe.

Once again the trumpet sent its call ringing round the halls of space. Then the White Knight rode forward. He came to a halt at a point overlooking the arena and as if at a given signal, the whole concourse of soldiers faced about and brought their swords to the engage. The White Knight cleft the air with his glittering blade and waved it from side to side, shattering the air with a myriad points of fire. Then he held the weapon steady before him. Each movement was meticulously followed by the soliders with perfect timing, creating wave after wave of living flame that swept out of the amphitheatre, carrying with it a force that would have shattered the Earth could it have manifested at that strength within the confines of the Earth's atmosphere. Then for a while the swords were still and rivers of power flowed from the points, out and down until they encompassed the Earth, closing in upon it, as a blanket smothers out fire.

Again the trumpet call and the flow of power died away. There was no sound but the rustle of swords being withdrawn to rest. A sigh of relief swept round the spectators for the vibration of that tremendous power had held them rigid. Facing about once more, the soldiers began to sing. Division by division they took up the mighty refrain in a grand cascade of sound. Never in the wildest dreams of Earth life was such music as this. Swelling in unison, the glorious voices sent their rhythmic tones rolling up the mountain side, until it seemed the waves must wash the very throne of God. For sheer majesty and breadth of sound it can surely never be surpassed, for it is the Eternal Hymn of Praise, which has been sung before the throne of God throughout the endless cycle, as it will be sung, for ever.

When the glorious refrain was over, the Master rode forward and blessed the assembly. Not one in that vast concourse but felt that he had received a special commendation from the all-embracing mind of this great Being. Each felt that he was at-one with this Master of Love and Power, working with Him, with but a single aim. Each felt that on this momentous occasion he had taken yet another step forward from which he would never retreat.

Then the Master turned His horse and rode away, followed by the shining throng. The martial music sounded once more and the divisions commenced to march out of the amphitheatre, swinging in perfect unison, marching with the proud tread of men who have conquered and overcome. At length the great arena was empty, the music died away, and nothing remained of that inspiring ceremony but the haunting memory of that glorious refrain which seemed to linger about the mountain that is Holy.

We hardly dare follow Michael and Ann into the future. They have grown beyond our compass. To us who still struggle in the currents of Earth, they seem great beings of wisdom and progress who have travelled beyond our ken. Already we have trespassed beyond the bounds of the illusion of time. Yet they were as we are; as they are we shall be. Now their experiences are such that we can only shade our eyes against brilliance that would blind us, seeing but the afterglow of their understanding of Truth, which, could we stand face to face with it, would drive us distracted with discontent at our present lot.

As they passed through Initiation after Initiation they found the memory of their pre-earthly existence coming back into prominence, each phase of their existence falling into place like the pieces of a giant puzzle. Each new unfoldment enabled them to emerge into a new freedom that made the last initiation seem like a prison cage. But these experiences are not for mortal ears and eyes to dwell upon, for their meaning would not be clear and their glory could not be sensed.

One last glimpse we may be permitted as the two travel onward through the arches of eternity. Bringing the far distant future back through aeons of time into the focus of the present, we see them take the last step of all, even though it be but a travesty of the Reality that is the last great Ultimation. But we must complete the circle, we must limn the journey back to the beginning, we must show that there is no future beyond our reaching, no past beyond our reckoning.

Freed now from the last vestige of that emotional body, which had proved such a revealer, in which so much had been accomplished, there is little of Self left to hold back these radiant twins. In readiness for the last Initiation of all, they array themselves in the robes of ceremony, creatures brilliant beyond our imaging. Accompanied by their beloved guide they make their way to a distant pinnacle, standing vastly alone in the depths of space. Filled with a new sense of at-one-ment with all things, living a life in common with the Universe, they stand there in contemplation of their lives as they had lived them. There is no regret, no sense of anything lacking, only a complete satisfaction in their achievement. Beyond pride, they know themselves to be good, beyond acquisitiveness they draw to themselves the love of all, beyond charity they give freely of all they possess. Then they turn to look forward into Infinity. Ah no, we cannot see what they see, we must leave it.

They stand there alone, in the silence of the Cosmos. Even Tendor has temporarily withdrawn his personality. And out of the stillness that is beyond silence, upon the breath of the Universe, there steals the music of the spheres. The sound of the Universe in action, the sound of great bodies travelling in their orbits, punctuated by the death of a star, glorified by the birth of a nebula. The eternal but ordered movements of the constellations form a great orchestral symphony which is the rhythm of Creation. And the hearts of both are filled because they are at-one with all these things, they are part of them, their consciousness has opened out to include all that is.

As they stand there in solemn meditation and at-one-ment their robes of distinction fall away from them. The last vestige of Self is sloughed off and they stand before their Maker in the nakedness of Pure Spirit. They experience a terrible loneliness, for with the absence of Self, they are bereft of a sounding board. There can be but one easement from this intolerable situation, at-one-ment with the Source to which they belong, not merely in contemplation, but in fact. Relieved of the tension that held them away from the Great Magnet, they feel themselves drawn irresistibly towards the glowing Heart of God. One flame of purity set out on this journey, one flame of purity they are once again. But there is something added, something gained. Before they burned with the pure light of Innocence, now they are alive with the radiant glow of Wisdom.

At length, the loneliness becomes unbearable, they yearn to break down the last illusion of separation which has held them away from a home which is rightfully theirs. As the Heavens open, they give a cry of pure ecstasy, for they gaze once more upon that which has drawn them throughout their absence. They enter in, and the Heart of God is made richer by their coming. His Plan is one step nearer completion, because two of His children have come home. And all the company of Heaven burst into a pæan of praise because the Father's Obligation is redeemed once again and hope is reborn in the hearts of men.

And a Voice cries out to Tendor, "Well done, thou good and faithful servant."